Sign Up Online

GMAS

Grade 3 ELA Practice

Georgia Milestones Assessment System Test Prep: Grade 3 English Language Arts Literacy (ELA) Practice Workbook and Full-length Online Assessments: GMAS Study Guide

Contributing Editor - Leigh Hargett
Contributing Editor - Anneda Nettleton
Contributing Editor - George Smith
Contributing Editor - Wendy Bundgaard
Executive Producer - Mukunda Krishnaswamy
Designer and Illustrator - Sowmya R.

First Edition - 2020

NGA Center/CCSSO are the sole owners and developers of the Common Core State Standards, which does not sponsor or endorse this product. © Copyright 2010. National Governors Association Center for Best Practices and Council of Chief State School Officers.

Georgia Department of Education is not affiliated to Lumos Learning. Georgia Department of Education, was not involved in the production of, and does not endorse these products or this site.

ISBN-10: 1-945730-78-1

ISBN-13: 978-1-945730-78-8

Printed in the United States of America

Last updated - July 2022

For permissions and additional information contact us

Lumos Information Services, LLC
PO Box 1575, Piscataway, NJ 08855-1575
http://www.LumosLearning.com

Email: support@lumoslearning.com
Tel: (732) 384-0146
Fax: (866) 283-6471

INTRODUCTION

About Lumos tedBook for GMAS Test Practice:
This book is specifically designed to improve student achievement on the GMAS. Students perform at their best on standardized tests when they feel comfortable with the test content as well as the test format. Lumos tedBook for GMAS test ensures this with meticulously designed practice that adheres to the guidelines provided by the GMAS for the number of questions, standards, difficulty level, sessions, question types, and duration.

About Lumos Smart Test Prep:
With more than a decade of experience and expertise in developing practice resources for standardized tests, Lumos Learning has developed the most efficient methodology to help students succeed on the state assessments (See Figure 1).

Lumos Smart Test Prep Methodology offers students realistic GMAS assessment rehearsal along with providing an efficient pathway to overcome each proficiency gap.

The process starts with students taking the online diagnostic assessment. This online diagnostic test will help assess students' proficiency levels in various standards. With the completion of this diagnostic assessment, Lumos generates a personalized study plan with a standard checklist based on student performance in the online diagnostic test. Parents and educators can use this study plan to remediate the proficiency gaps with targeted standards-based practice available in the workbook.

After student completes the targeted remedial practice, they should attempt the second online GMAS practice test. Upon finishing the second assessment, Lumos will generate another individualized study plan by identifying topics that require more practice. Based on these practice suggestions, further skill building activities can be planned to help students gain comprehensive mastery needed to ensure success on the state assessment.

Lumos Smart Test Prep Methodology

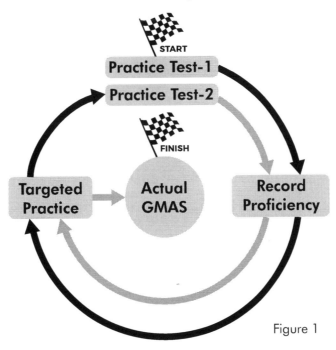

Figure 1

Table of Contents

Chapter 1
Lumos Smart Test Prep Methodology

Step 1: Access Online GMAS Practice Test

The online GMAS practice tests mirror the actual Georgia Milestones Assessment System (GMAS) in the number of questions, item types, test duration, test tools, and more.

After completing the test, your student will receive immediate feedback with detailed reports on standards mastery and a personalized study plan to overcome any learning gaps. With this study plan, use the next section of the workbook to practice.

Use the URL and access code provided below or scan the QR code to access the first GMAS practice test to get started.

URL	QR Code
Visit the URL below and place the book access code **www.lumoslearning.com/a/tedbooks** **Access Code: GMASG3E-64413-P**	

Step 2: Review the Personalized Study Plan Online

After students complete the online Practice Test 1, they can access their individualized study plan from the table of contents (Figure 2) Parents and Teachers can also review the study plan through their Lumos account (parent or teacher) portal.

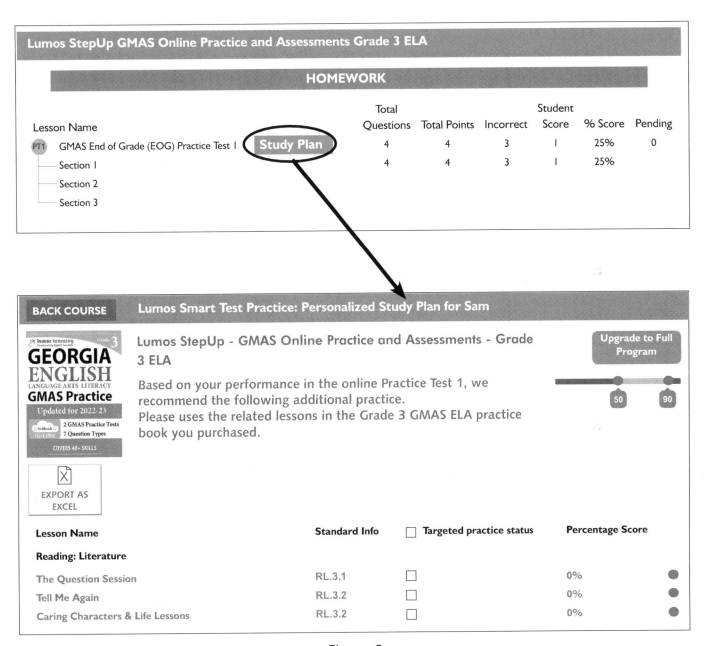

Figure 2

Step 3: Complete Targeted Practice

Using the information provided in the study plan report, complete the targeted practice using the appropriate lessons to overcome proficiency gaps. With lesson names included in the study plan, find the appropriate topics in this workbook and answer the questions provided. Students can refer to the answer key and detailed answers provided for each lesson to gain further understanding of the learning objective. Marking the completed lessons in the study plan after each practice session is recommended.(See Figure 3)

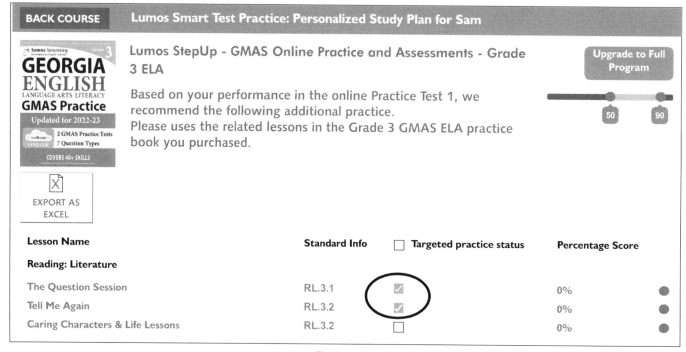

Figure 3

Step 4: Access the Practice Test 2 Online

After completing the targeted practice in this workbook, students should attempt the second GMAS practice test online. Using the student login name and password, login to the Lumos website to complete the second practice test.

Step 5: Repeat Targeted Practice

Repeat the targeted practice as per Step 3 using the second study plan report for Practice test 2 after completion of the second GMAS rehearsal.

Visit www.lumoslearning.com/a/lstp for more information on Lumos Smart Test Prep Methodology or Scan the QR Code

What if I buy more than one Lumos Study Program?

Step 1 → **Visit the URL given below and login to your account**

www.lumoslearning.com

Step 2 → **Click on 'My tedBooks' under the "Account" tab**

Place the Book Access Code and submit.

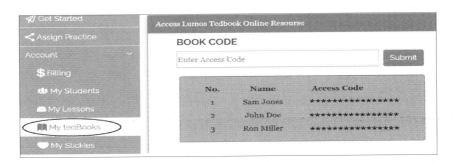

Step 3 → **Add the new book**

To add the new book for a registered student, choose the '**Existing Student**' button, select the student and submit.

To add the new book for a new student, choose the '**Add New Student**' button and complete the student registration.

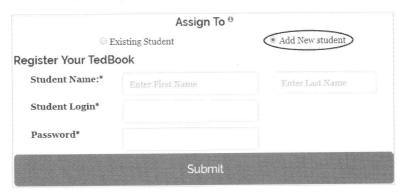

Test Taking Tips

1) **The day before the test,** make sure you get a good night's sleep.

2) **On the day of the test,** be sure to eat a good hearty breakfast! Also, be sure to arrive at school on time.

3) **During the test:**

- **Read each question carefully.**

  - Do not spend too much time on any one question. Work steadily through all questions in the section.
  - Attempt all the questions even if you are not sure of some answers.
  - If you run into a difficult question, eliminate as many choices as you can and then pick the best one from the remaining choices. Intelligent guessing will help you increase your score.
  - Also, mark the question so that if you have extra time, you can return to it after you reach the end of the section.
  - Some questions may refer to a graph, chart, or other kind of picture. Carefully review the infographics before answering the question.
  - Be sure to include explanations for your written responses and show all work.

- **While Answering Multiple-choice (EBSR) questions.**

  - Select the bubble corresponding to your answer choice.
  - Read all of the answer choices, even if think you have found the correct answer.

- **While Answering TECR questions.**

  - Read the directions of each question. Some might ask you to drag something, others to select, and still others to highlight. Follow all instructions of the question (or questions if it is in multiple parts)

Chapter 2 - Reading: Literature

The objective of the Reading Literature standards is to ensure that the student is able to read and comprehend literature (which includes stories, drama and poetry) related to Grade 3.

To help students master the necessary skills, information to help the student understand the concepts related to the standard is given. Along with this, we encourage the student to go through the resources available online on EdSearch to gain an in depth understanding of these concepts. The EdSearch page for each lesson can be accessed with the help of the URL or the QR code provided.

A small map is provided after each passage or text in which the student can enter the details as understood from the literary text. Doing this will help the student to refer to key points that help in answering the questions with ease.

Chapter 2

Lesson 1: The Question Session

In order to be able to answer questions from any story, it would be good to understand the various elements of the story. This will help you look for the answers in the story with ease.

To answer questions, we need to know Who, What, Where, When, and Why. The elements of a story help you to answer these questions.

The Elements (Parts) Of a Story

1. Plot: **What**

The plot is the main story of a literary work. There can be more than one plot in a story, and there can be one or more secondary (less important) plots (also called subplots).

2. Character(s): **Who**

The actions and thoughts and emotions of the main (major) character(s) have the most influence, are the most important, to the plot. There may be other less important characters (known as minor or secondary characters) in the story, but they will have less influence on the plot.

3. Setting(s): **Where and When**

The setting(s) for a story are the location(s) and/or time period(s) at or in which the story takes place. There can be more than one setting and more than one time period in the same story.

4. Supporting details: **Why**

The answer to "Why" is given as supporting details to the main plot or theme of the story in the text or passage.

You can scan the QR code given below or use the URL to access additional EdSearch resources including videos and mobile apps related to *The Question Session.*

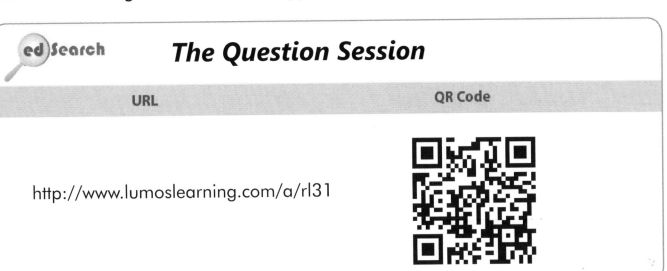

ed Search	*The Question Session*	
URL		**QR Code**
http://www.lumoslearning.com/a/rl31		

Question 1-3 are based on the story below.

After reading the story, enter the details in the map below. This will help you to answer the questions that follow.

Margaret was a simple lady who lived in a village with her husband, Robert. They had a daughter named Amy. Every day at sunrise, Margaret would wake up, cook, clean, and feed the cattle. Robert would milk the cows and then take the dogs for a long walk. Amy would study, help her mother for some time, and then get ready for school.

Amy studied in a school that was far away from her house, but she loved going to school. She went with her friends, Ingrid and Rebecca. They would walk together chatting, laughing, and singing songs as they went. They had to cross a river on the way. The only way they could cross it was by walking on a narrow bridge.
One day Margaret, Robert, Amy, and her friends were walking on the narrow bridge one behind the other. Amy and her friends were off to school, as usual, Margaret and Robert wanted to go to the market on the other side of the river to buy groceries for the house.

As they were crossing the narrow bridge, Rebecca slipped. She gave a frightened scream, clutching Ingrid, who was in front of her. Both of them lost their balance and fell into the river. Amy clutched her mother in fright. For a moment, she hesitated and then threw herself into the river after her friends, determined to save them.

Margaret screamed, and Robert jumped into the river. Some passers-by also jumped into the river and rescued the children, who were dripping wet, and shivering with fright.

That night Robert patted his daughter Amy and said, "You are a brave girl Amy, I'm proud of you."

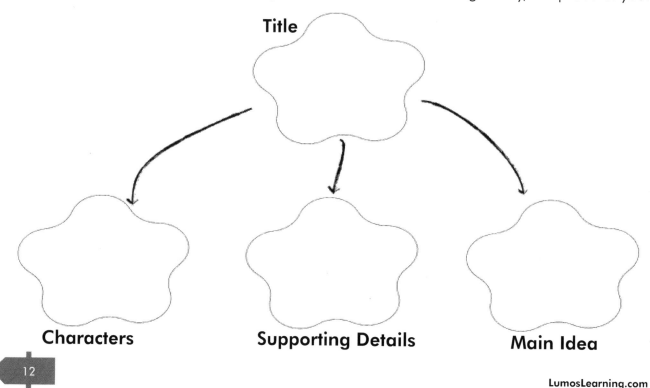

1. How is Margaret related to Amy?

   Ⓐ She is her cousin.
   Ⓑ She is her friend.
   Ⓒ She is her mother.
   Ⓓ She is her aunt.

2. Who slipped on the narrow bridge?

   Ⓐ Amy
   Ⓑ Margaret
   Ⓒ Robert
   Ⓓ Rebecca

3. Why did Robert and Margaret go along with the girls?

   Ⓐ They wanted to walk them to school.
   Ⓑ They wanted to go for a walk.
   Ⓒ They wanted to buy some groceries.
   Ⓓ They wanted to walk on the bridge.

Question 4 is based on the story below.

After reading the story, enter the details in the map below. This will help you to answer the questions that follow.

One day, a baby elephant was happily dancing through the jungle, nodding his head and lifting up his trunk to trumpet loudly.

The loud sound woke up a monkey who was sleeping in a tree nearby. He was very angry. He scolded the elephant and asked him to keep quiet.

"You silly animal," he said. "Can't you keep quiet? I'm sleeping."

"Oh, sorry," said the little elephant and walked on. After sometime, the little elephant reached a river and saw some beautiful swans there. He gazed at the beautiful birds. The swans looked at him and began to laugh.

"Oh! Look at that big creature," they said. "What a long nose, his ears are like fans, and look at his skin, it's much too big for him. He looks like a big wrinkled bag with all those folds!" They laughed at him and swam away.

The little elephant was very sad. He tried to smooth out his skin with his trunk but it was no good. He thought, "Why am I so ugly? Let me hide so that no one can see me."

He tried to hide himself in a thick bush but he disturbed some nests. The birds flew above his head crying loudly and tried to peck him.

Suddenly, he saw a big bear coming towards him. It was growling and appeared to be very angry. The little elephant was very frightened, and he trumpeted loudly. Just as he trumpeted, he heard a loud crashing and stomping. A herd of wrinkled elephants came charging to the rescue.

Seeing the herd, the frightened bear ran away.

The little elephant joyfully ran to the big elephants, thanked them, and said, "I wish I could be like you. You're so mighty and strong," he continued.

"But you are," replied the elephants. "You're a perfect little elephant." The little elephant danced for joy; he trumpeted loudly and walked away happily with the other elephants following behind.

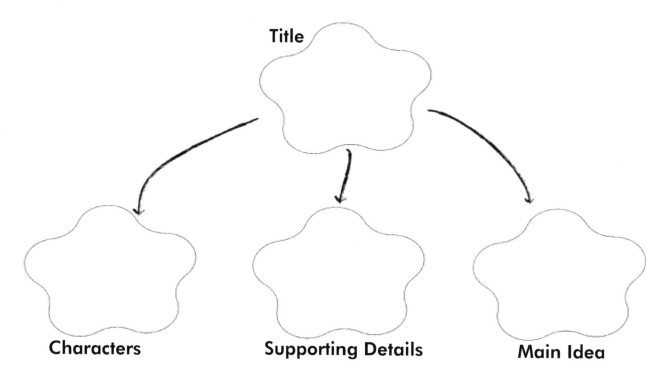

Title

Characters   Supporting Details   Main Idea

4. According to the story, why does an elephant's skin look 'wrinkly'?

  Ⓐ It is grey in color.
  Ⓑ It has too many folds.
  Ⓒ It is thick.
  Ⓓ It is hard.

Question 5-8 are based on the poem below.

Camels are bumpy,
Their backs are all lumpy,
Giraffes are long- legged and meek:
Bears are so growly,
Hyenas are howly,
Dolphins are slippery and sleek.

Kangaroos have a pocket,
But no way to lock it,
Their babies can look out and peep,
But monkeys are funny,
I wish I had money,
Enough to buy one and keep.

5. According to the poem, where is the camel's hump?

  Ⓐ on its stomach
  Ⓑ on its back
  Ⓒ underneath its stomach
  Ⓓ it has no hump

6. According to the poem, which animal is long-legged?

  Ⓐ Hyena
  Ⓑ Camel
  Ⓒ Giraffe
  Ⓓ Elephant

7. Part A

  What does the poem say about Dolphin?

7. Part B

What does the poem say causes dolphins to be slippery?

8. Read the Poem. Match each animal to its characteristic, put a tick mark against the characteristic for each animal.

Animals	Has Hump	Has Pocket	Slippery	Long legged
Kangaroo				
Camel				
Giraffe				
Dolphins				

Question 9 is based on the story below.

After reading the story, enter the details in the map below. This will help you to answer the questions that follow.

Once upon a time, there was a wealthy woman that had very poor eyesight. She decided to call a doctor to ask if he could restore her eyesight. The doctor promised to cure her but told her that she had to pay him a huge fee. He also told her that throughout the treatment she had to keep her eyes closed. The woman agreed to both requirements.

The doctor began the treatment in the woman's home. Every day the doctor stole something from the lady's house. The treatment lasted a lengthy period of time. Finally, when he had emptied her house, the doctor told her that he had finished her treatment, and that her eyesight was restored.

The woman was very happy that the treatment was over, but she refused to pay the doctor. The doctor was very angry that she refused to pay his hefty fee. He told her that he was taking her to court. She just laughed at him.

When the judge asked the woman to explain why she didn't pay the doctor, the woman said, "Sir, before the operation, I was partially blind, but at least I could see the things in my home." She continued, "But now after the treatment, I am unable to see anything in my home. The woman solemnly told the judge, I must be totally blind because I can see nothing."

16

The judge looked at the doctor, who hung his head in shame. The doctor realized that the woman knew that he had stolen all her things. He felt ashamed and returned everything he had stolen. The doctor also said that the woman did not owe him a fee for the treatment.

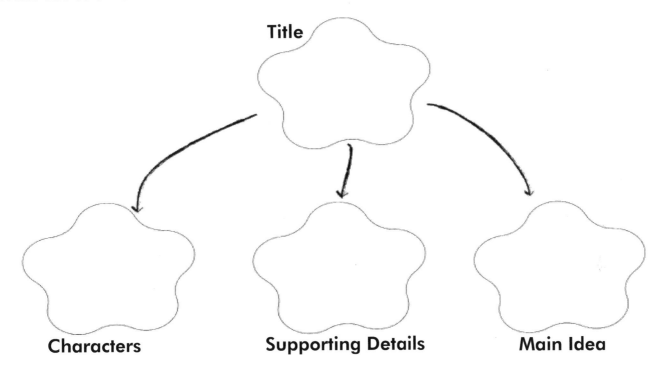

Title

Characters   **Supporting Details**   **Main Idea**

9. What was the old lady's eye sight like before her operation?

- Ⓐ   She was not able to see anything.
- Ⓑ   She could only see one thing.
- Ⓒ   She could see things but not very clearly.
- Ⓓ   She was totally blind.

Question 10 is based on the story below.

After reading the story, enter the details in the map below. This will help you to answer the questions that follow.

Brandon lived with his mother at one end of the forest. His school was at the other end of the forest. Every day he had to go through the forest to get to school and the forest was very scary.

One day he told his mother that he felt very scared to cross that forest.

His mother said, "Don't be scared" "Your brother lives in the forest. Whenever you get scared, you can always call him. He won't answer you but he will see that no harm comes to you."

Brandon said, "Why didn't you tell me about my brother earlier? What is his name?"

Mother said, "His name is Courage. Whenever you get frightened, call his name, and he will silently follow you to school and see that you come back home safely."

The next day Brandon was happy to get ready for school. He was not scared as he went through the forest on the way to school. That day, while coming home from school, he got scared when he heard the sounds of animals. Then he remembered his mother's words remembering him that his brother would protect him whenever he was frightened.

Brandon called out "Courage, Courage" with full confidence. Suddenly he began to feel better. He began to feel brave. He again called out, "Courage!, Courage!" He thought that his brother was silently following him, he began to sing softly and then loudly. He realized that he was not frightened after all. He crossed the forest confidently with courage.

The only traits we need to have to move ahead are confidence and courage in ourselves.

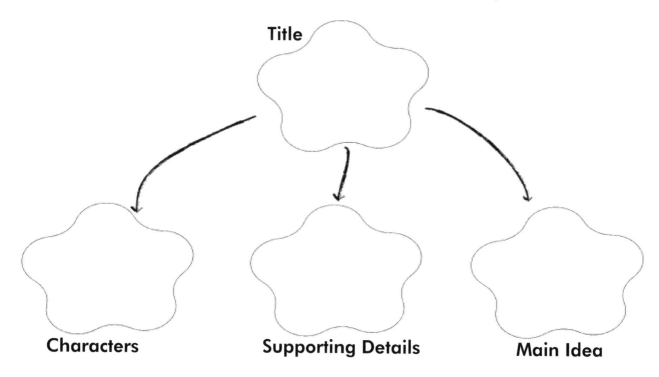

10. What is the best title for this story?

Chapter 2

Lesson 2: Tell Me Again

Publisher's Notes:

1. Determining the central message, lesson or moral: the central message, lesson or moral is the same as the main idea or theme of the text. This is the most important idea (or ideas) in a text. The main idea can be the purpose of the author in writing the text (for example, an attempt to persuade you to agree with the author's opinion, or to teach a lesson or a moral), or just to entertain you (for example, telling a funny story).

2. How the message is conveyed: conveyed means communicated. The author can communicate the message, lesson or moral in writing by telling about his/her or someone else's personal experience, or by teaching a lesson (which can be about a moral, such as what happens if someone steals something).The author can also include illustrations to help communicate his/her ideas.

Let us understand the concept with an example.

The Ant and the Grasshopper
Aesop's Fable

In a field, one summer's day, a grasshopper was hopping about, chirping and singing to its heart's content. A group of ants walked by, grunting as they struggled to carry plump kernels of corn. "Where are you going with those heavy things?" asked the grasshopper.

Without stopping, the first ant replied, "To our ant-hill. This is the third kernel I've delivered today."

"Why not come and sing with me," teased the grasshopper, "instead of working so hard?"

"We are helping to store food for the winter," said the ant, "and think you should do the same."

"Winter is far away and it is a glorious day to play," sang the grasshopper. But the ants went on their way and continued their hard work.

The weather soon turned cold. All the food lying in the field was covered with a thick white blanket of snow that even the grasshopper could not dig through.

Soon the grasshopper found itself dying of hunger. He staggered to the ants' hill and saw them handing out corn from the stores they had collected in the summer. He begged them for something to eat.

"What!" cried the ants in surprise, "haven't you stored anything away for the winter?"

What in the world were you doing all last summer?"

"I didn't have time to store any food," complained the grasshopper, "I was so busy playing music that before I knew it, the summer was gone."

The ants shook their head in disgust, turned their backs on the grasshopper and went on with their work.

Recount stories, determine the central message, lesson, or moral and explain how it is conveyed through key details in the text.

This is what you might write. The central message is: work hard to prepare for the future, especially if the future can bring danger. In this case, the danger for the grasshopper was a lack of food because of the change in seasons from summer to winter. The ants obeyed the central message and used the summer to prepare for the winter. The message was conveyed (communicated) to the reader in the following ways: "Why not come and sing with me," teased the grasshopper, "instead of working so hard?"; "We are helping to store food for the winter," said the ant, "and think you should do the same."; All the food lying in the field was covered with a thick white blanket of snow that even the grasshopper could not dig through. Soon the grasshopper found itself dying of hunger.; "What!" cried the ants in surprise, "haven't you stored anything away for the winter?"; "I didn't have time to store any food," complained the grasshopper.

You can scan the QR code given below or use the URL to access additional EdSearch resources including videos and mobile apps related to *Tell Me Again*.

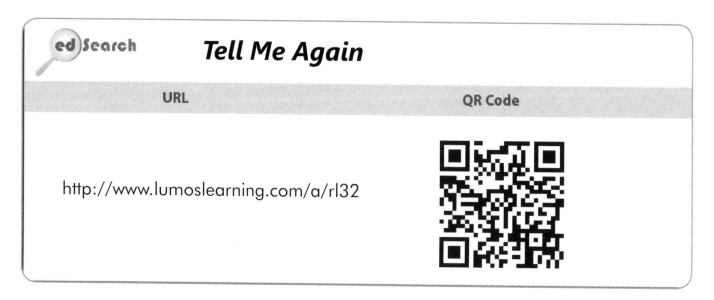

ed)Search   **Tell Me Again**

URL	QR Code
http://www.lumoslearning.com/a/rl32	

Question 1-3 are based on the story below.

After reading the story, enter the details in the map below. This will help you to answer the questions that follow.

One day, a baby elephant was happily dancing through the jungle, nodding his head and lifting his trunk to trumpet loudly.

The loud sound woke up a monkey who was sleeping in a tree nearby. He was very angry. He scolded the elephant and asked him to keep quiet.

"You silly animal," he said. "Can't you keep quiet? I'm sleeping."

"Oh, sorry," said the little elephant, and walked on. After some time, the little elephant reached a river and saw some beautiful swans there. He gazed at the beautiful birds. The swans looked at him and began to laugh.

"Oh! Look at that big creature," they said. "What a long nose, his ears are like fans, and look at his skin, it's much too big for him. He looks like a big wrinkled bag with all of those folds!" They laughed at him and swam away.

The little elephant was very sad. He tried to smooth out his skin with his trunk, but it was no good. He thought, "Why am I so ugly? Let me hide so that no one can see me."

He tried to hide in a thick bush, but he disturbed some nests. The birds flew above his head, crying loudly while trying to peck at him.

The little elephant ran for cover. He went behind a big rock to hide. Suddenly, he saw a big bear coming towards him. It was growling and appeared to be very angry. The little elephant was very frightened and trumpeted loudly. Just as he trumpeted, he heard a loud crashing and stomping. A herd of elephants came charging to the rescue.

Seeing the herd, the frightened bear ran away.

The little elephant joyfully ran to the big elephants, thanked them, and said, "I wish I could be like you. You're so mighty and strong," he continued.

"But you are," replied the elephants. "You're a perfect little elephant." The little elephant danced for joy; he trumpeted loudly and walked away happily with the other elephants following behind.

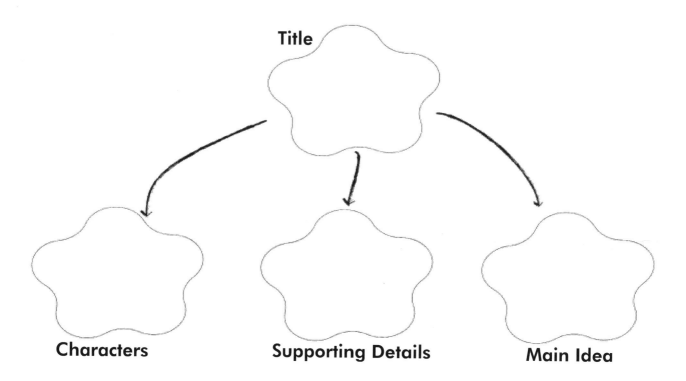

Title

Characters   **Supporting Details**   **Main Idea**

1. What caused the monkey to wake up in this story?

Ⓐ The wind was making a loud noise.
Ⓑ The elephant trumpeted loudly.
Ⓒ The monkey fell down.
Ⓓ The monkey was not asleep in the story.

2. Why did the swans laugh at the elephant?

Ⓐ They thought that the elephant looked ugly.
Ⓑ The elephant was happy.
Ⓒ The elephant was looking at them.
Ⓓ The elephant was dancing.

3. In this story, what caused the bear to run away?

Ⓐ He didn't want to see the monkey.
Ⓑ He was tired.
Ⓒ He was frightened by the herd of elephants.
Ⓓ He wanted to bring its friends.

Question 4 is based on the story below.

After reading the story, enter the details in the map below. This will help you to answer the questions that follow.

Brandon lived with his mother at one end of the forest. His school was at the other end of the forest. Every day he had to go through the forest to get to school and the forest was very scary.

One day he told his mother that he felt very scared to cross that forest.

His mother said, "Don't be scared" "Your brother lives in the forest. Whenever you get scared, you can always call him. He won't answer you but he will see that no harm comes to you."

Brandon said, "Why didn't you tell me about my brother earlier? What is his name?"

Mother said, "His name is Courage. Whenever you get frightened, call his name, and he will silently follow you to school and see that you come back home safely."

The next day Brandon was happy to get ready for school. He was not scared as he went through the forest on the way to school. That day, while coming home from school, he got scared when he heard the sounds of animals. Then he remembered his mother's words remembering him that his brother would protect him whenever he was frightened.

Brandon called out "Courage, Courage" with full confidence. Suddenly he began to feel better. He began to feel brave. He again called out, "Courage!, Courage!" He thought that his brother was silently following him, he began to sing softly and then loudly. He realized that he was not frightened after all. He crossed the forest confidently with courage.

The only traits we need to have to move ahead are confidence and courage in ourselves.

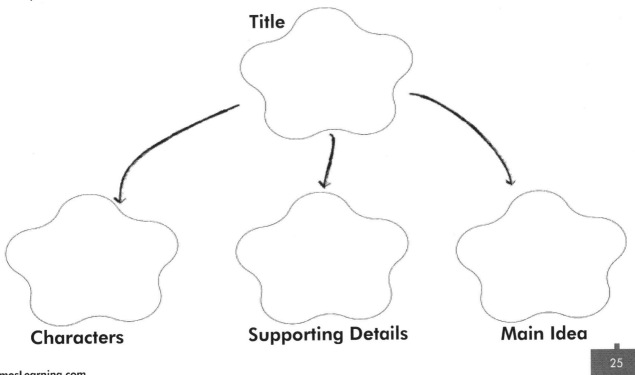

4. Who does Brandon's mother tell him lives in the forest?

Ⓐ A monster
Ⓑ His father
Ⓒ His brother
Ⓓ Fear

Question 5 is based on the poem below.

I quarreled with my brother
I don't know what about,
One thing led to another
And somehow we fell out.
The start of it was slight,
The end of it was strong,
He said he was right,
I knew he was wrong!

We hated one another.
The afternoon turned black.
Then suddenly my brother
Thumped me on the back,
And said, "Oh, come along!
We can't go on all night
I was in the wrong."
So he was in the right.

-by Eleanor Farjeon

5. Who is quarreling in the above poem?

Ⓐ The author with her brother.
Ⓑ The readers with their brothers.
Ⓒ The author with her mother.
Ⓓ None of these

Question 6 and 7 are based on the story below.

Margaret was a simple lady who lived in a village with her husband, Robert. They had a daughter named Amy. Every day at sunrise, Margaret would wake up, cook, clean, and feed the cattle. Robert would milk the cows and then take the dogs for a long walk. Amy would study, help her mother for some time, and then get ready for school.

Amy studied in a school which was far away from her house, but she loved going to school. She went with her friends, Ingrid and Rebecca. They would walk together chatting, laughing, and singing songs as they went. They had to cross a river on the way. The only way they could cross it was by walking on a narrow bridge.

One day Margaret, Robert, and Amy, and her friends were walking on the narrow bridge one behind the other. Amy and her friends were off to school as usual, and Margaret and Robert wanted to go to the market on the other side of the river to buy groceries for the house.

As they were crossing the narrow bridge, Rebecca slipped. She gave a frightened scream, clutching Ingrid, who was in front of her. Both of them lost their balance and fell into the river. Amy clutched her mother in fright. For a moment she hesitated and then threw herself into the river after her friends, determined to save them.

Margaret screamed, and Robert jumped into the river. Some passers-by also jumped into the river and rescued the children, who were dripping wet and shivering with fright.

That night Robert patted his daughter Amy and said, "You are a brave girl Amy, I'm proud of you."

6. According to the story, what did Robert do every morning?

Ⓐ Milk the cows.
Ⓑ Fetch milk from the shop.
Ⓒ Boil the milk.
Ⓓ Take the milk to sell at the market.

7. What did the girls have to cross on their way to school?

Ⓐ A narrow bridge.
Ⓑ A small stream.
Ⓒ A mango grove.
Ⓓ A big field.

Question 8-10 are based on the story below.

After reading the story, enter the details in the map below. This will help you to answer the questions that follow.

Tryouts for Madison

"I have to make the team," Madison said. Madison had thought of nothing but tryouts since the poster was displayed in the hall. She was new to the school. She understood that the other girls had an advantage, but what she lacked in experience, she made up for in effort and attitude. Being on the team would help her make new friends and feel like a part of a group.

The coach told her at the first practice to stretch daily, work on motions, and practice her jumps. This would develop flexibility. She wouldn't be as nervous if she could gain some height on her toe touches. She wanted her coach to know that she would be dedicated and work hard if she was on the team. Madison didn't mind-stretching. She actually found herself doing this while watching television, before and after meals, and before bedtime. While looking in a mirror, she would practice motions. The great thing about stretching and motion practice was that the hot temperatures would not be a factor in stopping her. She could do all the necessary moves in the comforts of air conditioning. Madison's parents could see her determination by the way she stretched and jumped numerous times a day.

Over the next two weeks, as summer faded into fall, Madison continued attending practices, stretching, and jumping. She was focused on being the best cheerleader at tryouts that she could be. She noticed that she was becoming as flexible as a straw. Her jumps were higher and her motions were nice and stiff.

At last, tryout day arrived! Madison quickly dressed in her tryout clothes and set off for the gym. She was smiling and whistling as she made her way to the gym. She had worked hard and practiced every day. Madison thought, "I hope that I do my best and that tryouts are fantastic!"

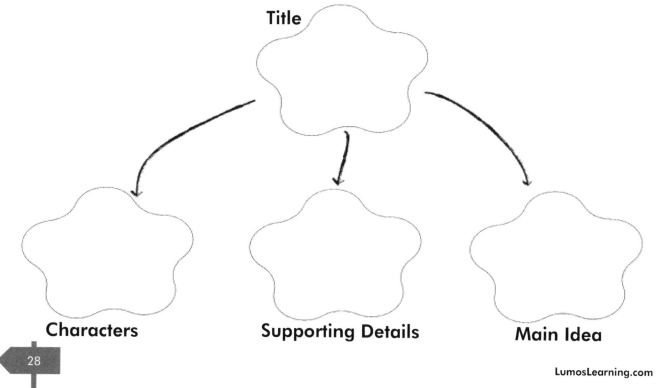

8. Why was Madison whistling when she entered the gym?

Ⓐ She made the team.
Ⓑ She felt good about her chances of making the team.
Ⓒ She whistles all the time.
Ⓓ She learned that everyone gets to be on the team.

9. Which character traits best describe Madison?

Ⓐ unfocused and compassionate
Ⓑ lazy and uncaring
Ⓒ brave and loyal
Ⓓ optimistic and hardworking

10. During which season of the year did the tryouts occur?

Ⓐ winter
Ⓑ fall
Ⓒ spring
Ⓓ summer

Question 11 is based on the story below.

Maggie's Dilemma?

Maggie has many things to accomplish over the weekend. She wants to go to a friend's house for a party on Sunday afternoon. If she doesn't get her chores and homework done, she is afraid that her parents will not let her attend the party.

As she is getting ready for bed, Friday night, she is worrying and wondering how she can do everything before the party on Sunday. Her mother tells her that she needs to prioritize her life. Maggie is not sure what that means. She thinks to herself, "What is prioritize? How does that help me in my life?"

Her older brother, Ronny, comes into her room. He asks her, "Hey, Sis, why the puzzled look? Why are you just sitting there on your bed looking around your room?"

"Ronny, what does it mean when Mom tells me I need to prioritize my life?"
"What's wrong with my life?"

Ron laughs and tells her that she has a tendency to try to do too much stuff in too little time. He suggests that she make a list of what she needs to do. Then, she needs to make a list of what she wants to do. Again, Maggie looks confused.

He takes out one of her notebooks and starts to write. She watches as he puts his name at the top of the list along with the words - Have to Do. Then he makes numbers going down each side. He writes, clean room as number 1. For number 2, he puts down take out the trash. Ron then writes down, mow the yard for number 3.

On another sheet of paper, he does the same thing, only this time after his name, he writes- Want to Do. On the second list, the number 1 is watch wrestling on TV. Number 2 is play video games.

Suddenly, Maggie gets it! "Oh, I see now. Prioritize means to put things in order of importance."

Her brother replies, "Duh, I knew I could help out!" Ron laughs along with Maggie. She is no longer puzzled and starts to write.

11. **Order the story by sequence of events that occurred. Select from the events given below and write in the order in which they occurred in the blank box given below.**

   A. **Maggie finally understands what she needs to do.**
   B. **Maggie asked her brother to explain what her mom had told her.**
   C. **Maggie didn't know if she could go to the party on Sunday if she didn't get all of her chores done before then.**
   D. **Maggie's brother helps her to understand what prioritizing means.**

Question 12 is based on the story below.

Bringing a Bear to School

Tyrone was so happy that his teacher said they were going to have a special celebration for a unit they had been studying on Bears in his class. They had been reading many bear books lately. Some of the books were about real bears and some were books about make-believe bears like Paddington and others. Mr. Clark, his teacher, wanted the students to relate to their own real-life experiences. The students were talking about the celebration during class one day.

Mr. Clark told them they could bring a stuffed bear from home if they wanted to or another stuffed animal for the day of the celebration. The girls were all excited. The boys were laughing and snickering about how dumb that idea was. They were saying only sissies would bring or have a stuffed toy. Tyrone's mouth frowned. He loved his Beary. He had Beary since he was just a tiny baby. Tyrone's grandfather had brought it to his mom on the day Tyrone was born. His grandfather had passed away several years later, and Tyrone held Beary all the time he thought about his grandfather. He even saved his allowance and special birthday money to buy his stuffed bear clothes. When Tyrone joined the soccer team, Beary got a soccer outfit. When he joined t-ball, Beary got a baseball uniform, too. So why were the boys making fun of having a stuffed bear? Tyrone did not understand.

The teacher sent home a note the weekend before the celebration explaining to parents what the next school day (Monday) would be like. Mr. Clark said that the students could bring their own stuffed animal if they chose to do so for a show and tell part of the celebration. They were even having zoo personnel come and share their experiences with the bears at the zoo. There would be Bear shaped cookies and cakes, too! Mr. Clark was also bringing his video of his trip to Russia where he saw many polar bears.

It sounded like so much fun! But, Tyrone was still hesitant on whether or not he should bring Beary to school. He wanted to show him off with his clothes and all. He wanted to tell the story of how his grandfather bought him the bear and how much it means to him still.

When Tyrone got home from school on Friday afternoon, he showed his mom the note from Mr. Clark. He had a puzzled look on his face. His mom said it sounded like the class was going to have a wonderful time on Monday. His sister, LaTasha, started laughing loudly. "Oh, please tell me you are not thinking of taking Beary?" she exclaimed.

"I was, but the other boys would probably make fun of me."

His mom said, "Why would they do that, Tyrone? Don't you think they have stuffed animals, too?"

"Maybe mom, but they would never admit it or bring them to school."

So all weekend long, Tyrone pondered what to do. Right before bedtime on Sunday night, he made his decision. Beary and his outfits were ready to go!

On Monday morning, Tyrone's mom decided she would take him to school herself rather than have him walk or ride the bus. When they arrived at his class, Mr. Clark was greeting all of the classmates. The entire classroom was decorated with bears of all sorts. On the front of Mr. Clark's desk was a beautiful stuffed bear. A sign in front said, "My Buddy!" Tyrone grinned from ear to ear as he joyfully took out Beary, dressed him in his baseball uniform, and put him on his desk. He made his own sign, "My Beary!"

Needless to say it was a great day for Tyrone. Several of the other boys had brought their stuffed animals and stuffed bears, too.

12. Order the story by sequence of events that occurred. Select from the events given below and write in the order in which they occurred in the blank box given below.

    A. Tyrone decided to take Beary to school.
    B. His sister, LaTasha, laughed at him.
    C. Mr. Clark had decorated the room in bears, including his own "Buddy" on his desk.
    D. The girls were excited.
    E. Tyrone had a great day at the celebration.
    F. Mr. Clark was going to have a celebration for the class after their unit on bears.

Question 13 and 14 are based on the story below.

OLD-FASHIONED FAIRY TALES
By Juliana Horatia Gatty Ewing

The following fairy tale is separated into 4 parts. Each part has questions that go along with the section, to help the reader have a better understanding of the tale. Also, for the reader, the selection has been numbered. Remember to read the selections more than one time for comprehension purposes.

While reading this fairy tale, keep in mind that it is written in what is called Old English. This means some words are used or spelled differently than the vocabulary we use today. Should you have difficulty with the words, use context clues to help. You may also ask your teacher, or use a dictionary to help you understand the meaning.

GOOD LUCK IS BETTER THAN GOLD.

Part 1

1. There was once upon a time a child who had Good Luck for his godfather.

2. "I am not Fortune," said Good Luck to the parents; "I have no gifts to bestow, but whenever he needs help I will be at hand."

3. "Nothing could be better," said the old couple. They were delighted. But what pleases the father often fails to satisfy the son: moreover, every man thinks that he deserves just a little more than he has got, and does not reckon it to the purpose if his father had less.

4. Many a one would be thankful to have as good reasons for contentment as he who had Good Luck for his godfather.

5. If he fell, Good Luck popped something soft in the way to break his fall; if he fought, Good Luck directed his blows, or tripped up his adversary; if he got into a scrape, Good Luck helped him out of it; and if ever Misfortune met him, Good Luck contrived to hustle her on the pathway till his godson got safely by.

6. In games of hazard the godfather played over his shoulder. In matters of choice he chose for him. And when the lad began to work on his father's farm the farmer began to get rich. For no bird or field-mouse touched a seed that his son had sown, and every plant he planted throve when Good Luck smiled on it.

7. The boy was not fond of work, but when he did go into the fields, Good Luck followed him.

8. "Your christening-day was a blessed day for us all," said the old farmer.

9. "He has never given me so much as a lucky sixpence," muttered Good Luck's godson.

10. "I am not Fortune—I make no presents," said the godfather.

11. When we are discontented, it is oftener to please our neighbours than ourselves. It was because the other boys had said—"Simon, the shoemaker's son, has an alderman for his godfather. He gave him a silver spoon with the Apostle Peter for the handle; but thy godfather is more powerful than any alderman"—that Good Luck's godson complained, "He has never given me so much as a bent sixpence."

Part 2

12. By and by the old farmer died, and his son grew up, and had the largest farm in the country. The other boys grew up also, and as they looked over the farmer's boundary-wall, they would say:

13. "Good-morning, Neighbour. That is certainly a fine farm of yours. Your cattle thrive without loss. Your crops grow in the rain and are reaped with the sunshine. Mischance never comes to your road. What you have worked for you enjoy. Such success would turn the heads of poor folk like us. At the same time, one would think a man need hardly work for his living at all who has Good Luck for his godfather."

14. "That is very true," thought the farmer. "Many a man is prosperous, and reaps what he sows, who had no more than the clerk and the sexton for gossips at his christening."

15. "What is the matter, Godson?" asked Good Luck, who was with him in the field.

16. "I want to be rich," said the farmer.

17. "You will not have to wait long," replied the godfather. "In every field you sow, in every flock you

rear there is increase without abatement. Your wealth is already tenfold greater than your father's."

18. "Aye, aye," replied the farmer. "Good wages for good work. But many a young man has gold at his command who need never turn a sod, and none of the Good People came to his christening. Fortunatus's Purse now, or even a sack or two of gold—"

19. "Peace!" cried the godfather; "I have said that I give no gifts."

20. Though he had not Fortunatus's Purse, the farmer had money and to spare, and when the harvest was gathered in, he bought a fine suit of clothes, and took his best horse and went to the royal city to see the sights.

21. The pomp and splendour, the festivities and fine clothes dazzled him.
22. "This is a gay life which these young courtiers lead," said he. "A man has nothing to do but to enjoy himself."

23. "If he has plenty of gold in his pocket," said a bystander.
24. By and by the Princess passed in her carriage. She was the King's only daughter. She had hair made of sunshine, and her eyes were stars.

25. "What an exquisite creature!" cried the farmer. "What would not one give to possess her?"
26. "She has as many suitors as hairs on her head," replied the bystander. "She wants to marry the Prince of Moonshine, but he only dresses in silver, and the King thinks he might find a richer son-in-law. The Princess will go to the highest bidder."

27. "And I have Good Luck for my godfather, and am not even at court!" cried the farmer; and he put spurs to his horse, and rode home.

Part 3

28. Good Luck was taking care of the farm.
29. "Listen, Godfather!" cried the young man. "I am in love with the King's daughter, and would want her to wife."

30. "It is not an easy matter," replied Good Luck, "but I will do what I can for you. Say that by good luck you saved the Princess's life, or perhaps better the King's—for they say he is selfish—"

31. "Tush!" cried the farmer. "The King is covetous, and wants a rich son-in-law."
32. "A wise man may bring wealth to a kingdom with his head, if not with his hands," said Good Luck, "and I can show you a district where the earth only wants mining to be flooded with wealth. Besides, there are a thousand opportunities that can be turned to account and influence. By wits and work, and with Good Luck to help him, many a poorer man than you has risen to greatness."

33. "Wits and work!" cried the indignant godson. "You speak well—truly! A hillman would have made a better godfather. Give me as much gold as will fill three meal-bins, and you may keep the rest of your help for those who want it."

34. Now at this moment by Good Luck stood Dame Fortune. She likes handsome young men, and there was some little jealousy between her and the godfather so she smiled at the quarrel.

35. "You would rather have had me for your gossip?" said she.
36. "If you would give me three wishes, I would," replied the farmer boldly, "and I would trouble you no more."
37. "Will you make him over to me?" said Dame Fortune to the godfather.
38. "If he wishes it," replied Good Luck. "But if he accepts your gifts, he has no further claim on me."
39. "Nor on me either," said the Dame. "Hark ye, young man, you mortals are apt to make a hobble of your three wishes, and you may end with a sausage at your nose, like your betters."

40. "I have thought of it too often," replied the farmer, "and I know what I want. For my first wish I desire imperishable beauty."

41. "It is yours," said Dame Fortune, smiling as she looked at him.
42. "The face of a prince and the manners of a clown are poor partners," said the farmer. "My second wish is for suitable learning and courtly manners, which cannot be gained at the plough-tail."

43. "You have them in perfection," said the Dame, as the young man thanked her by a graceful bow.
44. "Thirdly," said he, "I demand a store of gold that I can never exhaust."
45. "I will lead you to it," said Dame Fortune; and the young man was so eager to follow her that he did not even look back to bid farewell to his godfather.

Part 4

46. He was soon at court. He lived in the utmost pomp. He had a suit of armor made for himself out of beaten gold. No metal less precious might come near his person, except for the blade of his sword. This was obliged to be made of steel, for gold is not always strong enough to defend one's life or his honour. But the Princess still loved the Prince of Moonshine.

47. "Stuff and nonsense!" said the King. "I shall give you to the Prince of Gold."
48. "I wish I had the good luck to please her," muttered the young Prince. But he had not, for all his beauty and his wealth. However, she was to marry him, and that was something.

49. The preparations for the wedding were magnificent.
50. "It is a great expense," sighed the King, "but then I get the Prince of Gold for a son-in-law."

51. The Prince and his bride drove around the city in a triumphal procession. Her hair fell over her like sunshine, but the starlight of her eyes was cold.

52. In the train rode the Prince of Moonshine, dressed in silver, and with no color in his face.

53. As the bridal chariot approached one of the city gates, two black ravens hovered over it, and then flew away, and settled on a tree.

54. Good Luck was sitting under the tree to see his godson's triumph, and he heard the birds talking

above him.

55. "Has the Prince of Gold no friend who can tell him that there is a loose stone above the archway that is tottering to fall?" said they. And Good Luck covered his face with his mantle as the Prince drove through.

56. Just as they were passing out of the gateway the stone fell on to the Prince's head. He wore a casque of pure gold, but his neck was broken.

57. "We can't have all this expense for nothing," said the King: so he married his daughter to the Prince of Moonshine. If one can't get gold, one must be content with silver.

58. "Will you come to the funeral?" asked Dame Fortune of the godfather.
59. "Not I," replied Good Luck. "I had no hand in this matter."
60. The rain came down in torrents. The black feathers on the ravens' backs looked as if they had been oiled.
61. "Caw! caw!" said they. "It was an unlucky end."

13. What happens when the son goes into town? Circle the correct answer choice

Ⓐ He goes to a party and celebrates his wealth.
Ⓑ He saw the Princess and is intrigued to find out more about her.
Ⓒ He meets a beggar.
Ⓓ None of the above.

14. What did the farmer ask Dame Fortune to do? Write a sentence to explain your answer.

Question 15 is based on the story below.

FOREIGN LANDS

Up into the cherry tree
Who should climb but little me?
I held the trunk with both my hands
And looked abroad on foreign lands.

36

I saw the next-door garden lie,
Adorned with flowers, before my eye,
And many pleasant faces more
That I had never seen before.

I saw the dimpling river pass
And be the sky's blue looking-glass;
The dusty roads go up and down
With people tramping into town.

If I could find a higher tree
Farther and farther I should see,
To where the grown-up river slips
Into the sea among the ships.

To where the roads on either hand
Lead onward into fairyland,
Where all the children dine at five,
And all the playthings come alive.

- By Robert Louis Stevenson

15. Reading poetry can often help you to draw pictures in your mind. Reread the poem again and see if you can draw atleast one picture in your mind.
   Illustrate (draw) or write about what image or images come to mind when you read this poem."

Chapter 2

Lesson 3: Caring Characters & Life Lessons

You can scan the QR code given below or use the URL to access additional EdSearch resources including videos and mobile apps related to *Caring Characters & Life Lessons*.

 **Search**

Caring Characters & Life Lessons

URL	QR Code
http://www.lumoslearning.com/a/rl32	

Question 1 is based on the paragraph below.

A thirsty crow found a pitcher with just a little water in the bottom. His long, slender beak could just touch the water, but he could not get a drink. Looking around, the crow noticed many small stones lying nearby. Patiently, he picked up the stones one by one, and filled the pitcher until the water was high enough for him to get a drink.

1. What is the moral of this fable?

Ⓐ Haste makes waste.
Ⓑ Where there's a will, there's a way.
Ⓒ Look before you leap.
Ⓓ He who hesitates is lost.

Question 2 and 3 are based on the story below.

After reading the story, enter the details in the map below. This will help you to answer the questions that follow.

Eight-year-old Tess heard her parents talking about her little brother Andrew. She realized something was wrong. Andrew was very sick, and they did not have enough money for his treatment. Tess heard her daddy say, "Only a miracle can save him now."

Tess went to her bedroom and retrieved a jar from its hiding place. There were a few coins in it. She counted them carefully. She then made her way to the drug store. The pharmacist was too busy to pay attention to her. "And what do you want?" he asked, annoyed at her persistence. "Can't you see that I am talking to my brother? He is here from Chicago."

Tess persisted, "My brother's really sick .... and I want to buy a miracle. His name is Andrew. He has something bad growing inside of his head and my daddy says only a miracle can save him now. So, how much does a miracle cost?" Tess rambled.

The pharmacist's brother, a well-dressed man, stooped down and asked the girl. "What kind of miracle does your brother need?"

"Don't know," replied Tess, eyes welling up with tears. "I just know Mommy says he needs an operation. But my daddy can't pay for it. So, I want to use my money."

The man from Chicago asked, "How much money do you have?"

"One dollar and eleven cents," said Tess.

"Well, what a coincidence," smiled the man.

"One dollar and eleven cents is the exact price of a miracle for your little brother." He took her money in one hand and grasped Tess's hand in the other. "Take me to where you live. I want to see your brother and meet your parents. Let's see if I have the kind of miracle you need."

The well-dressed man was Carlton Armstrong, a neurosurgeon. He operated on Andrew without charging any money. It wasn't long until Andrew was home and well again. "I wonder how much the surgery cost?" said Mother.

Tess smiled to herself. She knew exactly how much the miracle cost— one dollar and eleven cents.... plus the immense faith of a little child.

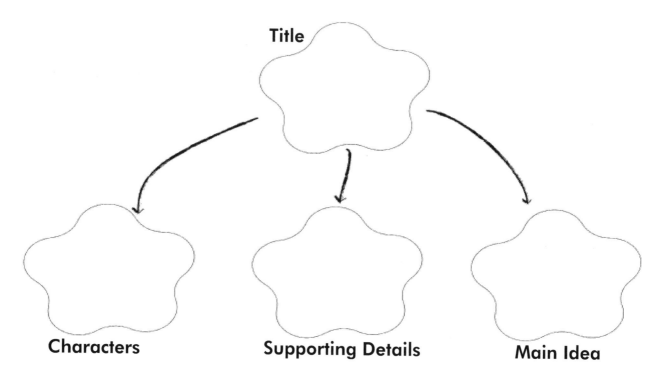

2. What is the message of this story?

Ⓐ Parents care for their kids.
Ⓑ Take good care of your health.
Ⓒ Worrying solves problems.
Ⓓ Miracles can happen when one has faith.

3. What is the moral of the above story?

Ⓐ Tess was an eight-year-old girl.
Ⓑ Sick people always get better by miracles.
Ⓒ Miracles always happen.
Ⓓ Persistence is more likely to get you what you want rather than doing nothing at all.

Question 4 is based on the fables below.

A.   Once a gazelle was running as fast as she could to outrun a lion who was pursuing her. She had a good lead and was probably going to outrun the lion when she came to a river. Although she could swim, the water looked cold and uninviting. She hesitated on the bank of the river, not wanting to jump in. While she debated, the lion overtook her, and she became his dinner.

B.   Once a gazelle was running as fast as she could to outrun a lion who was pursuing her. She had a good lead and was probably going to outrun the lion when she came to a river. Without looking, she jumped into the water where a crocodile was waiting, and she became his dinner.

4. Part A

What is the moral of Fable A?

Ⓐ He who hesitates is lost.
Ⓑ Look before you leap.
Ⓒ Running away never solves the problem.
Ⓓ One's actions do not determine one's fate.

4. Part B

What is the moral of Fable B?

Ⓐ He who hesitates is lost.
Ⓑ Look before you leap.
Ⓒ One's actions do not reflect one's fate.
Ⓓ Running away never solves the problem.

5. Which moral best completes the following story?

A dog that was prone to biting, was given a loud bell to wear around its neck. When anyone heard the bell, they quickly turned and went in the other direction. The dog was very proud of his bell until the old owl told him, _____.

Ⓐ Liars are not believed, even when they tell the truth.
Ⓑ Birds of a feather flock together.
Ⓒ Better half of a meal in freedom that a full meal in chains.
Ⓓ To be well known is not always to be admired.

6. Which moral best completes the following story?

The boy who guarded the sheep for the village was often bored and lonely. Once or twice, he called out, "Wolf!" just so the villagers would come out into the field to help him. He laughed to see them so excited. But one day, a wolf came to where the sheep were grazing. The boy called loudly, "Wolf! Wolf!" but no one from the village came to help him. _____

- Ⓐ Liars are not believed, even when they tell the truth.
- Ⓑ Birds of a feather flock together.
- Ⓒ Better half of a meal in freedom that a full meal in chains.
- Ⓓ To be well known is not always to be admired.

Question 7 and 8 are based on the fables below.

A.   The king's dinner was to be an elaborate affair, with many guests. In the kitchen, the cooks were rushing to prepare an elegant dinner. Extra chefs had been brought in from all over the kingdom and everyone was working very hard. The first dish on the menu was a delicate soup, full of fresh vegetables from the king's own garden. Each time a cook walked by and smelled the soup, he would taste it, and add just a pinch of salt to bring out the flavor. After each cook had added just a pinch of salt, the soup was served to the king, who sent it back to the kitchen. Too salty!

B.   The king's dinner was to be an elaborate affair, with many guests. In the kitchen, the cooks were rushing to prepare an elegant dinner. Extra chefs had been brought in from all over the kingdom and everyone was working very hard. The first dish on the menu was a delicate soup, full of fresh vegetables from the king's own garden. Many vegetables had to be chopped into tiny pieces, but because there were so many helpers in the kitchen, the soup was easy to prepare. When the king tasted the rich soup, he declared it to be a magnificent piece of work.

7. Which of the following is the moral of Fable A?

- Ⓐ Many hands make light work.
- Ⓑ Too many cooks spoil the broth.
- Ⓒ Never trust a cook who doesn't eat his own soup.
- Ⓓ A king can never be satisfied.

8. Which of the following is the moral of Fable B?

- Ⓐ Many hands make light work.
- Ⓑ Too many cooks spoil the broth.
- Ⓒ Never trust a cook who doesn't eat his own soup.
- Ⓓ A King can never be satisfied.

Question 9 is based on the poem below.

A spring morning
A strong breeze
Squirrels gaze lazily
Bud covered trees.
Many new born critters
An orange streaked dawn
Birds chirping happily
Wet lawn.
Rain coats and tees
Smell of fresh bloomed flowers
Buzzing of pollen seeking bees
Kites soaring in the sky.
Games at the park
Tractor drives across the field
Refreshing lemonade
What will this year's crops yield?
Dewy mornings
Afternoon rain showers
Muggy nights
Nature's beauty overpowers…
……Spring Happenings

9. What statement best summarizes this poem?

Ⓐ Spring is an uncomfortable season for some people.
Ⓑ Spring is about new life and new beginnings.
Ⓒ Spring comes after winter.
Ⓓ Spring is followed by summer.

Question 10 is based on the story below.

The Adventures of Huckleberry Finn by Mark Twain

Excerpt- public domain

I wanted to go and look at a place right about the middle of the island that I'd found when I was exploring; so we started and soon got to it, because the island was only three miles long and a quarter of a mile wide.

This place was a tolerable long, steep hill or ridge about forty feet high. We had a rough time getting to the top, the sides were so steep and the bushes so thick. We tramped and clumb around all over it, and by and by found a good big cavern in the rock, most up to the top on the side towards Illinois. The cavern was as big as two or three rooms bunched together, and Jim could stand up straight in it.

It was cool in there. Jim was for putting our traps in there right away, but I said we didn't want to be climbing up and down there all the time.

Jim said if we had the canoe hid in a good place, and had all the traps in the cavern, we could rush there if anybody was to come to the island, and they would never find us without dogs. And, besides, he said them little birds had said it was going to rain, and did I want the things to get wet?

So, we went back, and got the canoe, and paddled up abreast the cavern, and lugged all the traps up there. Then we hunted up a place close by to hide the canoe in, amongst the thick willows. We took some fish off of the lines and set them again, and begun to get ready for dinner.

The door of the cavern was big enough to roll a hogshead in, and on one side of the door the floor stuck out a little bit, and was flat and a good place to build a fire on. So we built it there and cooked dinner.

10. What details in the story tell you that the island was not very big? Write down the details that you find.

Question 11 is based on the story below.

Excerpt from Jo's Boys
Chapter 1 - Ten Years Later
by Louisa May Alcott

"If anyone had told me what wonderful changes were to take place here in ten years, I wouldn't have believed it." said Mrs. Jo to Mrs. Meg, as they sat on the piazza at Plumfield one summer day, looking about them with faces full of pride and pleasure.

"This is the sort of magic that money and kind hearts can work. I am sure Mr. Laurence could have no nobler monument than the college he so generously endowed; and a home like this will keep Aunt March's memory green as long as it lasts". Answered Mrs. Meg, always glad to praise the absent. "We used to believe in fairies, you remember, and plan what we'd ask for if we could have three wishes. Doesn't it seem as if mine had been really granted at last? Money, fame, and plenty of the work I love," said Mrs. Jo, carelessly rumpling up her hair as she clasped her hands over her head just as she used to do when a girl.

"I have had mine, and Amy is enjoying hers to her heart's content. If dear Marmee, John, and Beth were here, it would be quite perfect,"added Meg, with a tender quiver in her voice; for Marmee's place was empty now.

Jo put her hand on her sister's, and both sat silent for a little while, surveying the pleasant scene before them with mingled sad and happy thoughts.

It certainly did look as if magic had been at work, for quiet Plumfield was transformed into a busy little world. The house seemed more hospitable than ever, refreshed now with new paint, added wings, well-kept lawn and garden, and a prosperous air it had not worn when riotous boys swarmed everywhere and it was rather difficult for the Bhaers to make both ends meet. On the hill, where kites used to be flown, stood the fine college which Mr. Laurence's munificent legacy had built. Busy students were going to and fro along the paths once trodden by childish feet, and many young men and women were enjoying all the advantages that wealth, wisdom, and benevolence could give them.

11. **Visualize the scene described in this selection. If you were to make a drawing or painting, what would you do to be sure to include to help someone understand your thoughts? List 3 things to include based on the details of the passage.**

Question 12 is based on the poem below.

A GOOD PLAY

We built a ship upon the stairs,
All made of the back-bedroom chairs,
And filled it full of sofa pillows
To go a-sailing on the billows.
We took a saw and several nails,
And water in the nursery pails;
And Tom said, "Let us also take
An apple and a slice of cake";

—

Which was enough for Tom and me
To go a-sailing on, till tea.
We sailed along for days and days,
And had the very best of plays;
But Tom fell out and hurt his knee,
So there was no one left but me.

-By Robert Louis Stevenson
www.gutenburg.com public domain

12. After reading this poem, what can you conclude about what happened? Circle the correct answer choice.

Ⓐ Two boys were using their imagination while playing with make-believe ships on the stairs when one fell and was hurt.
Ⓑ The poet likes to build ships everywhere.
Ⓒ The boys played for days and days in the sea.
Ⓓ Both B and C.

Chapter 2

Lesson 4: Calling All Characters

Trait: a personal characteristic or quality of a person, plant or animal.
Example: a person might be conceited, selfish or generous.

Motivation: something that causes a person or animal to act in a certain way.
Example: Jack was so motivated to win the race that he spent all of this free time training. The dog learned tricks quickly because he knew he would get a reward.

Feelings: emotions, such as jealousy, joy, sadness.

Let us understand the concept with an example.

The Race
By Carla Gajewskey

Publisher's note: The original story has been edited with minor changes.

Jack knew he was the fastest rabbit in California. He also thought he was the most handsome rabbit in California. He was skinny like a green bean and his very tall ears stood straight up on his head. Because he was so skinny, he could hop through brush much faster than most other rabbits.

One day he saw a flyer inviting all rabbits to enter the 35th annual Rabbit Run. The winner would receive a golden trophy filled with wonderful juicy carrots. Jack signed up and practiced racing the entire week before the race. On the day of the race, all sizes, shapes and colors of rabbits showed up to the race. One rabbit, whose long ears hung to the ground, hopped up to Jack and said, "Hi, my name is Marty. I'm going to win that carrot cup for my Mama and her 7 baby rabbits. What is your name?"
Jack just said, "Jack."

Marty continued talking and talking. Jack just listened, but looked disturbed; he was not enjoying hearing Marty's continuous talking.

Race time. All the rabbits lined up at the starting line, with Marty lining up next to Jack. Marty wished Jack luck. The race started; Jack took off in a cloud of dust and took the lead, but when he looked back to see where the other rabbits were, he ran right into a thorn bush and got tangled up. The other rabbits began to pass him by; no one stopped to help Jack except Marty. Jack said, "Marty! What are you doing? You need to go and win the race for your Mama!" But Marty said, "You should always stop and help someone in need and everything else will work out." When Marty said this, Jack felt bad for feeling annoyed at Marty earlier.

Once he got free from the bush, Marty asked Jack if he wanted to the race. Jack said OK and smiled, and they asked another animal to be the starter. Jack took off in a cloud of dust but Marty not only passed him, but caught up and passed all the other racers and won the race. Jack caught up with him and asked him how he did it. Marty replied, "It's just the way I am made. My ears hang down so they don't catch the wind to slow me down when I run, like yours do." Jack congratulated Marty and started to walk off. Marty called after him, "Come have some juicy carrots with me!" Jack said, "I thought they were for your family?" Marty said, "They are! But friends are family too!"

Describe characters in a story (e.g., their traits, motivations, or feelings) and explain how their actions contribute to the sequence of events

This is what you might write.

Jack was very conceited ("Jack knew he was the fastest rabbit in California" and "He also thought he was the most handsome rabbit in California."). He was very motivated to win the Rabbit Run race, and did not want to be distracted, so he felt annoyed when Marty came up to him before the race and talked and talked. But then during the race Jack became tangled in the bush and all the other rabbits passed him by, except Marty, who showed kindness and caring by stopping to free Jack. This made Jack feel guilty for being annoyed at Marty when they first met. Jack realized that an act of kindness was more important than winning a race. Then, when the race was over, Jack congratulated Marty in a show of good sportsmanship. Marty again showed his caring and his generosity by offering to share his prize of carrots with Jack. Marty's actions taught Jack a lesson and probably changed Jack's behavior from then on.

You can scan the QR code given below or use the URL to access additional EdSearch resources including videos and mobile apps related to *Calling All Characters*.

Question 1 is based on the story below.

After reading the story, enter the details in the map below. This will help you to answer the questions that follow.

Margaret was a simple lady who lived in a village with her husband, Robert. They had a daughter named Amy. Every day at sunrise, Margaret would wake up, cook, clean, and feed the cattle. Robert would milk the cows and then take the dogs for a long walk. Amy would study, help her mother for some time, and then get ready for school.

Amy studied in a school that was far away from her house, but she loved going to school. She went with her friends, Ingrid and Rebecca. They would walk together chatting, laughing, and singing songs as they went. They had to cross a river on the way. The only way they could cross it was by walking on a narrow bridge.

One day Margaret, Robert, Amy, and her friends were walking on the narrow bridge one behind the other. Amy and her friends were off to school, as usual, Margaret and Robert wanted to go to the market on the other side of the river to buy groceries for the house.

As they were crossing the narrow bridge, Rebecca slipped. She gave a frightened scream, clutching Ingrid, who was in front of her. Both of them lost their balance and fell into the river. Amy clutched her mother in fright. For a moment, she hesitated and then threw herself into the river after her friends, determined to save them.

Margaret screamed, and Robert jumped into the river. Some passers-by also jumped into the river and rescued the children, who were dripping wet, and shivering with fright.

That night, Robert patted his daughter Amy, and said, "You are a brave girl Amy, I'm proud of you."

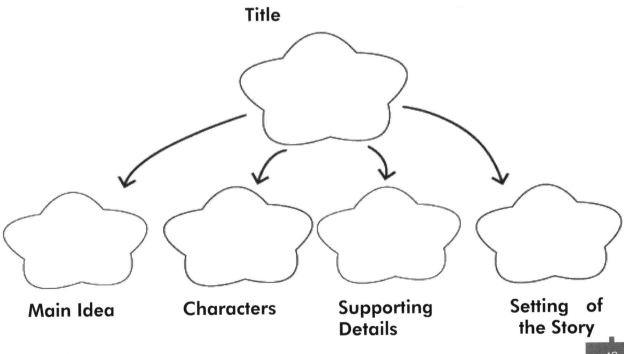

1. Part A

In this story, Amy was scared but she jumped into the river. What caused Amy to ignore her fear?

Ⓐ Amy wanted to show off.
Ⓑ Amy wanted to escape.
Ⓒ Amy wanted to save her friends.
Ⓓ Amy wanted to join the fun.

1. Part B

Why did Robert jump into the river?

Ⓐ He wanted to save the girls.
Ⓑ He wanted to go for a swim.
Ⓒ He wanted to bathe in the river.
Ⓓ He was feeling hot.

Question 2 and 3 are based on the story below.

After reading the story, enter the details in the map below. This will help you to answer the questions that follow.

One day, a baby elephant was happily dancing through the jungle, nodding his head and lifting his trunk to trumpet loudly.

The loud sound woke up a monkey who was sleeping in a tree nearby. He was very angry. He scolded the elephant and asked him to keep quiet.

"You silly animal," he said. "Can't you keep quiet? I'm sleeping."

"Oh, sorry," said the little elephant, and walked on. After some time, the little elephant reached a river and saw some beautiful swans there. He gazed at the beautiful birds. The swans looked at him and began to laugh.

"Oh! Look at that big creature," they said. "What a long nose, his ears are like fans, and look at his skin, it's much too big for him. He looks like a big wrinkled bag with all of those folds!" They laughed at him and swam away.

The little elephant was very sad. He tried to smooth out his skin with his trunk, but it was no good. He thought, "Why am I so ugly? Let me hide so that no one can see me."

He tried to hide in a thick bush, but he disturbed some nests. The birds flew above his head, crying loudly while trying to peck at him.

The little elephant ran for cover. He went behind a big rock to hide. Suddenly, he saw a big bear coming towards him. It was growling and appeared to be very angry. The little elephant was very frightened and trumpeted loudly. Just as he trumpeted, he heard a loud crashing and stomping. A herd of elephants came charging to the rescue you. You're so mighty and strong," he continued.

"But you are," replied the elephants. "You're a perfect little elephant." The little elephant danced for joy, he trumpeted loudly, and walked away happily with the other elephants following behind.

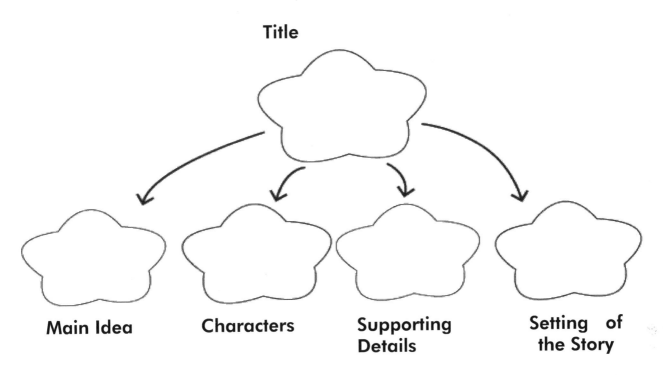

Title

Main Idea   **Characters**   **Supporting Details**   **Setting of the Story**

2. **Which of the little elephant's actions showed it was happy?**

Ⓐ It danced along happily.
Ⓑ It was walking thoughtfully.
Ⓒ It was swaying from side to side.
Ⓓ It was sleeping peacefully.

3. **Why does the little elephant tell the other elephants, "I wish I could be like you"?**

Ⓐ He loved the elephants.
Ⓑ He admired them because they were mighty and strong.
Ⓒ He was not an elephant.
Ⓓ He was frightened of them.

Question 4 is based on the story below.

After reading the story, enter the details in the map below. This will help you to answer the questions that follow.

Once upon a time, there was a wealthy woman that had very poor eyesight. She decided to call a doctor to ask if he could restore her eyesight. The doctor promised to cure her but told her that she had to pay him a huge fee. He also told her that throughout the treatment she had to keep her eyes closed. The woman agreed to both requirements.

The doctor began the treatment in the woman's home. Every day the doctor stole something from the lady's house. The treatment continued a lengthy period of time. Finally, when he had emptied her house, the doctor told her that he had finished her treatment and that her eyesight was restored. The woman was very happy that the treatment was over, but she refused to pay the doctor. The doctor was very angry that she refused to pay his hefty fee. He told her that he was taking her to court. She just laughed at him.

When the judge asked the woman to explain why she didn't pay the doctor, the woman said, "Sir, before the operation, I was partially blind, but at least I could see the things in my home." She continued, "But now after the treatment, I am unable to see anything in my home. The woman solemnly told the judge, I must be totally blind because I can see nothing."

The judge looked at the doctor, who hung his head in shame. The doctor realized that the woman knew that he had stolen all her things. He felt ashamed and returned everything he had stolen. The doctor also said the woman did not owe him a fee for the treatment.

Title

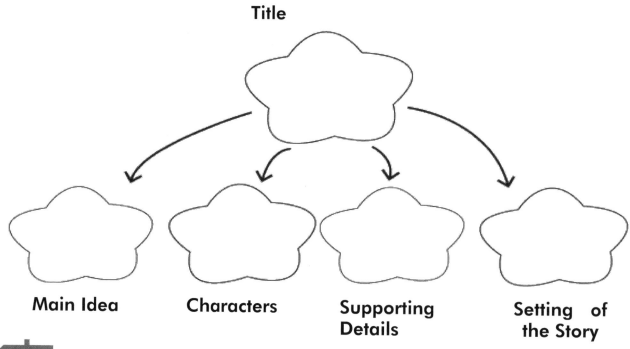

Main Idea   Characters   Supporting Details   Setting of the Story

4. Why did the doctor tell the old woman, "You must keep your eyes closed during the treatment"?

Ⓐ He wanted her to relax.
Ⓑ He did not want her to see him stealing the things from her house.
Ⓒ He could perform the operation better.
Ⓓ She would get her eyesight faster if she closed her eyes.

Question 5 is based on the story below.

After reading the story, enter the details in the map below. This will help you to answer the questions that follow.

Brandon lived with his mother at one end of the forest. His school was at the other end of the forest. Every day he had to go through the forest to get to school and the forest was very scary.

One day he told his mother that he felt very scared to cross that forest. His mother said, "Don't be scared" "Your brother lives in the forest. Whenever you get scared, you can always call him. He won't answer you but he will see that no harm comes to you."

"Why did you not tell me about my brother earlier? What is his name?"

Mother said, "His name is Courage. Whenever you get frightened, call his name, and he will silently follow you to school and see that you come back home safely."

The next day Brandon was happy to get ready for school. He was not scared as he went through the forest on the way to school. That day, while coming home from school, he got scared when he heard the sounds of animals. He then remembered his mother's words that his brother would protect him whenever he was frightened. Brandon called out "Courage, Courage" with full confidence. Suddenly he began to feel better. He began to feel brave. He again called out, "Courage!, Courage!" He thought that his brother was silently following him, he began to sing softly and then loudly. He realized that he was not frightened after all. He crossed the forest confidently with courage.

The only thing we need to have is confidence and courage in ourselves to move ahead.

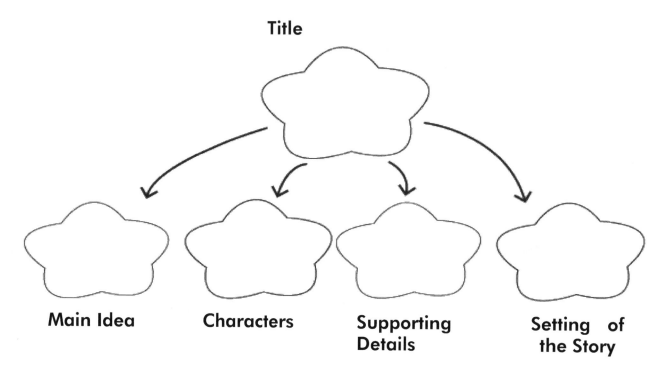

Title

Main Idea **Characters** **Supporting Details** **Setting of the Story**

5. Why did Brandon begin to feel brave?

- Ⓐ He fought with the animals and won.
- Ⓑ He began to walk around the forest instead of through the forest.
- Ⓒ He found courage and confidence.
- Ⓓ He stopped going to school.

Question 6 is based on the paragraph below.

How can I describe the creature that I have taken such pains to form? He was horrifying in every way. So wild were my thoughts that I seemed to see him everywhere. When at last I encountered him again, he said, "Remember, you have made me bigger and more powerful than you. Do not try to harm me. Be kind to me, as you should. Remember that I am your creature. I ought to be your son, but you rejected me for no reason. I was once good and kind, but everywhere I went people hated and feared me because of my hideous appearance. Misery has made me evil."

6. Which of the following does NOT describe the monster?

- Ⓐ He was frightening.
- Ⓑ He was strong.
- Ⓒ He was gentle.
- Ⓓ He was large.

Question 7 is based on the story below.

After reading the story, enter the details in the map below. This will help you to answer the questions that follow.

My First Trip to the Beach

About three weeks ago, Jeremiah's parents surprised him with some news. They were taking him to the beach. He was excited and couldn't wait to tell all of his friends at school.

Soon enough, Friday afternoon arrived. Jeremiah, his sister, his parents, and his nanny all loaded into the car, and set out for the long drive to Destin, Florida. Listening to DVD's grew old rather quickly. A nap was sure to allow Jeremiah to get closer to Florida without growing bored from the ride.

When he awoke from his nap, it was time to stop for dinner. He exited the car, excited to stretch his legs. "Come on, Jeremiah," exclaimed his nanny. He was glad that she had been able to come to the beach. This was also going to be her first time seeing the ocean.

After a quick meal at a fast-food restaurant, the family piled back into the car.

The family arrived at their condo, almost too tired to enjoy the peaceful sound of the ocean. As Jeremiah headed to bed, he knew that the beach would be his to explore in a few hours. He stretched out his small frame across the twin-sized bed and soon fell asleep. He awoke a few hours later, hearing his dad outside on the balcony.

When Jeremiah finally saw the view in the daylight, he was in awe. Beautiful green waters lay off in the distance. They seemed to go on and on, as far as his eyes could see. The sand reminded him of snow.

"Wanna go for a walk?" asked his dad.

Jeremiah smiled, "Yes!" Running back inside, he threw his shoes on. His dad said that he didn't want to try to wear those in the soft, grainy sand. He dressed, and then off they went.

"What's this?" asked Jeremiah, pointing to a loose mound of sand.

"This is a sand dune, it keeps the buildings safe," his dad replied.

"Oh, okay…" Jeremiah and his dad walked along the ocean's edge. There were few words spoken, but the looks on their faces expressed feelings of happiness, as they walked along the beautiful water's edge.

Title

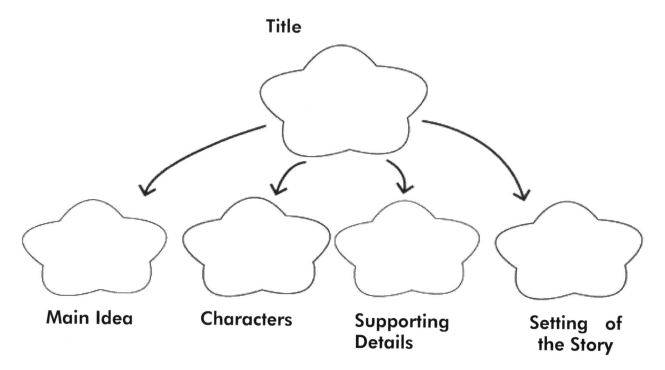

Main Idea **Characters** **Supporting Details** **Setting of the Story**

7. Which statement BEST describes Jeremiah?

Ⓐ He had traveled a lot.
Ⓑ He was not familiar with the beach.
Ⓒ He was very moody.
Ⓓ He always had to have his way.

Question 8 and 9 are based on the story below.

After reading the story, enter the details in the map below. This will help you to answer the questions that follow.

Danny had always been a different kind of child, so I wasn't real happy when Xavier started hanging out with him. I didn't really know how to handle the situation, but I didn't want to be one of those parents who told him he had to stop. When Xavier told me about playing with Danny that first day at recess, I remember thinking, "Oh no…"

It has been about a month since that day, and every afternoon I still ask if anyone lost recess today. It is my way of finding out if Danny or Xavier got into any trouble. This way it doesn't seem like I am pointing the finger at Danny. Those first few times that I asked, it seemed that Xavier would usually tell me something silly that Danny did to get in trouble: throws pit balls, spit wads, pour milk onto another student's mashed potatoes, run in the hallway, etc. Not bad things, just things that showed disrespect. As the days passed, either Xavier realized that I was fed up with Danny's silliness or wasn't Danny getting into as much trouble.

I have agreed to let Danny spend the night tonight. The boys are excited about sleeping outside in the tent, and I have arranged for them to make S'mores, have a small campfire, and enjoy the comforts of almost being alone in the wilderness. "Mom, where are you? This is Danny." I stare at Danny. He looks sweet enough. His short haircut makes him look much younger than eight, well, assuming that he is the same age as Xavier.

"Hi, Mrs."
"Just call me Ann. Danny, do you want to see Xavier's room?" I asked.

Danny smiled at me and I was hooked. His crystal blue eyes lit up, and his left cheek had a small, but noticeable dimple. I patted Danny on the back. "We are glad you came to visit," I stated. I walked the boys down the hallway to Xavier's room.

"What's this?" Xavier asked.
"Since this is your first official camp out, I thought you needed the right pajamas. I just guessed your size, Danny; let's hope they fit." Danny scooped the pajamas up, while Xavier shrugged.

"Is this the bathroom?" I nodded. Moments later, Danny returned, wearing his new pajamas. They were a little large, but they would do. The boy that I had pegged to be the troublemaker seemed so sweet. He threw his tiny arms around me. "These are great…" said Danny. I could see the tears in his eyes, and I pulled him even closer.

"I am glad that you like them, Danny," I stated.

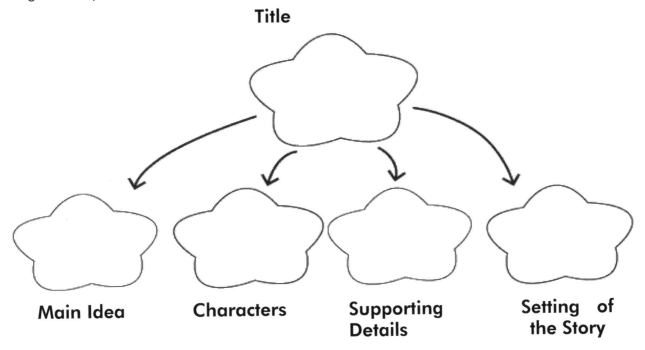

Title

Main Idea   **Characters**   **Supporting Details**   **Setting of the Story**

8. Which word BEST describes Xavier's mom?

Ⓐ harsh
Ⓑ unforgiving
Ⓒ open-minded
Ⓓ sad

9. How were Danny and Xavier different?

Ⓐ Danny often gets in trouble, while Xavier follows the rules.
Ⓑ Danny follows the rules, while Xavier often gets in trouble.
Ⓒ Xavier lives with his mom, but Danny does not.
Ⓓ Both boys are very much alike, which is why their mom wanted them to be friends.

Question 10 and 11 are based on the story below.

Maggie's Dilemma?

Maggie has many things to accomplish over the weekend. She wants to go to a friend's house for a party on Sunday afternoon. If she doesn't get her chores and homework done, she is afraid that her parents will not let her attend the party.

As she is getting ready for bed, Friday night, she is worrying and wondering how she can do everything before the party on Sunday. Her mother tells her that she needs to prioritize her life. Maggie is not sure what that means. She thinks to herself, "What is prioritize? How does that help me in my life?"

Her older brother, Ronny, comes into her room. He asks her, "Hey, Sis, why the puzzled look? Why are you just sitting there on your bed looking around your room?"

"Ronny, what does it mean when Mom tells me I need to prioritize my life?"
"What's wrong with my life?"

Ron laughs and tells her that she has a tendency to try to do too much stuff in too little time. He suggests that she make a list of what she needs to do. Then, she needs to make a list of what she wants to do. Again, Maggie looks confused.

He takes out one of her notebooks and starts to write. She watches as he puts his name at the top of the list along with the words - Have to Do. Then he makes numbers going down each side. He writes, clean room as number 1. For number 2, he puts down take out the trash. Ron then writes down, mow the yard for number 3.

On another sheet of paper, he does the same thing, only this time after his name, he writes- Want to Do. On the second list, the number 1 is watch wrestling on TV. Number 2 is play video games.

Suddenly, Maggie gets it! "Oh, I see now. Prioritize means to put things in order of importance."

Her brother replies, "Duh, I knew I could help out!" Ron laughs along with Maggie. She is no longer puzzled and starts to write.

10. What was the problem that Maggie was having? Select the correct answer by circling it.

Ⓐ She kept her room too messy.
Ⓑ She couldn't decide what her brother wanted her to do.
Ⓒ Maggie did not know how she could do everything she needed to do and wanted to do over the weekend.
Ⓓ None of the above.

11. What do you think Maggie will do next?
   Write at least 3 sentences to tell what you think she will do next based on this story. Be sure to use complete sentences in your answer.

Question 12 is based on the story below.

Bringing a Bear to School

Tyrone was so happy that his teacher said they were going to have a special celebration for a unit they had been studying on Bears in his class. They had been reading many bear books lately. Some of the books were about real bears and some were books about make-believe bears like Paddington and others. Mr. Clark, his teacher, wanted the students to relate to their own real-life experiences. The students were talking about the celebration during class one day.

Mr. Clark told them they could bring a stuffed bear from home if they wanted to or another stuffed animal for the day of the celebration. The girls were all excited. The boys were laughing and snickering about how dumb that idea was. They were saying only sissies would bring or have a stuffed toy. Tyrone's mouth frowned. He loved his Beary. He had Beary since he was just a tiny baby. Tyrone's grandfather had brought it to his mom on the day Tyrone was born. His grandfather had passed away several years later, and Tyrone held Beary all the time he thought about his grandfather. He even saved his allowance and special birthday money to buy his stuffed bear clothes. When Tyrone joined the soccer team, Beary got a soccer outfit. When he joined t-ball, Beary got a baseball uniform, too. So why were the boys making fun of having a stuffed bear? Tyrone did not understand.

The teacher sent home a note the weekend before the celebration explaining to parents what the next school day (Monday) would be like. Mr. Clark said that the students could bring their own stuffed animal if they chose to do so for a show and tell part of the celebration. They were even having zoo personnel come and share their experiences with the bears at the zoo. There would be Bear shaped cookies and cakes, too! Mr. Clark was also bringing his video of his trip to Russia where he saw many polar bears.

It sounded like so much fun! But, Tyrone was still hesitant on whether or not he should bring Beary to school. He wanted to show him off with his clothes and all. He wanted to tell the story of how his grandfather bought him the bear and how much it means to him still.

When Tyrone got home from school on Friday afternoon, he showed his mom the note from Mr. Clark. He had a puzzled look on his face. His mom said it sounded like the class was going to have a wonderful time on Monday. His sister, LaTasha, started laughing loudly. "Oh, please tell me you are not thinking of taking Beary?" she exclaimed.

"I was, but the other boys would probably make fun of me."
His mom said, "Why would they do that, Tyrone? Don't you think they have stuffed animals, too?"
"Maybe mom, but they would never admit it or bring them to school."

So all weekend long, Tyrone pondered what to do. Right before bedtime on Sunday night, he made his decision. Beary and his outfits were ready to go!

On Monday morning, Tyrone's mom decided she would take him to school herself rather than have him walk or ride the bus. When they arrived at his class, Mr. Clark was greeting all of the classmates. The entire classroom was decorated with bears of all sorts. On the front of Mr. Clark's desk was a beautiful stuffed bear. A sign in front said, "My Buddy!" Tyrone grinned from ear to ear as he joyfully took out Beary, dressed him in his baseball uniform, and put him on his desk. He made his own sign, "My Beary!"

Needless to say it was a great day for Tyrone. Several of the other boys had brought their stuffed animals and stuffed bears, too.

12. In your own words, write a sentence explaining what Beary means to Tyrone and why. Use the evidence in the story for your answer.

Chapter 2

Lesson 5: A Chain of Events

You can scan the QR code given below or use the URL to access additional EdSearch resources including videos and mobile apps related to *A Chain of Events*.

 **ed)Search**

A Chain of Events

URL	QR Code
http://www.lumoslearning.com/a/rl33	

Question 1 is based on the story below.

One day, a baby elephant was happily dancing through the jungle, nodding his head and lifting his trunk to trumpet loudly.

The loud sound woke up a monkey who was sleeping in a tree nearby. He was very angry. He scolded the elephant and asked him to keep quiet.

"You silly animal," he said. "Can't you keep quiet? I'm sleeping."

"Oh, sorry," said the little elephant, and walked on. After some time, the little elephant reached a river and saw some beautiful swans there. He gazed at the beautiful birds. The swans looked at him and began to laugh.

"Oh! Look at that big creature," they said. "What a long nose, his ears are like fans, and look at his skin, it's much too big for him. He looks like a big wrinkled bag with all of those folds!" They laughed at him and swam away.

The little elephant was very sad. He tried to smooth out his skin with his trunk, but it was no good. He thought, "Why am I so ugly? Let me hide so that no one can see me."

He tried to hide in a thick bush, but he disturbed some nests. The birds flew above his head, crying loudly while trying to peck at him.

The little elephant ran for cover. He went behind a big rock to hide. Suddenly, he saw a big bear coming towards him. It was growling and appeared to be very angry. The little elephant was very frightened and trumpeted loudly. Just as he trumpeted, he heard a loud crashing and stomping. A herd of elephants came charging to the rescue.

Seeing the herd, the frightened bear ran away.

The little elephant joyfully ran to the big elephants, thanked them, and said, "I wish I could be like you. You're so mighty and strong," he continued.

"But you are," replied the elephants. "You're a perfect little elephant." The little elephant danced for joy; he trumpeted loudly and walked away happily with the other elephants following behind.

1. Choose the correct set of words to fill in the blank.

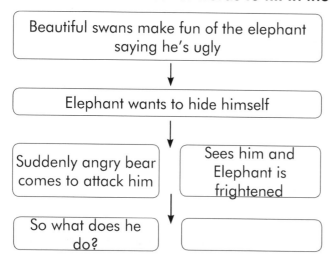

- Ⓐ He asks the bear to leave him.
- Ⓑ He began to trumpet loudly.
- Ⓒ He ran as fast as he could.
- Ⓓ He was crying.

Question 2 is based on the story below.

Margaret was a simple lady who lived in a village with her husband, Robert. They had a daughter named Amy. Every day at sunrise, Margaret would wake up, cook, clean, and feed the cattle. Robert would milk the cows and then take the dogs for a long walk. Amy would study, help her mother for some time, and then get ready for school.

Amy studied in a school that was far away from her house, but she loved going to school. She went with her friends, Ingrid and Rebecca. They would walk together chatting, laughing, and singing songs as they went. They had to cross a river on the way. The only way they could cross it was by walking on a narrow bridge.

One day Margaret, Robert, Amy, and her friends were walking on the narrow bridge one behind the other. Amy and her friends were off to school, as usual, Margaret and Robert wanted to go to the market on the other side of the river to buy groceries for the house.

As they were crossing the narrow bridge, Rebecca slipped. She gave a frightened scream, clutching Ingrid, who was in front of her. Both of them lost their balance and fell into the river. Amy clutched her mother in fright. For a moment she hesitated and then threw herself into the river after her friends, determined to save them.

Margaret screamed, and Robert jumped into the river. Some passers-by also jumped into the river and rescued the children, who were dripping wet and shivering with fright.

That night Robert patted his daughter Amy and said, "You are a brave girl Amy, I'm proud of you."

2. What happened after Rebecca grabbed Ingrid on the bridge?

   Ⓐ Margaret and Robert went on the other side of the river.
   Ⓑ Robert screamed.
   Ⓒ The girls fell into the river.
   Ⓓ Margaret helped her family by cooking and cleaning.

3. Which of the following answers best shows the chain of events?

(1) I was very mad at my sister for eating the cookie.
(2) "Why did you eat the last cookie?" I asked.
(3) Sister ate the last cookie in the cookie jar.
(4) "Sorry," she said, "I was really hungry."

   Ⓐ 3,1,4,2
   Ⓑ 3,1,2,4
   Ⓒ 1,2,3,4
   Ⓓ 2,3,4,1

Question 4 is based on the poem below.

I quarreled with my brother
I don't know what about,
One thing led to another
And somehow we fell out.
The start of it was slight,
The end of it was strong,
He said he was right,
I knew he was wrong!
We hated one another.
The afternoon turned black.
Then suddenly my brother
Thumped me on the back.
And said, "Oh, come along!
We can't go on all night-
I was in the wrong."
So he was in the right.

-by Eleanor Farjeon

4. Which event happened last in the poem?

   Ⓐ The two brothers argued.
   Ⓑ One brother apologized to the other.
   Ⓒ The weather turned rainy.
   Ⓓ The two brothers played together.

Question 5 is based on the passage below.

Cell Phones in the Classroom

A familiar ringtone sounds in the classroom directing everyone's attention to a shy student in the back row. Several years ago, this would have seemed a bit strange, but not today. A recent study showed that one in three third-grade students have a cell phone. With so many students having access to technology devices, a lot of talks have gone into deciding whether to use them as learning tools or to ban them from the classroom.

Let's think about cell phones' role as learning tools. Annie needs a calculator but forgot hers. She takes out her cell phone and can use the calculator app on the phone. Just across the room, Johnny is trying to spell the word "similar," so he uses the dictionary app on his phone to find the correct spelling. Mitchell, has completed all of his work early, so he decides to use the multiplication app on his phone to review multiplication facts in a fun and interactive way. These devices are causing teachers and other school officials to see that cell phones give students access to resources that actually save schools money.

While cell phones may sound great, not every school district is ready to lift the cell phone ban. There are still those that have major concerns. One concern is what to do about students who do not have a cell phone. Another worry is how to make sure students are using the phone as a learning tool instead of texting and social media. Additional concerns arise with how to address when a phone is broken or stolen while at school. Certainly, the list of problems that some schools have goes on and on.

The answer isn't clear for schools across the United States. Some schools are starting to lift the cell phone ban, but others are keeping it in place. As students pack backpacks with cell phones, the discussion of having them in the classroom will certainly continue.

5. **According to the passage, what happened before Mitchell opened the multiplication app on his phone?**

   Ⓐ His teacher told him to play outside.
   Ⓑ He completed all of his assignments.
   Ⓒ He got bored.
   Ⓓ He heard an alarm.

Question 8 is based on the story below.

Once upon a time, there was a wealthy woman that had very poor eyesight. She decided to call a doctor to ask if he could restore her eyesight. The doctor promised to cure her but told her that she had to pay him a huge fee. He also told her that throughout the treatment she had to keep her eyes closed. The woman agreed to both requirements.

The doctor began the treatment in the woman's home. Every day the doctor stole something from the lady's house. The treatment lasted a lengthy period of time. Finally, when he had emptied her house, the doctor told her that he had finished her treatment and that her eyesight was restored.

The woman was very happy that the treatment was over, but she refused to pay the doctor. The doctor was very angry that she refused to pay his hefty fee. He told her that he was taking her to court. She just laughed at him.

When the judge asked the woman to explain why she didn't pay the doctor, the woman said, "Sir, before the operation, I was partially blind, but at least I could see the things in my home." She continued, "But now after the treatment, I am unable to see anything in my home. The woman solemnly told the judge, I must be totally blind because I can see nothing."

The judge looked at the doctor, who hung his head in shame. The doctor realized that the woman knew that he had stolen all her things. He felt ashamed and returned everything he had stolen. The doctor also said the woman did not owe him a fee for the treatment.

8. Choose the correct sentence that concludes the chain of events.

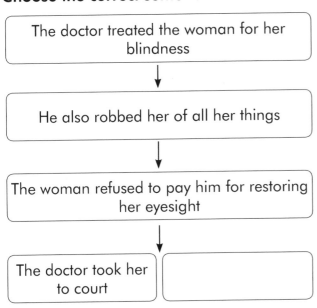

Ⓐ   The judge made the old woman pay the doctor his fee.
Ⓑ   The doctor paid the woman his fee.
Ⓒ   The doctor refused to take his fees.
Ⓓ   The doctor returned everything he had stolen.

Question 9 is based on the paragraph below.

An astronomer used to go out every night to observe stars. Often, he would be seen with a telescope in one hand and a notebook in the other. One evening, while he wandered through the suburbs with his attention fixed on the sky, he accidentally fell into a deep uncovered well. He cried out loudly for help. As he waited to be rescued, he moaned and howled about his sores and bruises. His neighbor was passing by and happened to hear his wailing and weeping. He quickly helped him out of the well. After he came to know how the accident happened, this is what he said to the astronomer: "Hark you old fellow, why in striving to pry into heaven, do you not manage to see what is on earth?"

9. Which event happened first in the story?

Ⓐ A neighbor heard the astronomer fall in a well.
Ⓑ The neighbor helped the astronomer out of the well.
Ⓒ The neighbor yelled at the astronomer for not paying attention.
Ⓓ The astronomer went for a walk.

Question 10 is based on the story below.

After reading the story, enter the details in the map below. This will help you to answer the questions that follow.

I Don't Want To Go

Emily zipped up her suitcase, sighed loudly, and then lugged it out to the Family Utility Vehicle. "Why do I have to go?" she asked.
"This is a family vacation," replied her dad.

Sure it was, she thought. The idea of spending three entire days and nights sleeping in a tent out in the wilderness that was named after the explorer Daniel Boone did not appeal to her girly side. "Mom, can we stay…?"

Before she could finish, Emily's younger brother came bolting out the door, his suitcase overflowing, and his momentum almost knocking her to the ground. "Let's go, let's go."

Emily climbed into the backseat, her MP3 player blasting loudly; at least she had some piece of civilization left. As they drove for what seemed like forever, Emily enjoyed peering out the window. As they got farther and farther away from the city, she began to catch glimpses of rabbits, squirrels, and various birds that she wasn't used to seeing. The tall buildings and annoying noises of the city began to be replaced by a peaceful quiet. She turned her music off, but kept the ear buds in place, as she didn't want anyone to know that she was enjoying the ride. Finally, she saw the sign: Welcome to the Daniel Boone National Forest.

"Can we hike to the falls?" her brother asked.
She exited the vehicle, declared that she was ready for a walk. She had heard about Cumberland Falls but had never actually seen them. Some of her classmates had mentioned that they were smaller, but

a lot like Niagara Falls. She had no desire to let the others know she was excited, but she hoped that her dad would say that they could go exploring.

Looking around her, she saw huge mountains that seemed to tower above the river below. This was much different from the small subdivision that she called home. Just maybe the next three days wouldn't be so bad. As she removed her earbuds, she smiled, as a small deer crossed the pathway several hundred feet in the distance. The first live deer that she had ever seen was when she was twelve. " Wow, this is really amazing! Let's take that walk, Dad."
"Really?" he asked.

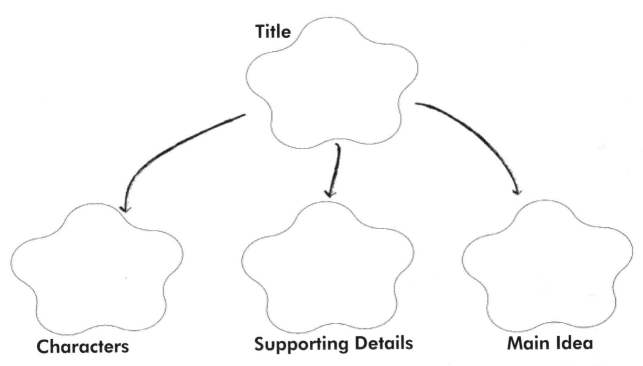

10. What happened to get Emily more interested in her camping trip with the family?

Ⓐ She listened to her MP3 player.
Ⓑ She saw a lot of wild animals that she was not used to seeing.
Ⓒ Her dad told her about a trip when he used to go camping with his parents.
Ⓓ Her brother started crying because he did not want her to be sad.

Question 11 is based on the story below.

Christopher's Magic Reading Tricks!

There are many ways to help you in understanding things you read.
Here are some examples of ways that Christopher uses to help him in his reading.

The first one is what his teacher calls prior knowledge. This means that as you read you think -what do I already know if anything about this topic? Christopher says it helps him remember if he has ever read anything about it before. Then he uses that and tries to learn something new as he reads.

The second way is to question as you read. Think to yourself- what is the author trying to tell me, before, during and after you read? Christopher likes to say- "Self, what is it I am trying to learn as I read this? Can I repeat it after I read it?"

The third and Christopher says the most fun is to make a picture in your mind while you read. He says that if it is a story, you can even make a movie in your mind! Teachers use the term visualize your reading.

The fourth strategy or technique that Christopher learned from his teacher is to infer. This one means that Christopher has to use clues in the reading to figure out what is going on or what the author really means in the story.

The most favorite way for Christopher to get more out of what he has read is to summarize the reading. He tells his friends who may be struggling with this to tell what's important in a sentence or two after you read.

Christopher likes to reread his passages or stories more than one time when he knows he is going to be tested over them or asked questions about them. He says he also takes notes and sometimes uses more than one way to help him read better.

He had a hard time with reading when he was in first and second grade, but now since he uses these "magic tricks" to reading, he loves reading!

11. What is Christopher's favorite reading trick? Write your answer in the box given below.

Question 12 is based on the story below.

Bringing a Bear to School

Tyrone was so happy that his teacher said they were going to have a special celebration for a unit they had been studying on Bears in his class. They had been reading many bear books lately. Some of the books were about real bears and some were books about make-believe bears like Paddington and others. Mr. Clark, his teacher, wanted the students to relate to their own real-life experiences. The students were talking about the celebration during class one day.

Mr. Clark told them they could bring a stuffed bear from home if they wanted to or another stuffed animal for the day of the celebration. The girls were all excited. The boys were laughing and snickering about how dumb that idea was. They were saying only sissies would bring or have a stuffed toy. Tyrone's mouth frowned. He loved his Beary. He had Beary since he was just a tiny baby. Tyrone's grandfather had brought it to his mom on the day Tyrone was born. His grandfather had passed away several years later, and Tyrone held Beary all the time he thought about his grandfather. He even saved his allowance and special birthday money to buy his stuffed bear clothes. When Tyrone joined the soccer team, Beary got a soccer outfit. When he joined t-ball, Beary got a baseball uniform, too. So why were the boys making fun of having a stuffed bear? Tyrone did not understand.

The teacher sent home a note the weekend before the celebration explaining to parents what the next school day (Monday) would be like. Mr. Clark said that the students could bring their own stuffed animal if they chose to do so for a show and tell part of the celebration. They were even having zoo personnel come and share their experiences with the bears at the zoo. There would be Bear shaped cookies and cakes, too! Mr. Clark was also bringing his video of his trip to Russia where he saw many polar bears.

It sounded like so much fun! But, Tyrone was still hesitant on whether or not he should bring Beary to school. He wanted to show him off with his clothes and all. He wanted to tell the story of how his grandfather bought him the bear and how much it means to him still.

When Tyrone got home from school on Friday afternoon, he showed his mom the note from Mr. Clark. He had a puzzled look on his face. His mom said it sounded like the class was going to have a wonderful time on Monday. His sister, LaTasha, started laughing loudly. "Oh, please tell me you are not thinking of taking Beary?" she exclaimed.

"I was, but the other boys would probably make fun of me."
His mom said, "Why would they do that, Tyrone? Don't you think they have stuffed animals, too?"
"Maybe mom, but they would never admit it or bring them to school."

So all weekend long, Tyrone pondered what to do. Right before bedtime on Sunday night, he made his decision. Beary and his outfits were ready to go!

On Monday morning, Tyrone's mom decided she would take him to school herself rather than have him walk or ride the bus. When they arrived at his class, Mr. Clark was greeting all of the classmates. The entire classroom was decorated with bears of all sorts. On the front of Mr. Clark's desk was a beautiful stuffed bear. A sign in front said, "My Buddy!" Tyrone grinned from ear to ear as he joyfully took out Beary, dressed him in his baseball uniform, and put him on his desk. He made his own sign, "My Beary!"

Needless to say it was a great day for Tyrone. Several of the other boys had brought their stuffed animals and stuffed bears, too.

12. Why did Mr. Clark decide to have a celebration for his class? Circle the correct answer choice.

Ⓐ It was his birthday and he wanted the students to have fun.

Ⓑ He liked celebrations.

Ⓒ The class was finishing a unit on bears and he wanted to wrap it up with real life experiences for the children.

Ⓓ None of the above.

Question 13 is based on the story below.

Blue Hole

Sarah loved to go swimming at the local "Blue Hole" near her grandmother's house. The Blue Hole was nicknamed that because it was so crystal blue year round. It was located at the deep end of a creek bed. Regardless of whether it was winter, spring, summer or fall, the Blue Hole was ice cold, as well.

One early Saturday spring morning, Sarah, her friend Blaire, and her younger cousin Cody, were headed to the Blue Hole on their bikes. The traffic suddenly picked up and the old country gravel road was full of cars and trucks, even a few motorcycles. The kids all pulled off the road and stopped. "What is going on?" asked Sarah. Blaire replied, "I have no clue, no one is hardly ever on this road!" Just then Cody blurted out, "Look up ahead! Everyone is stopping at the Blue Hole. We will never get to swim now!"

Sure enough over 20 to 30 vehicles were stopped ahead and people were scrambling to the creek. "What do you think is happening?" questioned Sarah.

The kids dropped their bikes by the side of the road and ran ahead.

There it was! A baby calf had fallen into the icy Blue Hole and firefighters were struggling to get her out. News reporters were all around, as well. According to the reporter, the calf had been in the creek earlier that morning since before daybreak, but not at the Blue Hole end. The calf had gradually followed other people toward the deep end. Once there, she panicked and was unable to gain footing to get out.

The firefighters had been working to try to lasso her for over 2 hours, and were not having any luck. About that time, everyone heard a loud MOOOO! Over and over again and getting closer! It was the mother cow. She was looking for her baby! Instantly, the calf leaped to the edge of the creek bank. The mother cow came through the bushes rushing toward her baby. She licked and licked on her and the baby leaned against its mother. All was well, safe and sound!

The crowd of bystanders cheered along with Sarah, Blaire and Cody. They went and got their bikes where they had left them. Looking at each other in a confused manner, the friends couldn't decide what to do next. Cody grinned and said, "Enough excitement today, let's just go riding!"

13. What detail shows the emotions of the characters once the baby calf was safe? Circle the correct answer.

Ⓐ The crowd of bystanders cheered along with Sarah, Blaire and Cody.
Ⓑ "What is going on?" asked Sarah.
Ⓒ Cody grinned and said, "Enough excitement today, let's just go riding!"
Ⓓ None of the above.

Question 14 is based on the story below.

Excerpt from Jo's Boys
Chapter 1 - Ten Years Later
by Louisa May Alcott

"If anyone had told me what wonderful changes were to take place here in ten years, I wouldn't have believed it." said Mrs. Jo to Mrs. Meg, as they sat on the piazza at Plumfield one summer day, looking about them with faces full of pride and pleasure.

"This is the sort of magic that money and kind hearts can work. I am sure Mr. Laurence could have no nobler monument than the college he so generously endowed; and a home like this will keep Aunt March's memory green as long as it lasts". Answered Mrs. Meg, always glad to praise the absent.

"We used to believe in fairies, you remember, and plan what we'd ask for if we could have three wishes. Doesn't it seem as if mine had been really granted at last? Money, fame, and plenty of the work I love," said Mrs. Jo, carelessly rumpling up her hair as she clasped her hands over her head just as she used to do when a girl.

"I have had mine, and Amy is enjoying hers to her heart's content. If dear Marmee, John, and Beth were here, it would be quite perfect,"added Meg, with a tender quiver in her voice; for Marmee's place was empty now.

Jo put her hand on her sister's, and both sat silent for a little while, surveying the pleasant scene before them with mingled sad and happy thoughts.

It certainly did look as if magic had been at work, for quiet Plumfield was transformed into a busy little world. The house seemed more hospitable than ever, refreshed now with new paint, added wings, well-kept lawn and garden, and a prosperous air it had not worn when riotous boys swarmed everywhere and it was rather difficult for the Bhaers to make both ends meet. On the hill, where kites used to be flown, stood the fine college which Mr. Laurence's munificent legacy had built. Busy students were going to and fro along the paths once trodden by childish feet, and many young men and women were enjoying all the advantages that wealth, wisdom, and benevolence could give them.

14. Who are the main characters in this selection? Remember main characters are those that are most important. Write a sentence explaining your answer.

Question 15 is based on the passage below.

Playing Video Games

Scotty loves to play video games! I mean he plays every chance he gets. He even plays when he should be doing his homework, chores or going to bed! It has gotten so bad that his parents are considering a punishment to teach him a lesson.

Scotty doesn't understand why they are upset with him and is trying to figure out what he can do so that he doesn't get his video game machine taken away. He has asked his friends for their ideas on the subject, too. He even asked his counselor at school. Scotty has been seeing her since his grades started dropping. The counselor told him it is very simple, give up the game playing on his own and get back to doing homework, chores, and going to bed on time.

To Scotty, the ideas his counselor told him are good, but he is very reluctant to do it. So one of his friends, Hailey, has offered to help. She is going to make him a chart of time spent on playing games compared to time spent on his responsibilities. He agrees to give it a try.

The following is his chart for the first week.

	Monday	Tuesday	Wednesday	Thursday	Friday	Saturday	Sunday	Totals
Playing Video Games	4 hours	4 hours	3 hours	3 hours	2 hours	3 hours	3 hours	22 hours
Doing Home-work	30 min	30 min	1 hour	1 hour	1 hour	none	none	4 hours
Doing Chores	15 min	15 min	45 min	45 min	45 min	2 hours	1 hour	5 hours 45 min
Going to Bed On Time	Not done	Not done	Not done	Done	Not done	Done	Done	Went to bed on time 3 days

15. Has Scotty's attitude toward doing his homework and chores improved or not? Select the correct answer choice and write it in the box given below.

Ⓐ His attitude has not improved during the first week.
Ⓑ His attitude has shown some improvement.
Ⓒ There is no change in his behavior.

Chapter 2

Lesson 6: Figurative Language Expressions

Literal language: an expression of language using the strict meanings of a word or phrase.
Nonliteral language: an expression of language, such as simile, metaphor, or personification, by which the usual or literal meaning of a word is not employed.

Examples of events described using *nonliteral* and *literal* expressions:

1. My father bought two new cars and a boat this weekend.
He is **made of money**.

Nonliteral
Humans are made of flesh and bone, not money. It implies he is rich.
He is **very rich**.

Literal
Rich means having a lot of something, such as money.

2. My brother was tossing a ball in the house when he broke my mom's favorite vase.
I told him that when she gets home, **he will be toast**.

Nonliteral
Humans cannot be turned into toast – toast is heated bread. It is another way of saying he will be in big trouble.

Literal. I told him that when she gets home, **he will be in big trouble**.

3. I said to my friend: "You have to deal with the bully and let him know your true feelings. You can't **beat around the bush**."

Nonliteral
There is not a bush sitting there that the speaker needs to beat with a stick. Actually, the expression originated in England and meant that some members of a group hunting game birds would beat the bushes to flush the birds out so they could be captured, which was the whole point of the hunt. It implies that someone is evading making a point or taking some action directly.

Literal. You must talk to the bully directly, confront him, face to face.

78

You can scan the QR code given below or use the URL to access additional EdSearch resources including videos and mobile apps related to *Figurative Language Expressions.*

ed)Search	**Figurative Language Expressions**
URL	**QR Code**
http://www.lumoslearning.com/a/rl34	

1. What is the meaning of the phrase "can't go on"?

   Ⓐ Cannot go back
   Ⓑ Cannot switch it on
   Ⓒ Cannot continue
   Ⓓ Cannot stop fighting

2. What does the underlined phrase mean in this stanza?

I quarreled with my brother
I don't know what about,
One thing led to another
And somehow we fell out.
The start of it was slight,
The end of it was strong,
He said he was right,
I knew he was wrong!
~Eleanor Farjeon

   Ⓐ had a disagreement
   Ⓑ fell down
   Ⓒ fainted
   Ⓓ were pushed out

3. What is the meaning of the word "charging up" in the following sentence?

Just as he trumpeted, he heard a loud crashing and stamping. A herd of wrinkled elephants came charging up.

   Ⓐ walked away
   Ⓑ walked slowly forward
   Ⓒ came up to dance
   Ⓓ rushed forward to attack

4. What is the meaning of the underlined phrase?

My grandfather bought two new cars and a boat last Saturday. He is made of money!

   Ⓐ poor
   Ⓑ rich
   Ⓒ a thief
   Ⓓ a banker

5. What is the meaning of the underlined phrase?

My little sister won't leave me alone when I try to work on my homework. She was so annoying last night that I told her to <u>take a hike</u>!

- Ⓐ   go outside and take a walk in the woods
- Ⓑ   go to your room
- Ⓒ   go away
- Ⓓ   stop talking

6. What does the underlined phrase mean?

Jonah thought I cheated when we were playing a video game against each other, but I told him <u>I won fair and square</u>.

- Ⓐ   cheating
- Ⓑ   dishonestly
- Ⓒ   honestly
- Ⓓ   in the last minute

7. What does the underlined phrase mean?

My cousin broke my aunt's favorite coffee cup. I told him, "When your mom finds out you did this, <u>you're toast</u>!"

- Ⓐ   making breakfast
- Ⓑ   need to lie
- Ⓒ   in big trouble
- Ⓓ   going to have to explain

8. What does the underlined phrase mean?

I hate to be told what to do! Whenever someone tells me how to act, I <u>dig my heels</u> in and do what I want to do!

- Ⓐ   put my feet on the floor
- Ⓑ   dig a hole
- Ⓒ   give something a try
- Ⓓ   refuse to do something

9. What does the underlined phrase in the sentence mean?

Even though it was the final inning of the baseball game and the score was tied, the batter <u>kept his cool</u> when he came up to bat. He calmly hit a home run giving his team enough runs to win the game.

Ⓐ drank some cold water
Ⓑ took a break
Ⓒ stayed calm
Ⓓ played great

Question 10 is based on the story below.

Antonio walked into the house. He was feeling overwhelmed, and just didn't know what to do about his latest problem. His mom noticed his sad face and asked him to sit down. "What's that cloud hanging over your head, son?" He just shrugged. "Been a bad day?" He nodded. She pulled her son closer and said, "Tomorrow is a new day." He smiled. His mom had a way of saying these silly expressions. They never meant what he thought they did at first, but they always made him smile.

"Has that new kid been walking around with a chip on his shoulder again?"

He chuckled out loud, picturing in his mind the new student walking around with a huge concrete block or some other "chip" on his shoulder. "Guess so…."

"Don't beat around the bush with him anymore, son….just tell him how you feel."

Antonio returned his mom's hug, squeezing her as hard as he could.

"Mom, you sure do have a way with words." The two smiled happily. "What's for dinner? I could eat a horse."

10. What did Antonio's mom mean when she asked him about the cloud hanging over his head?

Ⓐ She wanted to know if he felt sick.
Ⓑ She wanted to know why he was so sad.
Ⓒ She wanted to know if he had any homework.
Ⓓ She wanted to know if it was going to rain soon.

Question 11-13 are based on the passage below.

Water! Water! Safe and clean.

Did you know that as humans, we are full of water in our bodies? Yes, we are! We do know that we must have water to stay alive. We never think about it being a problem to have plenty of water to drink, bathe, wash clothes, and do dishes or even to water our yards. In past years, many environmentalists (people who study our surroundings and who worry about our lands), have warned us that we are not taking good care of our natural resources, water being one of those. We have seen pollution in rivers, streams and wetlands. This will eventually have a negative impact on our easy access to good clean water.

So, here is the question posed to you. What can you do to help? You might think to yourself, "Me, I am just a kid!" You can help. Keep your lawns and driveways free of litter. Water your yard only every 3-5 days. Be sure to turn off water hoses immediately after use.

Volunteer to help on a weekly basis to go around and pick up litter in your town. Make a list of where you find litter the most and get your friends or class in on the project. Picking up litter will help our water to stay cleaner, too. The less litter we have the fewer possibilities for trash to enter our waterways.

Do not use plastic bottles or bags. Get your parents to use the cloth bags when they shop for groceries. If you do use plastic, be sure to recycle it. Plastic is bad for our communities and can cause multiple types of pollution.

When showering or bathing, time your shower or bath. Make a chart and have your family do the same. Not only will you save our precious water resources, but you will save your family money on the monthly water bill, as well.

When you wash clothes in the washing machine, do not overfill your water. Either wash smaller loads, or a larger load when necessary. Most washing machines have a level to help you not overuse water.

Water is one of our greatest natural resources. We need it! It is up to all of us to be responsible to keep it plentiful and clean.

11. Litter can end up in our _____ and cause pollution to our water. Select all the correct answers that fits into the sentence above.

    Ⓐ rivers
    Ⓑ streams
    Ⓒ wetlands

12. **Instead of plastic bags, get your parents to use the _____ bags when they buy groceries.**

13. **Water is a _____ resource.**

Question 14 is based on the story below.

Christopher's Magic Reading Tricks!

There are many ways to help you in understanding things you read.
Here are some examples of ways that Christopher uses to help him in his reading.

The first one is what his teacher calls prior knowledge. This means that as you read you think -what do I already know if anything about this topic? Christopher says it helps him remember if he has ever read anything about it before. Then he uses that and tries to learn something new as he reads.

The second way is to question as you read. Think to yourself- what is the author trying to tell me, before, during and after you read? Christopher likes to say- "Self, what is it I am trying to learn as I read this? Can I repeat it after I read it?"

The third and Christopher says the most fun is to make a picture in your mind while you read. He says that if it is a story, you can even make a movie in your mind! Teachers use the term visualize your reading.

The fourth strategy or technique that Christopher learned from his teacher is to infer. This one means that Christopher has to use clues in the reading to figure out what is going on or what the author really means in the story.

The most favorite way for Christopher to get more out of what he has read is to summarize the reading. He tells his friends who may be struggling with this to tell what's important in a sentence or two after you read.

Christopher likes to reread his passages or stories more than one time when he knows he is going to be tested over them or asked questions about them. He says he also takes notes and sometimes uses more than one way to help him read better.

He had a hard time with reading when he was in first and second grade, but now since he uses these "magic tricks" to reading, he loves reading!

14. Match the magic reading trick with its definition. Write the definition from Table 1 against each magic trick.

> ## Table 1
> A. Use what you already know to learn more.
> B. Tell what's important in a sentence or two.
> C. Ask yourself what is the author trying to tell me?
> D. Read the story or passage again.
> E. Make pictures or movies in your mind about the story.
> F. Use the clues in reading to figure out what is really going on.

Definition	Magic Tricks for reading
Infer	F. Use the clues in reading to figure out what is really going on.
Prior Knowledge	
Summarize	
Visualize	
Question	
Reread	

Question 15 is based on the paragraph below.

NASA facts and terms

NASA, National Aeronautics and Space Administration began in 1958. This occurred one year after the Soviets launched Sputnik 1. Sputnik 1 was the first artificial satellite in the entire world. This began what was known as the "space race" between Russia and the United States. NASA has excelled in many areas of space science. The greatest is that of having manned (human) space missions.

Here is a list of those:
U.S. Manned Space Programs

- Mercury: the first U.S. program for human spaceflight
- Gemini: the first two-man crews, longer missions
- Apollo: the first spaceflights to the moon
- Skylab: a place where humans lived and worked in space for extended periods of time
- Apollo-Soyuz: first international manned spaceflight
- Space shuttle: the first reusable spacecraft
- International Space Station: an effort to create a permanent orbiting laboratory in space

The following vocabulary helps you to better understand when reading about NASA and its accomplishments. Study the vocabulary, match the vocabulary to definitions. Then fill in the blanks using the context sentences.

Aeronautics - Science dealing with the operation of aircraft.

Astronaut - A person who pilots a spacecraft or works in space; a space traveler, particularly one from the United States. For example, Alan B Shepard Jr was the commander of several NASA space missions.

Johnson Space Center - The headquarters for all U.S. manned spacecraft projects conducted by NASA; the location of the Mission Control Center for manned space flights.

Kennedy Space Center - The launch facility for all U.S. space missions that carry crews.

Launch vehicle - A powerful rocket used to launch a spacecraft or satellite into space.

NASA (National Aeronautics & Space Administration) - The government agency whose mission is to research and develop safe and meaningful ways to explore space.

Orbit - The path of a spacecraft or a heavenly body as it revolves around a planet or other body.

Space shuttle - A reusable space vehicle that takes off like a rocket and lands like an airplane.

Space station - An orbiting spacecraft designed to be occupied by teams of astronauts or cosmonauts over a long period.

15. **Match the vocabulary with the definition. Write the correct definition against each of the words given.**

> A. headquarters of US manned spacecraft projects and location of Mission Control
> B. the science of space craft operation
> C. government agency in charge of space exploration
> D. launch facility in Cape Canaveral, FL
> E. orbiting space craft designed for occupancy for long period of time
> F. a reusable space craft, takes off like a rocket, lands like a plane
> G. powerful rocket used to launch space craft or satellite
> H. a person who operates spacecraft or works in space, from US
> I. path of a spacecraft or heavenly body as it goes around a planet

Definition	Vocabulary
NASA	C. government agency in charge of space exploration
Launch vehicle	
Aeronautics	
Astronaut	
Space shuttle	
Orbit	
Johnson Space Center	
Kennedy Space Center	
Space Station	

Chapter 2

Lesson 7: Parts of a Whole

Let us understand the concept with an example.

The Boy from Africa

Chapter 2 tells about what life was like for a young boy named Makuna growing up poor in a village in Africa. His school room was a shack with no walls and very few books. Both parents had died of disease and Makuna was raised by his grandmother.

Chapter 3 tells about a person named Joyce who taught at an elementary school in the United States. Many of her students immigrated (moved from another country) to her town from the same village that Makuna was living in. She heard sad stories from them about conditions in that African village.

Chapter 4 tells about Joyce's decision to raise money and food supplies for the village and to travel there herself to deliver them. And that is what happened; she convinced many people to donate money and groceries and she went to the village and delivered the money and groceries. While there, she met Makuna and felt very sad for him, and wished she could adopt him and bring him home with her.

Chapter 4 tells how Joyce managed to legally adopt Makuna and bring him to the United States. It describes how he made a lot of adjustments to his new life in the United States.

Your assignment: Write a review of the story telling what you thought about it and explaining how each chapter depends on the previous chapters.

Here is what you might write.

I think Joyce is a very caring person. She is a teacher, which means she cares about helping children learn. And, when she heard her students tell sad stories about the African village in which they had lived before coming to the United States, she cared enough to help that village by convincing people in her town to donate money and groceries to the village, and then she made the trip to deliver them. Another example of her caring was adopting Makuna and bringing him here where he could have a healthier life and better schooling.

The chapters are in what is called chronological order – that is, in the order in which events took place over a period of time, and the information in one chapter leads into the next chapter. The first chapter introduced Makuna and what his life was like in the African village. The second chapter introduced Joyce and explained how she heard about Makuna's village. The introductions of Makuna and Joyce in Chapters 1 and 2 were needed because the remaining chapters include both people. Chapter 4 tells about Joyce's trip to Africa that came about because of what her students told her in Chapter 3, and was where she met Makuna. Chapter 4 tells about Joyce deciding to adopt Makuna, after meeting him in Chapter 4, and bringing him to the United States.

You can scan the QR code given below or use the URL to access additional EdSearch resources including videos and mobile apps related to *Parts of a Whole*.

ed Search	**Parts of a Whole**
URL	**QR Code**
http://www.lumoslearning.com/a/rl35	

Question 1 is based on the poem below.

Camels are bumpy,
Their backs are all lumpy,
Giraffes are long- legged and meek:
Bears are so growly,
Hyenas are howly,
Dolphins are slippery and sleek.

Kangaroos have a pocket,
But no way to lock it,
Their babies can look out and peep,
But monkeys are funny
I wish I had money,
Enough to buy one and keep.

1. The above poem has two _____ .

 Ⓐ stanzas
 Ⓑ paragraphs
 Ⓒ passages
 Ⓓ parts

Question 2 is based on the paragraph below.

An astronomer used to go out every night to observe stars. Often, he would be seen with a telescope in one hand and a notebook in the other. One evening, while he wandered through the suburbs with his attention fixed on the sky, he accidentally fell into a deep uncovered well. He cried out loudly for help. As he waited to be rescued, he moaned and howled about his sores and bruises. His neighbor was passing by and happened to hear his wailing and weeping. He quickly helped him out of the well. After he came to know how the accident happened, this is what he said to the astronomer: "Hark you old fellow, why in striving to pry into heaven, do you not manage to see what is on earth?"

2. What line from the paragraph tells the reader where the astronomer lived?

 Ⓐ One evening, while he wandered through the suburbs.
 Ⓑ He quickly helped him out of the well.
 Ⓒ He would often be seen with a telescope in one hand and a notebook in the other.
 Ⓓ It does not tell us where he lived.

Question 3 is based on the story below.

PART II. THE FIREBRAND IN THE FOREST

When the two women saw that the wolf had the firebrand, they were very angry, and straightway they ran after him.

"Catch it and run!" cried the wolf, and he threw it to the deer. The deer caught it and ran.
"Catch it and run!" cried the deer, and he threw it to the bear. The bear caught it and ran.
"Catch it and fly!" cried the bear, and he threw it to the bat. The bat caught it and flew.
"Catch it and run!" cried the bat, and he threw it to the squirrel. The squirrel caught it and ran.

"Oh, serpent," called the two old women, "you are no friend to the First Americans. Help us. Get the firebrand away from the squirrel."

As the squirrel ran swiftly over the ground, the serpent sprang up and tried to seize the firebrand. He did not get it, but the smoke went into the squirrel's nostrils and made him cough. He would not let go of the firebrand, but ran and ran till he could throw it to the frog.

When the frog was running away with it, the squirrel for the first time thought of himself, and he found that his beautiful bushy tail was no longer straight, for the fire had curled it up over his back.

"Do not be sorry," called the young First American across the pond. "Whenever a First American boy sees a squirrel with his tail curled up over his back, he will throw him a nut."

PART III. THE FIREBRAND IN THE POND

All this time the firebrand was burning, and the frog was going to the pond as fast as he could. The old women were running after him, and when he came to the water, one of them caught him by the tail.

"I have caught him!" she called.
"Do not let him go!" cried the other.

"No, I will not," said the first; but she did let him go, for the little frog tore himself away and dived into the water. His tail was still in the woman's hand, but the firebrand was safe, and he made his way swiftly across the pond.

"Here it is," said the frog.
"Where?" asked the young First American. Then the frog coughed, and out of his mouth came the firebrand. It was small, for it had been burning all this time, but it set fire to the leaves and twigs, and soon the First Americans were warm again. They sang and they danced about the flames.

This is from the work *How Fire Was Brought to the First Americans* by Cyrus MacMillian.

3. What are the bold parts of this selection called?

- Ⓐ titles
- Ⓑ parts
- Ⓒ headings
- Ⓓ topics

Question 4-6 are based on the story below.

My First Trip to the Beach

About three weeks ago, Jeremiah's parents surprised him with some news. They were taking him to the beach. He was excited and couldn't wait to tell all of his friends at school.

Soon enough, Friday afternoon arrived. Jeremiah, his sister, his parents, and his nanny all loaded into the car, and set out for the long drive to Destin, Florida. Listening to DVD's grew old rather quickly. A nap was sure to allow Jeremiah to get closer to Florida without growing bored from the ride.

When he awoke from his nap, it was time to stop for dinner. He exited the car, excited to stretch his legs. "Come on, Jeremiah," exclaimed his nanny. He was glad that she had been able to come to the beach. This was also going to be her first time seeing the ocean.

After a quick meal at a fast-food restaurant, the family piled back into the car.

The family arrived at their condo, almost too tired to enjoy the peaceful sound of the ocean. As Jeremiah headed to bed, he knew that the beach would be his to explore in a few hours. He stretched out his small frame across the twin-sized bed and soon fell asleep. He awoke a few hours later, hearing his dad outside on the balcony.

When Jeremiah finally saw the view in the daylight, he was in awe. Beautiful green waters lay off in the distance. They seemed to go on and on, as far as his eyes could see. The sand reminded him of snow.

"Wanna go for a walk?" asked his dad.
Jeremiah smiled, "Yes!" Running back inside, he threw his shoes on. His dad said that he didn't want to try to wear those in the soft, grainy sand. He dressed, and then off they went.

"What's this?" asked Jeremiah, pointing to a loose mound of sand.
"This is a sand dune, it keeps the buildings safe," his dad replied.

"Oh, okay..." Jeremiah and his dad walked along the ocean's edge. There were few words spoken, but the looks on their faces expressed feelings of happiness, as they walked along the beautiful water's edge.

4. Why did Jeremiah NOT wear shoes to the beach?

Ⓐ His dad told him that they would get lost in the ocean.
Ⓑ His dad advised him against trying to walk through the sand with shoes on.
Ⓒ His mom told him that she did not want them to get dirty.
Ⓓ He had forgotten to pack shoes for the beach.

5. Why were the sand dunes located on the beach, according to Jeremiah's dad?

Ⓐ They were there to keep people from walking on the beach.
Ⓑ They were there to protect the buildings from the ocean's water.
Ⓒ Some other kids on the beach had built a huge sand mound.
Ⓓ They did not see sand dunes, except in pictures.

6. Why did the family have a quick fast-food meal?

Ⓐ They were ready to get back home.
Ⓑ They were not very hungry.
Ⓒ They wanted to save time, so they could get to the beach sooner.
Ⓓ It was the only restaurant that they could find open.

Question 7 is based on the story below.

Amber entered the small grocery store. She looked at the list that her mom had sent with her. She knew that she only had enough money to buy the milk, bread, and eggs that were on the list. Quickly, she grabbed the items and paid for them.

Eying the candy on her way out, she picked up a pack of gum, looked around and saw that no one was watching her. It had been weeks since she had chewed gum, and she thought that it would be okay. She had walked a long way to the store and felt that she deserved a little treat.

Amber walked through the double doors staring at the bright green package of chewing gum in her hand. She immediately turned back around, walked back inside, and returned the gum to its spot on the display stand. The cashier smiled and nodded, but did not say a word.

7. Why did Amber put the gum back on the shelf?

Ⓐ Amber realized that she should not steal it.
Ⓑ The cashier told her that she was going to have to return it.
Ⓒ Her mom made her return it.
Ⓓ The police were watching her.

Question 8 is based on the passage below.

Dear Diary,

I just returned from my first trip to the beach. It was different than I expected. The water scared me a bit, but I tried to act cool in front of my little sister. I couldn't let her know how much the crashing waves scared me.

Building sand castles in the sparkling white grains of sand was a blast, and I even had a chance to bury my sister. This is every brother's dream, right? Well, not really, and she was able to break free from the sand wall that I had built around her.

My favorite place wasn't at beach, it was sitting on the balcony. I loved looking down at the emerald green waters. Maybe when we do go back again, I won't be afraid to wander out a little farther into the water. Dad seemed to enjoy it a lot. Mom was a lot like me. She just wanted to stay close to the shore.

Jeremiah

P. S. Oh, I almost forgot to tell you that we went looking for crabs three nights in a row, but we did not have any luck. It was still fun. My fear of the ocean seemed to disappear in the night.

8. What was one thing that made Jeremiah really enjoy his visit to the beach?

   Ⓐ Finding a lot of crabs in his evening walks on the beach.
   Ⓑ Building sand castles and burying his sister in the sand.
   Ⓒ Swimming in the ocean.
   Ⓓ Tearing down the sand dunes that were built near the condo.

Directions: Read the following play. Then answer the questions that follow.

BROCK: (Brock enters the stage.) What a great day it is.
TERRY: (Snarls)What's good about it?
BROCK: (Laughs) I found something outside on the playground.
TERRY: (Rolls eyes).
MRS. ADAMS: (Walks over). Good morning, boys.
BROCK AND TERRY: Good morning.
MRS. ADAMS: (MOTIONS). Sit down, boys.
TERRY: (Pushes Brock.)
BROCK: Why'd you do that? (In a rather loud voice).
TERRY: (Throws hands into the air and pushes Brock again).
MRS. ADAMS: (Runs over). Boys, is this how we want to start off the week?
TERRY: (Sighs.) But, Brock says it is a great day, and…

MRS. ADAMS: (Looks confused). You are upset, just because Brock is happy?
TERRY: (Shakes head no).
BROCK: I don't know what's wrong with him.
TERRY: (Reaches into his pocket.) My mom gave me twenty dollars to pay for my lunch bill, but I can't find it. She is going to be really mad.
BROCK: (Smiles)
MRS. ADAMS: When did you last have the money?
BROCK: (Reaches into his pocket.) Remember that I told you I found something?
TERRY: (Nods).
BROCK: (Hands money to Terry). I found this outside. I bet you dropped it.
TERRY: (Hugs Brock).

9. What made Terry act so mean towards his friend, Brock?

Ⓐ He lost the money that he needed to pay his lunch bill.
Ⓑ Brock said something mean to him at recess.
Ⓒ Brock stole Terry's lunch money.
Ⓓ Terry wasn't feeling good and wanted to get in trouble, so the school would send him home.

Question 10 is based on the story below.

Jasmine nervously left the car. She and her parents had been riding for what seemed like days, but after ten hours, they were finally here. She carefully studied the old farmhouse. "Are you ready?" her dad asked. Jasmine only shrugged. She had talked with her "G", as the kind lady had referred to herself, a few times on the phone, but at the age of eight, she had never actually met her grandma. It seemed that work, school, or illness had kept her away.

Jasmine's parents had told her stories about her "G" and that she had met her when she was only a few months old, but in Jasmine's mind this was the first time. She exited the car and was greeted by a petite, black-haired lady, standing in the doorway. Her smile looked familiar. It seemed to be a combination of her own and the warm smile that her dad seldom showed, but that warmed her heart, over and over.

Her "G" had scooped her up. "Come on in here, Jasmine." Jasmine felt a bit nervous, but she walked into the house with her grandmother's arms still around her. I bet you are tired of sitting. "How long have you had my beautiful granddaughter cooped up in that car?" asked her "G".
Jasmine's dad replied, "It has been a while."

"Come on, honey. There is so much that I want to show you," her grandma cooed. Jasmine followed her grandmother through the house. It seemed that they exited one doorway, only to enter another. "Here is a surprise for you," her grandma stated. Looking down, Jasmine saw the most beautiful locket. She picked it up, nervously. "I have been saving this for you. It was your great granny's...my mom's." Jasmine pulled it closer for a better view.
"Let me put it on you, you beautiful girl."

10. Why did Jasmine's "G" wait so long to give her the locket?

Ⓐ G's own mom had given her permission to give it to Jasmine.
Ⓑ It was the first time that they had ever met.
Ⓒ She had misplaced the locket and finally found it, so she was able to pass it on to Jasmine.
Ⓓ It was the first time that she had seen her granddaughter who was now old enough to understand the specialty of a locket.

Question 11 is based on the story below.

OLD-FASHIONED FAIRY TALES
By Juliana Horatia Gatty Ewing

The following fairy tale is separated into 4 parts. Each part has questions that go along with the section, to help the reader have a better understanding of the tale. Also, for the reader, the selection has been numbered. Remember to read the selections more than one time for comprehension purposes.

While reading this fairy tale, keep in mind that it is written in what is called Old English. This means some words are used or spelled differently than the vocabulary we use today. Should you have difficulty with the words, use context clues to help. You may also ask your teacher, or use a dictionary to help you understand the meaning.

GOOD LUCK IS BETTER THAN GOLD.

Part 1

1. There was once upon a time a child who had Good Luck for his godfather.

2. "I am not Fortune," said Good Luck to the parents; "I have no gifts to bestow, but whenever he needs help I will be at hand."
3. "Nothing could be better," said the old couple. They were delighted. But what pleases the father often fails to satisfy the son: moreover, every man thinks that he deserves just a little more than he has got, and does not reckon it to the purpose if his father had less.

4. Many a one would be thankful to have as good reasons for contentment as he who had Good Luck for his godfather.

5. If he fell, Good Luck popped something soft in the way to break his fall; if he fought, Good Luck directed his blows, or tripped up his adversary; if he got into a scrape, Good Luck helped him out of it; and if ever Misfortune met him, Good Luck contrived to hustle her on the pathway till his godson got safely by.

6. In games of hazard the godfather played over his shoulder. In matters of choice he chose for him. And when the lad began to work on his father's farm the farmer began to get rich. For no bird or field-mouse touched a seed that his son had sown, and every plant he planted throve when Good

Luck smiled on it.

7. The boy was not fond of work, but when he did go into the fields, Good Luck followed him.

8. "Your christening-day was a blessed day for us all," said the old farmer.

9. "He has never given me so much as a lucky sixpence," muttered Good Luck's godson.

10. "I am not Fortune—I make no presents," said the godfather.

11. When we are discontented, it is oftener to please our neighbours than ourselves. It was because the other boys had said—"Simon, the shoemaker's son, has an alderman for his godfather. He gave him a silver spoon with the Apostle Peter for the handle; but thy godfather is more powerful than any alderman"—that Good Luck's godson complained, "He has never given me so much as a bent sixpence."

Part 2

12. By and by the old farmer died, and his son grew up, and had the largest farm in the country. The other boys grew up also, and as they looked over the farmer's boundary-wall, they would say:

13. "Good-morning, Neighbor. That is certainly a fine farm of yours. Your cattle thrive without loss. Your crops grow in the rain and are reaped with the sunshine. Mischance never comes to your road. What you have worked for you enjoy. Such success would turn the heads of poor folk like us. At the same time, one would think a man need hardly work for his living at all who has Good Luck for his godfather."

14. "That is very true," thought the farmer. "Many a man is prosperous, and reaps what he sows, who had no more than the clerk and the sexton for gossips at his christening."

15. "What is the matter, Godson?" asked Good Luck, who was with him in the field.

16. "I want to be rich," said the farmer.

17. "You will not have to wait long," replied the godfather. "In every field you sow, in every flock you rear there is increase without abatement. Your wealth is already tenfold greater than your father's."

18. "Aye, aye," replied the farmer. "Good wages for good work. But many a young man has gold at his command who need never turn a sod, and none of the Good People came to his christening. Fortunatus's Purse now, or even a sack or two of gold—"

19. "Peace!" cried the godfather; "I have said that I give no gifts."

20. Though he had not Fortunatus's Purse, the farmer had money and to spare, and when the harvest was gathered in, he bought a fine suit of clothes, and took his best horse and went to the royal city to see the sights.

21. The pomp and splendour, the festivities and fine clothes dazzled him.

22. "This is a gay life which these young courtiers lead," said he. "A man has nothing to do but to enjoy himself."

23. "If he has plenty of gold in his pocket," said a bystander.

24. By and by the Princess passed in her carriage. She was the King's only daughter. She had hair made of sunshine, and her eyes were stars.

25. "What an exquisite creature!" cried the farmer. "What would not one give to possess her?"

26. "She has as many suitors as hairs on her head," replied the bystander. "She wants to marry the Prince of Moonshine, but he only dresses in silver, and the King thinks he might find a richer son-in-law. The Princess will go to the highest bidder."

27. "And I have Good Luck for my godfather, and am not even at court!" cried the farmer; and he put spurs to his horse, and rode home.

Part 3

28. Good Luck was taking care of the farm.

29. "Listen, Godfather!" cried the young man. "I am in love with the King's daughter, and would want her to wife."

30. "It is not an easy matter," replied Good Luck, "but I will do what I can for you. Say that by good luck you saved the Princess's life, or perhaps better the King's—for they say he is selfish—"

31. "Tush!" cried the farmer. "The King is covetous, and wants a rich son-in-law."

32. "A wise man may bring wealth to a kingdom with his head, if not with his hands," said Good Luck, "and I can show you a district where the earth only wants mining to be flooded with wealth. Besides, there are a thousand opportunities that can be turned to account and influence. By wits and work, and with Good Luck to help him, many a poorer man than you has risen to greatness."

33. "Wits and work!" cried the indignant godson. "You speak well—truly! A hillman would have made a better godfather. Give me as much gold as will fill three meal-bins, and you may keep the rest of your help for those who want it."

34. Now at this moment by Good Luck stood Dame Fortune. She likes handsome young men, and there was some little jealousy between her and the godfather so she smiled at the quarrel.

35. "You would rather have had me for your gossip?" said she.

36. "If you would give me three wishes, I would," replied the farmer boldly, "and I would trouble you no more."

37. "Will you make him over to me?" said Dame Fortune to the godfather.

38. "If he wishes it," replied Good Luck. "But if he accepts your gifts, he has no further claim on me."

39. "Nor on me either," said the Dame. "Hark ye, young man, you mortals are apt to make a hobble of your three wishes, and you may end with a sausage at your nose, like your betters."

40. "I have thought of it too often," replied the farmer, "and I know what I want. For my first wish I desire imperishable beauty."

41. "It is yours," said Dame Fortune, smiling as she looked at him.

42. "The face of a prince and the manners of a clown are poor partners," said the farmer. "My second wish is for suitable learning and courtly manners, which cannot be gained at the plough-tail."

43. "You have them in perfection," said the Dame, as the young man thanked her by a graceful bow.

44. "Thirdly," said he, "I demand a store of gold that I can never exhaust."

45. "I will lead you to it," said Dame Fortune; and the young man was so eager to follow her that he did not even look back to bid farewell to his godfather.

Part 4

46. He was soon at court. He lived in the utmost pomp. He had a suit of armor made for himself out of beaten gold. No metal less precious might come near his person, except for the blade of his sword. This was obliged to be made of steel, for gold is not always strong enough to defend one's life or his honour. But the Princess still loved the Prince of Moonshine.

47. "Stuff and nonsense!" said the King. "I shall give you to the Prince of Gold."

48. "I wish I had the good luck to please her," muttered the young Prince. But he had not, for all his beauty and his wealth. However, she was to marry him, and that was something.

49. The preparations for the wedding were magnificent.

50. "It is a great expense," sighed the King, "but then I get the Prince of Gold for a son-in-law."

51. The Prince and his bride drove around the city in a triumphal procession. Her hair fell over her like sunshine, but the starlight of her eyes was cold.

52. In the train rode the Prince of Moonshine, dressed in silver, and with no color in his face.

53. As the bridal chariot approached one of the city gates, two black ravens hovered over it, and then flew away, and settled on a tree.

54. Good Luck was sitting under the tree to see his godson's triumph, and he heard the birds talking above him.

55. "Has the Prince of Gold no friend who can tell him that there is a loose stone above the archway that is tottering to fall?" said they. And Good Luck covered his face with his mantle as the Prince drove through.

56. Just as they were passing out of the gateway the stone fell on to the Prince's head. He wore a casque of pure gold, but his neck was broken.

57. "We can't have all this expense for nothing," said the King: so he married his daughter to the Prince of Moonshine. If one can't get gold, one must be content with silver.

58. "Will you come to the funeral?" asked Dame Fortune of the godfather.

59. "Not I," replied Good Luck. "I had no hand in this matter."
60. The rain came down in torrents. The black feathers on the ravens' backs looked as if they had been oiled.
61. "Caw! caw!" said they. "It was an unlucky end."

11. Part A

What happened to the Prince of Gold at the end?

11. Part B

Write a sentence explaining why this happened.

Question 12 is based on the poem below.

FOREIGN LANDS

Up into the cherry tree
Who should climb but little me?
I held the trunk with both my hands
And looked abroad on foreign lands.

I saw the next-door garden lie,
Adorned with flowers, before my eye,
And many pleasant faces more
That I had never seen before.

I saw the dimpling river pass
And be the sky's blue looking-glass;
The dusty roads go up and down
With people tramping into town.
If I could find a higher tree

Farther and farther I should see,
To where the grown-up river slips
Into the sea among the ships.

To where the roads on either hand
Lead onward into fairyland,
Where all the children dine at five,
And all the playthings come alive.

-- By Robert Louis Stevenson

12. In your own words, explain the rhyming pattern that the poet Robert Louis Stevenson uses in this poem.

Question 13 is based on the story below.

CHAPTER I: Looking-Glass House
Excerpt taken from Alice in Wonderland, Through the Looking Glass

One thing was certain, that the white kitten had nothing to do with it:—it was the black kitten's fault entirely. For the white kitten had been having its face washed by the old cat for the last quarter of an hour (and bearing it pretty well, considering); so you see that it couldn't have had any hand in the mischief.

The way Dinah washed her children's faces was this: first she held the poor thing down by its ear with one paw, and then with the other paw she rubbed its face all over, the wrong way, beginning at the nose: and just now, as I said, she was hard at work on the white kitten, which was lying quite still and trying to purr—no doubt feeling that it was all meant for its good.

But the black kitten had been finished with earlier in the afternoon, and so, while Alice was sitting curled up in a corner of the great arm-chair, half talking to herself and half asleep, the kitten had been having a grand game of romps with the ball of worsted Alice had been trying to wind up, and had been rolling it up and down till it had all come undone again; and there it was, spread over the hearth-rug, all knots and tangles, with the kitten running after its own tail in the middle.
'Oh, you wicked little thing!' cried Alice, catching up the kitten, and giving it a little kiss to make it un-

derstand that it was in disgrace. 'Really, Dinah ought to have taught you better manners! You ought, Dinah, you know you ought!' she added, looking reproachfully at the old cat, and speaking in as cross a voice as she could manage—and then she scrambled back into the arm-chair, taking the kitten and the worsted with her, and began winding up the ball again. But she didn't get on very fast, as she was talking all the time, sometimes to the kitten, and sometimes to herself. Kitty sat very demurely on her knee, pretending to watch the progress of the winding, and now and then putting out one paw and gently touching the ball, as if it would be glad to help, if it might.

'Do you know what to-morrow is, Kitty?' Alice began. 'You'd have guessed if you'd been up in the window with me—only Dinah was making you tidy, so you couldn't. I was watching the boys getting in sticks for the bonfire—and it wants plenty of sticks, Kitty! Only it got so cold, and it snowed so, they had to leave off. Never mind, Kitty, we'll go and see the bonfire to-morrow.' Here Alice wound two or three turns of the worsted round the kitten's neck, just to see how it would look: this led to a scramble, in which the ball rolled down upon the floor, and yards and yards of it got unwound

13. By using the details in the story, what do you think is the setting of the story? Write a sentence that supports your answer.

Question 14 is based on the story below.

The Adventures of Huckleberry Finn by Mark Twain

Excerpt- public domain

I wanted to go and look at a place right about the middle of the island that I'd found when I was exploring; so we started and soon got to it, because the island was only three miles long and a quarter of a mile wide.

This place was a tolerable long, steep hill or ridge about forty feet high. We had a rough time getting to the top, the sides were so steep and the bushes so thick. We tramped and clumb around all over it, and by and by found a good big cavern in the rock, most up to the top on the side towards Illinois. The cavern was as big as two or three rooms bunched together, and Jim could stand up straight in it. It was cool in there. Jim was for putting our traps in there right away, but I said we didn't want to be climbing up and down there all the time.

Jim said if we had the canoe hid in a good place, and had all the traps in the cavern, we could rush there if anybody was to come to the island, and they would never find us without dogs. And, besides, he said them little birds had said it was going to rain, and did I want the things to get wet?

So, we went back, and got the canoe, and paddled up abreast the cavern, and lugged all the traps up there. Then we hunted up a place close by to hide the canoe in, amongst the thick willows. We took some fish off of the lines and set them again, and begun to get ready for dinner.

The door of the cavern was big enough to roll a hogshead in, and on one side of the door the floor stuck out a little bit, and was flat and a good place to build a fire on. So we built it there and cooked dinner.

14. **In this excerpt from Huckleberry Finn, where does the setting of the story take place? Circle the correct answer choice.**

   Ⓐ The setting is in Huck's backyard.
   Ⓑ The setting is on a grassy hillside.
   Ⓒ The setting is on an island in a cavern.
   Ⓓ None of the above.

Question 15 is based on the poem below.

"A Little Road Not Made Of Man"
By Emily Elizabeth Dickinson

A little road not made of man,
Enabled of the eye,
Accessible to thill of bee,
Or cart of butterfly.

If town it have, beyond itself,
'T is that I cannot say;
I only sigh, -- no vehicle
Bears me along that way.

15. **Which are the correct rhyming words in patterns from the poem? Circle the correct answer choice.**

   Ⓐ man, can, eye, bee.
   Ⓑ eye, butterfly, say, way.
   Ⓒ butterfly, sigh, eye, way.
   Ⓓ road, cart, eye, butterfly.

Chapter 2

Lesson 8: Who's Talking Now?

Let us understand the concept with an example.

Point of view: opinion, a way of looking at an issue or event. If writing your own opinion, you can choose to use the pronouns "I" or "we" or "us." If telling someone what to do, use the pronouns "you" or "your." If giving opinions to or about a group, use the pronouns "they" or "them."

Curriculum: the list of courses given by an educational institution (school or college).

I am a newspaper reporter for a newspaper in a small town. Recently, the school board decided to eliminate the art and music programs from the curriculum of the elementary school in town. The reasons given by the school board were:

Need to reduce costs
These courses were less important than other courses like English, Math and Science
Eliminating these courses would allow for more time to be spent on English, Math and Science
Kid's parents can pay for lessons from art and music teachers who work privately outside the school district.

Your assignment: You love music and art and don't want to have them eliminated from the curriculum. You need to make up reasons why they should be kept.

Here is what you might write.

I love music and art. Art allows me to be creative, to make artwork that is completely original. I can bring my artwork home and hang it in my house, or have it hung in school. Science and math force me to follow formulas and steps that are already produced; there is nothing we produce that the rest of the school would be interested in seeing, except a science project once a year. We have a lot of homework in English, Math and Science; we don't need more. We need a break from them to do courses that are pure fun, like art and music. In music, we can pick songs that are fun to sing, and we can even make up our own songs or change the words. We can perform songs in a concert for the school. You can hardly ever do that in math or science. As far as having private teachers, these lessons cost more money for a family than having art and music teachers whose salaries are paid by everyone in town. I hope the school board can find some other way to lower their costs.

You can scan the QR code given below or use the URL to access additional EdSearch resources including videos and mobile apps related to *Who's Talking Now?*

 Who's Talking Now?

URL	QR Code
http://www.lumoslearning.com/a/rl36	

Question 1 is based on the poem below.

I had a silver buckle,
I sewed it on my shoe,
And 'neath a sprig of mistletoe
I danced the evening through!
I had a bunch of cowslips,
I hid 'em in a grot,
In case the elves should come by night
And me remember not.
I had a yellow ribbon,
I tied it in my hair,
That, walking in the garden,
The birds might see it there.
I had a secret laughter,
I laughed it near the wall:
Only the ivy and the wind
May tell of it at all.

By Walter de la Mare (1873-1956), under the pseudonym Walter Ramal, title unknown, from Songs of Childhood, published 1902.

1. Who is the narrator of this poem?

Ⓐ   the birds
Ⓑ   an elf
Ⓒ   I (the writer, author)
Ⓓ   the ivy

Question 2 is based on the paragraph below.

Pearl reached in her pocket for the coins, but she could not feel them. Desperately, she pulled everything out of her pocket. She found a chocolate wrapper, a bus pass, her student ID card, lipstick, mascara, and her cell phone. There were NO coins!

2. Who is telling this story about Pearl?

Ⓐ   Pearl
Ⓑ   Pearl's mother
Ⓒ   a narrator
Ⓓ   the bus driver

Question 3 is based on the poem below.

The Goose that Laid the Golden Egg

A man once had a goose I'm told,
Which had laid each day an egg of gold.
Now if this treasure were well spent,
It might make any one content.
But no! This man desired more;
And though of eggs he had rich store;
He thought one day the goose he'd kill,

And then at once his pockets fill.
So chasing goosey round and round,
She soon was caught and firmly bound
He opened her from neck to tail
And then his folly did bewail.
For not a single egg was there,
And thus he lost this treasure rare.

3. Who is telling the story in this poem? Mark "Yes" or "No" against each character.

	Yes	No
The man	○	○
The goose	○	○
A narrator, outside of the story	○	○
The golden eggs	○	○

Question 4 is based on the story below.

I Don't Want To Go

Emily zipped up her suitcase, sighed loudly, and then lugged it out to the Family Utility Vehicle. "Why do I have to go?" she asked.

"This is a family vacation," replied her dad.

Sure it was, she thought. The idea of spending three entire days and nights sleeping in a tent out in the wilderness that was named after the explorer Daniel Boone did not appeal to her girly side. "Mom, can we stay...?"

Before she could finish, Emily's younger brother came bolting out the door, his suitcase overflowing, and his momentum almost knocking her to the ground. "Let's go, let's go."

Emily climbed into the backseat, her MP3 player blasting loudly; at least she had some piece of civilization left. As they drove for what seemed like forever, Emily enjoyed peering out the window. As they got farther and farther away from the city, she began to catch glimpses of rabbits, squirrels, and various birds that she wasn't used to seeing. The tall buildings and annoying noises of the city began to be replaced by a peaceful quiet. She turned her music off, but kept the ear buds in place, as she didn't want anyone to know that she was enjoying the ride. Finally, she saw the sign: Welcome to the Daniel Boone National Forest.

"Can we hike to the falls?" her brother asked.

She exited the vehicle, declared that she was ready for a walk. She had heard about Cumberland Falls but had never actually seen them. Some of her classmates had mentioned that they were smaller, but a lot like Niagara Falls. She had no desire to let the others know she was excited, but she hoped that her dad would say that they could go exploring.

Looking around her, she saw huge mountains that seemed to tower above the river below. This was much different from the small subdivision that she called home. Just maybe the next three days wouldn't be so bad. As she removed her earbuds, she smiled, as a small deer crossed the pathway several hundred feet in the distance. The first live deer that she had ever seen was when she was twelve. " Wow, this is really amazing! Let's take that walk, Dad."

"Really?" he asked.

4. What point of view is this story written in?

Ⓐ First person spoken through Emily's voice.
Ⓑ First person spoken through Emily's dad's voice.
Ⓒ Third person spoken through an outside narrator.
Ⓓ First person spoken through Emily's brother's voice.

Question 5 is based on the paragraph below.

May 24, 2012
Dear Diary,

I just returned from my first trip to the beach. It was different than I expected. The water scared me a bit, but I tried to act cool in front of my little sister. I couldn't let her know how much the crashing waves scared me.

Building sand castles in the sparkling white grains of sand was a blast, and I even had a chance to bury my sister. That has to be every brother's dream, right? Well, not really, and she was able to break free from the sand wall that I had built up around her.

My favorite place wasn't at the beach, but sitting in the balcony. I loved looking down at the emerald green waters. Maybe when we go back again, I won't be afraid to wander out a little farther into the water. Dad sure did seem to enjoy that a lot. Mom was a lot like me. She just wanted to stay close to the shore.

Jeremiah

P. S. Oh, I almost forgot to tell you that we went looking for crabs three nights in a row, but we did not have any luck. It was still fun. My fear of the ocean seemed to disappear in the night.

5. From what point of view is this story presented?

- Ⓐ Jeremiah's point of view (first person)
- Ⓑ Dad's point of view (first person)
- Ⓒ Narrator point of view (third person)
- Ⓓ Mom's point of view (first person)

Question 6 is based on the story below.

Danny had always been a different kind of child, so I wasn't real happy when Xavier started hanging out with him. I didn't really know how to handle the situation, but I didn't want to be one of those parents that told him he had to stop. When Xavier told me about playing with Danny that first day at recess, I remember thinking, "Oh no…"

It has been about a month since that day, and I still ask every afternoon if anyone lost recess today. It is my way of finding out if Danny or Xavier got into any trouble. This way it doesn't seem so much like I am pointing the finger at Danny. Those first few times that I asked, it seemed that Xavier was always telling me something silly that Danny did to get in trouble: spit wads, pouring his milk into another student's mashed potatoes, running in the hallway, etc. Not bad things, just things that showed disrespect. As the days passed, either Xavier has realized that I am fed up with Danny's silliness or he isn't getting in trouble as much.

I have agreed to let Danny spend the night tonight. The boys are excited about sleeping outside in the tent, and I have arranged for them to make S'mores, have a small campfire, and enjoy the comforts of almost being alone in the wilderness. "Mom, where are you? This is Danny." I stare at Danny. He looks sweet enough. His short haircut makes him look much younger than his age of eight, well, assuming that he is the same age as Xavier.

"Hi, Mrs."
"Just call me Ann. Danny, do you want to see Xavier's room?" I asked.

Danny smiled at me and I was hooked. His crystal blue eyes lit up, and his left cheek had a small, but noticeable dimple. I patted Danny on the back. "We are glad you came to visit," I stated. I walked the boys down the hallway to Xavier's room.

"What's this?" Xavier asked.
"Since this is your first official camp out, I thought you needed the right pajamas. I just guessed your size, Danny, let's hope they fit." Danny scooped the pajamas up, while Xavier just shrugged.

"Is this the bathroom?" I nodded. Moments later, Danny returned, wearing his new pajamas. They were a little large, but they would do. The boy that I had pegged to be the troublemaker seemed so sweet. He threw his tiny arms around me. "These are great..." said Danny. I could see the tears in his eyes, and I pulled him even closer.

"I am glad you like them, Danny," I stated.

6. From what point of view is this story presented?

Ⓐ   Danny's point of view (first person)
Ⓑ   Xavier's point of view (first person)
Ⓒ   Narrator's point of view (third person)
Ⓓ   Ann's point of view (first person)

Question 7 is based on the paragraph below.

I am not feeling good about this at all. I had so much homework last night that I couldn't study for my science test. My stomach is tied in knots, tighter than the ones on my shoestrings. Maybe it won't be as bad as I expect. I mean, let's face it, science is science! I listen in class, I do all of my homework assignments, and I participate in the review games. It will be okay. I am not going to panic! I am not going to panic!

7. From what point of view is this story presented?

Ⓐ   Student's point of view (first person)
Ⓑ   Parent's point of view (first person)
Ⓒ   Teacher's point of view (first person)
Ⓓ   Other's point of view (third person)

Question 8 is based on the paragraph below.

An astronomer used to go out every night to observe stars. Often, he would be seen with a telescope in one hand and a notebook in the other. One evening, while he wandered through the suburbs with his attention fixed on the sky, he accidentally fell into a deep uncovered well. He cried out loudly for help. As he waited to be rescued, he moaned and howled about his sores and bruises. His neighbor was passing by and happened to hear his wailing and weeping. He quickly helped him out of the well. After he came to know how the accident happened, this is what he said to the astronomer: "Hark you old fellow, why in striving to pry into heaven, do you not manage to see what is on earth?"

8. Who is telling this story?

Ⓐ   someone outside of the story
Ⓑ   the astronomer
Ⓒ   the astronomer's wife
Ⓓ   the neighbor

Question 9 is based on the story below.

Robert Bruce, King of Scotland, was hiding in a hut in the forest. His enemies were seeking him far and wide. Six times he had met them in battle, and six times he had failed. Hope and courage were gone. Bruce had given up all as lost. He was about to run away from Scotland and to leave the country in the hands of his enemies.

Full of sorrow, he lay stretched on a pile of straw in the poor woodchopper's hut. While he lay there thinking, he noticed a spider spinning her web.

The spider was trying to spin a thread from one beam of the cottage to another. It was a long way between the beams, and Bruce saw how hard a task it was for her to do. "She will never do it," thought the king. The little spider tried it once and failed. She tried it twice and failed. The king counted each attempt.

She had tried it six times and had failed each time.
"She is like me," thought the king. "I have tried six battles and failed. She has tried to reach the beam six times and failed."

Then staring up from the straw, he cried, "I will hang my fate upon the little spider. If she swings the seventh time and fails, then I will give up all for lost. If she swings the seventh time and wins, I will call my men together once more for a battle with the enemy and never give up, much like the little spider."

The spider tried the seventh time, letting herself down upon her slender thread. She swung out bravely. "Look! look!" shouted the king. "She has reached it. The thread hangs between the two beams. If the spider can do it, I can do it."

Bruce got up from the straw with new strength and sent his men from village to village, calling the people to arms. The brave soldiers answered his call and came trooping in. At length, his army was ready to fight, and when the king led them in a great battle against the enemy, this time, like the spider, Bruce won.

This is an excerpt taken from 'The Beacon Second Reader' which was written by James Fassett.

9. How would this story be different if the spider was telling the story?

- Ⓐ Robert Bruce would not be talking.
- Ⓑ The reader would hear the spider's thoughts.
- Ⓒ The spider would have given up trying to make its web.
- Ⓓ The spider's web would have been larger.

Question 10 is based on the story below.

Gerry walked around enjoying nature. This was his favorite time of day. In less than an hour, the activity would slow down as the zoo closed for the day. The visitors would go home and the zoo workers would spend extra time with the animals. Many times, the workers would offer special treats. Before this could happen, Gerry had to make it through until closing. Looking up, he spotted a family walking close to the edge of the enclosure.

"Let's see the giraffe, Grandma!" one of the two little boys shouted loudly. "I want to see him," the other one yelled. "If you are not quiet, you will scare him off," the grandmother cautioned. She reached into her basket to pull out a handful of lettuce. Gerry couldn't help but move a little closer. It was his favorite kind of lettuce.

The first boy whispered quietly. "Can I have some lettuce? He is coming this way." After getting a handful of the green vegetable, the boy held it over the edge of the enclosure. "Here he comes."

Gerry closed his eyes and chewed the delicious treat in pleasure. This was definitely his favorite time of day.

10. Who is the narrator of the story?

- Ⓐ The narrator is the giraffe.
- Ⓑ The narrator is the grandma with a basket.
- Ⓒ The narrator is NOT a character in the story.
- Ⓓ The narrator is another animal that lives in the forest.

Question 11 is based on the paragraph below.

Water! Water! Safe and clean.

Did you know that as humans, we are full of water in our bodies? Yes, we are! We do know that we must have water to stay alive. We never think about it being a problem to have plenty of water to drink, bathe, wash clothes, and do dishes or even to water our yards. In past years, many environmentalists (people who study our surroundings and who worry about our lands), have warned us that we are not taking good care of our natural resources, water being one of those. We have seen pollution in rivers, streams and wetlands. This will eventually have a negative impact on our easy access to good clean water.

So, here is the question posed to you. What can you do to help? You might think to yourself, "Me, I am just a kid!" You can help. Keep your lawns and driveways free of litter. Water your yard only every 3-5 days. Be sure to turn off water hoses immediately after use.

 Volunteer to help on a weekly basis to go around and pick up litter in your town. Make a list of where you find litter the most and get your friends or class in on the project. Picking up litter will help our water to stay cleaner, too. The less litter we have the fewer possibilities for trash to enter our waterways.

 Do not use plastic bottles or bags. Get your parents to use the cloth bags when they shop for groceries. If you do use plastic, be sure to recycle it. Plastic is bad for our communities and can cause multiple types of pollution.

When showering or bathing, time your shower or bath. Make a chart and have your family do the same. Not only will you save our precious water resources, but you will save your family money on the monthly water bill, as well.

When you wash clothes in the washing machine, do not overfill your water. Either wash smaller loads, or a larger load when necessary. Most washing machines have a level to help you not overuse water.

Water is one of our greatest natural resources. We need it! It is up to all of us to be responsible to keep it plentiful and clean.

11. **Now, brainstorm ways that you can help to save our natural water resources. Write down your ideas below. List at least 4 ideas.**

Question 12 is based on the paragraph below.

Eating Healthy- A good start to staying strong!

Most health professionals encourage people to eat vegetables and fruit on a daily basis!

Some great vegetables include broccoli, okra, spinach, lettuce, green beans, peas, and cabbage. Try new vegetables now and then. It will help you to develop better eating habits. Who knows, you might even like them. I know when I was a kid, I was very leery of okra and spinach. Now, I love them!

Other vegetables include carrots, squash and sweet potatoes. Most kids do not like vegetables, except for carrots and green beans. Again, try a bite every now and then. Most people may not realize it, but there are some fruit like apricots, cantaloupes, and mangos that can take the place of a vegetable in your meals.

It is important in eating to pick vegetables and fruit that have been prepared with little or no added fat, sugar or salt. Fresh fruits and fresh vegetables are the best when the season is right and they are available in your area.

Most vegetables and fruit have little or no fat in them. Try to stay clear of high fat foods when you eat such as French fries, onion rings, and salads with large amounts of dressing, and/ or those fruits served with heavy creams. The same goes for fruit that is in cans or containers with heavy syrup as they have more sugar. More amounts of sugar can add unwanted calories which will make you gain weight.

Everyone knows that most kids do not buy the food, but that their parents do make those choices in stores. So next time you have a chance talk to your mom or dad or whoever does the grocery shopping. Ask them if you can go along or ask them to be sure to pick out fresh fruit whenever possible. Frozen fruit can be a good selection, too, as it is usually just packed with water.

Use your reading skills and read labels before you buy or eat. Share that information with your parents, too.

Healthy bodies need fiber found in vegetables and fruit. Juices on the other hand, do not contain the needed fiber.

Be sure to stay clear of those punches or fruit drinks that are not 100% fruit, too. Usually, they are sources of that heavy syrup and sugar additives that may taste good, but do not benefit your health.

Eating healthy is always a good choice!

12. **What would be the best way to make sure you are eating healthy in regards to fruits and vegetables? Circle the correct answer choice.**

Ⓐ Check your weight daily.
Ⓑ Chart what you eat on a daily basis noting if the vegetables and/or fruit were low in fat and sugar.
Ⓒ Eat tasty food and do not worry.
Ⓓ None of the above.

Question 13 is based on the paragraph below.

Who says guys only cook on the grill

My grandma, mom and sister always do the cooking in the kitchen at our house. It is very good in-deed, do not get me wrong. Sometimes, however, I would like to cook on the stove, too! Dad says that guys do the grilling on the bbq pit outside. Why can't we cook inside, too?

So one day I asked Dad, "Dad, what would you like for supper tonight?" He replied, "Gee, Howard, I would really love hamburger steak with onions, but your mom doesn't want to cook that."

I announced, "Please, let me try to cook it!" Mom and Dad looked at each other and nodded yes.

I was so elated! First thing I did was ask Mom if she had everything we needed. She said she had no idea what we needed. So I looked on our computer under recipes and found several. I began to read off the ingredients. Some she had already and some she said we do not use. I decided to combine a couple of recipes and make my own. Here it is!

Ingredients for the hamburger steak patties:

1 to 1 ½ lbs of hamburger meat- preferably the ground chuck
3-4 tablespoons of cooking oil, we use canola
1 large egg
2/3 cups of really fine chopped onions
1 teaspoon of Worchester sauce- spicy sauce if you would rather
A pinch of salt
A pinch of garlic powder
A pinch of black pepper
About 1/3-1/2 cup of all-purpose flour- use that to coat the patties to brown

Now, the gravy:

Instead of making homemade gravy, Dad and I decided I could use the package of onion gravy mix- I used 2 packages!
A half of an onion sliced real thin, long slices!
A little more Worchester sauce for flavor- a splash or two

Directions:

Take the ingredients for the hamburger steak patties and mix them together- do not add the flour. Form large patties, it will probably make at least 5-6. Flatten as much as you can, but not too thin. Now pat the flour on each side of the patties. In a very large frying pan or skillet, heat your cooking oil until it starts to bubble just a bit. Now place the patties in the oil and cook on each side for about 4-5 minutes until brown. Remove them from the frying pan. Lay aside, but keep warm. (Warning, do not try to flatten your patties, as it will cause them to fall apart. One of mine did fall apart.)

While the pan is still hot and on, add the thinly sliced onions. Let them cook until they start to turn a little brown. Now, lower the flame and add the gravy mix according to the package. Turn the flame back up and let it come to a low boil. Be sure to use a spoon or ladle and stir the gravy while it is cooking.

Let the gravy mix cook on low for about 5 minutes. Add more water a little at a time if it thickens too fast. Now take the patties and add them to the gravy mix. Cover with a lid and cook for no more than 20 minutes on low.

Enjoy! We did! Yes, now my grandma, mom and sister let me cook inside any time I want to try a new recipe! Who says guys only cook on the grill?

13. Part A
If you were to cook a meal for your family, what would you like to cook?
What do you think your ingredients list might look like?

Part B
List 4 ingredients you think you might need.

Question 14 is based on the paragraph below.

School Rules

The students at Morgan Lane Elementary are very upset with some of the new rules. Starting this year, they can no longer have rolling carts to carry their books, lunches, and personal items. The school board became concerned about what some kids might be hiding in the backpacks and rolling carts. Also, last spring, one of the students was hurt when another student's cart hit them in the hallway. Parents are a little upset, but they understand that for safety and security of the students and staff, this is a good idea. The new rule states that only clear see-through backpacks will be allowed. Even students' lunches have to be able to be seen.

This is not making the students happy at all. Mrs. Logan's third-graders have been talking about it all morning. Most of them had already bought their carts and colored backpacks before the rule was adopted by the school board. So here on the first day of school, they are lugging around everything. The stores ran out of the clear see-through backpacks quickly. Some parents just couldn't afford to purchase additional items at such a late date when they had already bought others before.

Needless to say all of this chatter in class, has made it rough for Mrs. Logan to teach on the first day.

She has decided to stop her lesson and have a class discussion. She is using a chart to show good reasons for the changes and to show students concerns about the changes. It also shows possible alternatives or solutions for problems that are being brought up by the students.

Here is what the chart looks like so far.

Positive Effects of New Rule	Negative Effects of New Rule	Possible Alternatives or Solutions
Fewer accidents with carts	Students who are small in size cannot carry backpacks without injury to their backs.	Put in lockers for students so they do not have to worry about carrying so much that is visible to all.
No worries about things that are unrelated to school being in backpacks	Handicap students unable to get around with backpacks	Hold an awareness session to fully explain situations behind the decision
Students and staff are better protected.	Feeling of unrest and not trusting students.	Allow small non-see through bags for personal items.

14. Give two reasons why you feel the rule is good, 2 more reasons why it is a problem and 2 more solutions. Write your answer in the box below.

Chapter 2

Lesson 9: I Can See It Now

Let us understand the concept with an example.

Conveyed: communicated.

Aspects of a character: his/her traits (generous, selfish, cheerful).

Aspects of a setting: details such as color, dimensions, scenery, climate.

The Award

Even though I am much older than the typical college student, I decided to take a musical theater course at a local college just for the fun of it. During the course, I learned songs and dance steps from a real show, which were used to present that show at the end of the course by everyone in the class.

During the course I had to work harder to learn the words to the songs and to learn the dance steps than all of the other students, most of whom had taken singing and dancing lessons recently. But what an exciting feeling it was to finally feel comfortable singing the songs and performing the dance steps in the show, and best of all, to have my classmates vote me "Most Improved." The photograph shows me receiving the award for "Most Improved."

My assignment: To select an illustration (a photo in this case) that makes an important contribution to the text.

This is what I wrote.

While the text states that it was an exciting feeling to perform in the show and to receive the "Most Improved" award, the illustration (in this case, a photo) adds more realism to how I felt by actually showing me smiling and looking proud. Including the photo makes a more dramatic impression on the reader of the emotions I felt than just describing them with words.

You can scan the QR code given below or use the URL to access additional EdSearch resources including videos and mobile apps related to *I Can See It Now.*

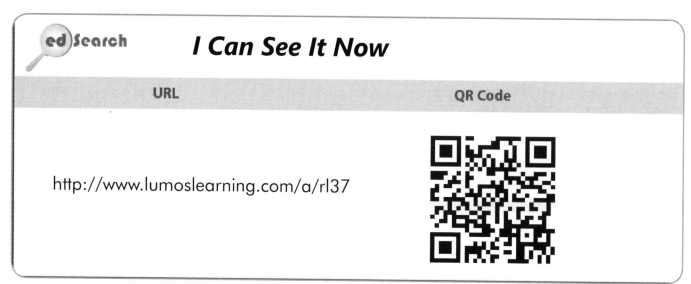

URL	QR Code
http://www.lumoslearning.com/a/rl37	

Question 1-5 are based on the graph below.

Hamburgers	Corn dogs	Pizza	Spaghetti	Mac & Cheese

Look at the graph above and answer the following questions about the lunch menu at Curbside School.

1. What is the most popular item on the lunch menu?

 Ⓐ Hamburgers
 Ⓑ Corn dogs
 Ⓒ Pizza
 Ⓓ Spaghetti
 Ⓔ Mac & cheese

2. What addition to the graph would make it easier for you to decide which item is liked almost as much as spaghetti?

 Ⓐ Pictures
 Ⓑ Headings
 Ⓒ Food descriptions
 Ⓓ Numbers

3. Which item is the students' second favorite?

  Ⓐ Hamburgers
  Ⓑ Corn dogs
  Ⓒ Pizza
  Ⓓ Spaghetti
  Ⓔ Mac & cheese

4. What should the lunch ladies at Curbside School serve most often to keep the students happy?

  Ⓐ Hamburgers
  Ⓑ Corn dogs
  Ⓒ Pizza
  Ⓓ Spaghetti
  Ⓔ Mac & cheese

5. If the lunch ladies at Curbside School drop one item from the lunch menu, what item should be removed?

  Ⓐ Hamburgers
  Ⓑ Corn dogs
  Ⓒ Pizza
  Ⓓ Spaghetti
  Ⓔ Mac & cheese

6. I think this story will be a _____. The mood will be _____. I can tell this because _____.

  Ⓐ A comedy, the mood will be funny, because the picture is a spaceship and spaceships are always funny.
  Ⓑ A fantasy, the mood will be mysterious, because spaceships are intriguing.
  Ⓒ A tragedy, the mood will be sad, because the picture is scary.
  Ⓓ A scary tale, the mood will be frightening, because most people are scared of spaceships.

7. I think this story will be a _____. The mood will be _____. I can tell this because _____.

  Ⓐ The story will be a tragedy; the mood will be sad, dogs don't like wearing hats.
  Ⓑ The story will be a narrative; the mood will be happy, the dogs are smiling
  Ⓒ The story will be nonfiction; the mood will be gloomy, it is a true story about a dog that is very ill.
  Ⓓ The story is an autobiography; the mood will be informative, because dogs like to tell their life histories.

8. I think this story will be a _____. The mood will be _____. I can tell this because _____.

  Ⓐ The story will be a comedy; the mood will be sad, because the little girl looks upset.
  Ⓑ The story will be non-fiction; the mood will be funny, because the little girl is laughing.
  Ⓒ The story will be a narrative; the mood will be serious, because the little girl is thinking.
  Ⓓ The story will be a fantasy; the mood will be thrilling, because the little girl looks scared.

9. **I think this story will be a** _____. **The mood will be** _____. **I can tell this because** _____.

Ⓐ The story will be an autobiography; the mood will be serious, because the dragon will be telling his life story.

Ⓑ The story will be a comedy; the mood will be funny, because the dragon looks like he likes to tell jokes.

Ⓒ The story will be a fantasy; the mood will be scary, because the dragon looks fierce.

Ⓓ The story will be a narrative, the mood will be informational, because the imaginary creature wants to tell the reader about dragons.

10. **What event is represented by the below logos?**

Ⓐ The Olympic games
Ⓑ A theatrical performance
Ⓒ A concert
Ⓓ A business conference

Question 11 is based on the paragraph below.

Students Likes and Dislikes

Mrs. Landry, the librarian at Happy Lane Elementary School was trying to get information about what topics her students wanted to read about. She was designing a reading plan and wanted to be sure that most of the students liked the book selections she was going to use. So, Mrs. Landry developed a chart to show the students likes and dislikes.

The following chart depicts what the third-grade students reported to her on their questionnaire form.

	Adventure	Families	Pets	Hobbies	Mystery	History
Likes	50	107	119	115	100	9
Dislikes	69	12	0	4	19	110

11. What books should Mrs. Landry not choose to have the students read? Highlight the correct answer.

Ⓐ Mrs. Landry should not choose books about pets or families.
Ⓑ Mrs. Landry should choose all the books because the students like all of them.
Ⓒ Mrs. Landry should not choose mystery books.
Ⓓ Mrs. Landry should not choose books about history.

Question 12 and 13 are based on the passage below.

States in the US

Look at the map. Then read the list of states in ABC order. Note that the states of Hawaii and Alaska are not shown in the correct location. The reason for this is simple. Alaska is located on the end of Canada far above Washington to the left. One side of Alaska is located on the Pacific Ocean. It is not connected to the rest of the US. The state of Hawaii is a group of islands located in the Pacific Ocean and again is not adjoined to the US. Thus it, too, would not fit correctly on this map. The Pacific Ocean is on the left of the map in blue, the Gulf of Mexico is on the bottom in blue and flows into the Atlantic Ocean on the right in blue.

The Fifty States in ABC Order:

Alabama, Alaska, Arizona, Arkansas, California,
Colorado, Connecticut
Delaware, Florida, Georgia, Hawaii, Idaho, Illinois,
Indiana
Iowa, Kansas, Kentucky, Louisiana, Maine,
Maryland, Massachusetts, Michigan.
Minnesota, Mississippi, Missouri, Montana,

Nebraska, Nevada,
New Hampshire, New Jersey, New Mexico, New York,
North Carolina, North Dakota, Ohio,
Oklahoma, Oregon, Pennsylvania, Rhode Island,
South Carolina,
South Dakota, Tennessee, Texas,
Utah, Vermont, Virginia, Washington, West Virginia,
Wisconsin, Wyoming.

Carefully review all that you read, and see before answering the questions below.

After reviewing the facts given, the map and the list of states in ABC order, answer the questions.

12. Which states have the Pacific Ocean as their borders? List them.
   HINT: There are five.

13. **Which states have the Gulf of Mexico as borders? List them.**
HINT: There are 5.

Question 14 is based on the passage below.

Playing Video Games

Scotty loves to play video games! I mean he plays every chance he gets. He even plays when he should be doing his homework, chores or going to bed! It has gotten so bad that his parents are considering a punishment to teach him a lesson.

Scotty doesn't understand why they are upset with him and is trying to figure out what he can do so that he doesn't get his video game machine taken away. He has asked his friends for their ideas on the subject, too. He even asked his counselor at school. Scotty has been seeing her since his grades started dropping. The counselor told him it is very simple, give up the game playing on his own and get back to doing homework, chores, and going to bed on time.

To Scotty, the ideas his counselor told him are good, but he is very reluctant to do it. So one of his friends, Hailey, has offered to help. She is going to make him a chart of time spent on playing games compared to time spent on his responsibilities. He agrees to give it a try.

14. **Based on this chart, complete the chart totals. For "Going to Bed On Time", count the days he did go to bed on time.**

	Monday	Tuesday	Wednesday	Thursday	Friday	Saturday	Sunday	Totals
Playing Video Games	4 hours	4 hours	3 hours	3 hours	2 hours	3 hours	3 hours	
Doing Homework	30 min	30 min	1 hour	1 hour	1 hour	none	none	
Doing Chores	15 min	15 min	45 min	45 min	45 min	2 hours	1 hour	
Going to Bed On Time	Not done	Not done	Not done	Done	Not done	Done	Done	

Chapter 2

Lesson 10: Alike and Different

Theme: the main idea of a story.
Setting: the time and place in which the story takes place.
Plot: the most important actions, plans or events taking place in a story that support the main idea or theme of the story.
Supporting statements: text that explains or adds more detail to the theme (main idea). For instance, giving examples.

Cheater Pants and Junie B. Jones and the Mushy, Gushy Valentine by Barbara Park, both starring Junie B. Jones in the Junie B. Jones series, will be used as examples for how you might meet the requirements of this standard.

Publisher's Note: Here are some suggestions for how you might write a text that does what the standard asks for.
1. Before you can compare and contrast anything, you must first identify the themes (main ideas), settings (times and places) plots and supporting statements.
2. After doing step 1, you need to figure out what is the same or similar about the themes, settings and plots, in both stories, and what is different about them.

Here is an example of what you might write.

Cheater Pants tells a story about two times Junie cheated in school, once by copying an essay a classmate wrote for homework and another about copying another classmate's test answer that the classmate purposely showed to her. While these two events are important to the story, they are not the main theme; the main theme is telling the reader how Junie and the classmate felt after they had cheated, how they were punished, and how they felt when the story ended. I think the author planned the main theme to discourage readers from cheating by showing them the negative emotions they would feel.

Junie B. Jones and the Mushy, Gushy Valentine tells about a special day that Junie's teacher planned for the class to celebrate Valentine's Day. The children were all excited as they and the teacher talked about what they would do on that day, just as you would be if it happened in your school. But just as in Cheater Pants, the main theme is not about the event itself; instead it is about something else. In this story, it is about how an event that was supposed to celebrate a day where everyone shared love and kindness was turned into competition and bragging and insults that the students caused among themselves.

But the theme also allowed for something happy to happen at the end. I think the author wanted to send a message that even an event that stands for love and sharing (Valentine's Day) can be spoiled if children forget what the purpose of the day is, and allow selfish and unpleasant behavior to spoil it, except that the ending shows that it is possible for Junie and a classmate to experience the true meaning of Valentine's Day.

A setting is both time and place. The place was at the same school for both stories, but the Cheater story took place in first grade and the Valentine story took place in kindergarten, with different teachers and different classmates. Also, parts of both stories took place in Junie's house with her parents. For Cheater, the time could have been anytime during the school year; for Valentine, it was the days before and the day of Valentine's Day.

What about the plots? The most important events in Cheater Pants were: Junie did not do her written homework; she was worried because in school the next day the teacher made each student read what they wrote, and as she feared, the teacher figured out that Junie had copied a classmate's homework without the classmate knowing it. She also felt shame and humiliation when the teacher punished her, and sent a note to her parents who also punished her for what she did. But then she forgot to study for a spelling test and when a classmate saw her struggling over a word, held his paper so she could copy the answer. Both were not caught, but felt so guilty that they confessed to the teacher who praised them for their honesty. The plot describes the mostly negative feelings the two had but ended with a positive feeling.

For Junie B. Jones and the Mushy, Gushy Valentine, the most important events were: the excitement that happened when the teacher told them about plans for a Valentine's Day celebration in the classroom; the excitement of cutting out hearts and pasting them on the box that the students would drop their Valentine's Day cards into; the competition between Junie and a classmate to see who could cut out the most hearts; the bragging competition about who would get the most cards; Junie selecting a skunk card for a classmate she did not like; Junie's disappointment at getting one less card than her classmates; Junie's joy when the beautiful missing card is found; Junie's search for the secret admirer who sent it; and the joy the sender and Junie felt when his identity was discovered. This plot changed from happy feelings to negative feelings to happy feelings at the end.

You can scan the QR code given below or use the URL to access additional EdSearch resources including videos and mobile apps related to *Alike and Different*.

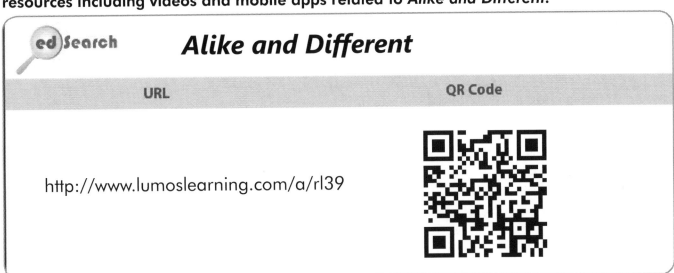

ed)Search

Alike and Different

URL	QR Code
http://www.lumoslearning.com/a/rl39	

Question 1 and 2 are based on the story below.

One day, a baby elephant was happily dancing through the jungle, nodding his head and lifting his trunk to trumpet loudly.

The loud sound woke up a monkey who was sleeping in a tree nearby. He was very angry. He scolded the elephant and asked him to keep quiet.

"You silly animal," he said. "Can't you keep quiet? I'm sleeping."

"Oh, sorry," said the little elephant, and walked on. After some time, the little elephant reached a river and saw some beautiful swans there. He gazed at the beautiful birds. The swans looked at him and began to laugh.

"Oh! Look at that big creature," they said. "What a long nose, his ears are like fans, and look at his skin, it's much too big for him. He looks like a big wrinkled bag with all of those folds!" They laughed at him and swam away.

The little elephant was very sad. He tried to smooth out his skin with his trunk, but it was no good. He thought, "Why am I so ugly? Let me hide so that no one can see me."

He tried to hide in a thick bush, but he disturbed some nests. The birds flew above his head, crying loudly while trying to peck at him.

The little elephant ran for cover. He went behind a big rock to hide. Suddenly, he saw a big bear coming towards him. It was growling and appeared to be very angry. The little elephant was very frightened and trumpeted loudly. Just as he trumpeted, he heard a loud crashing and stomping. A herd of elephants came charging to the rescue.

Seeing the herd, the frightened bear ran away.

The little elephant joyfully ran to the big elephants, thanked them, and said, "I wish I could be like you. You're so mighty and strong," he continued.

"But you are," replied the elephants. "You're a perfect little elephant." The little elephant danced for joy; he trumpeted loudly and walked away happily with the other elephants following behind.

1. What was different about the little elephant from the other animals?

Ⓐ He is smaller than the other animals.
Ⓑ He looks different than the other animals.
Ⓒ He is weaker than the other animals.
Ⓓ He is quieter than the other animals.

2. Who is the little elephant most like in this story?

Ⓐ The other elephants
Ⓑ The bear
Ⓒ The birds
Ⓓ The monkey

Question 3 is based on the paragraph below.

An astronomer used to go out every night to observe stars. Often, he would be seen with a telescope in one hand and a notebook in the other. One evening, while he wandered through the suburbs with his attention fixed on the sky, he accidentally fell into a deep uncovered well. He cried out loudly for help. As he waited to be rescued, he moaned and howled about his sores and bruises. His neighbor was passing by and happened to hear his wailing and weeping. He quickly helped him out of the well. After he came to know how the accident happened, this is what he said to the astronomer: "Hark you old fellow, why in striving to pry into heaven, do you not manage to see what is on earth?"

3. How is the neighbor different than the astronomer?

Ⓐ The neighbor is more interested in the sky than the astronomer is.
Ⓑ The astronomer is awake at night while the neighbor is asleep.
Ⓒ The astronomer likes to read, but the neighbor does not.
Ⓓ The neighbor is concerned with things on earth while the astronomer is concerned with things in the sky.

Question 4 is based on the passages below.

Read BOTH passages. Then answer the question that follows.

Passage 1 - I Don't Want To Go

Emily zipped up her suitcase, sighed loudly, and then lugged it out to the Family Utility Vehicle. "Why do I have to go?" she asked.

"This is a family vacation," replied her dad.

Sure it was, she thought. The idea of spending three entire days and nights sleeping in a tent out in the wilderness that was named after the explorer Daniel Boone did not appeal to her girly side. "Mom, can we stay...?"

Before she could finish, Emily's younger brother came bolting out the door, his suitcase overflowing, and his momentum almost knocking her to the ground. "Let's go, let's go."

Emily climbed into the backseat, her MP3 player blasting loudly; at least she had some piece of civilization left. As they drove for what seemed like forever, Emily enjoyed peering out the window. As they got farther and farther away from the city, she began to catch glimpses of rabbits, squirrels, and various birds that she wasn't used to seeing. The tall buildings and annoying noises of the city began to be replaced by a peaceful quiet. She turned her music off, but kept the ear buds in place, as she didn't want anyone to know that she was enjoying the ride. Finally, she saw the sign: Welcome to the Daniel Boone National Forest.

"Can we hike to the falls?" her brother asked.

She exited the vehicle, declared that she was ready for a walk. She had heard about Cumberland Falls but had never actually seen them. Some of her classmates had mentioned that they were smaller, but a lot like Niagara Falls. She had no desire to let the others know she was excited, but she hoped that her dad would say that they could go exploring.

Looking around her, she saw huge mountains that seemed to tower above the river below. This was much different from the small subdivision that she called home. Just maybe the next three days wouldn't be so bad. As she removed her earbuds, she smiled, as a small deer crossed the pathway several hundred feet in the distance. The first live deer that she had ever seen was when she was twelve. " Wow, this is really amazing! Let's take that walk, Dad."

"Really?" he asked.

Passage 2

Jasmine nervously left the car. She and her parents had been riding for what seemed like days, but after ten hours, they were finally here. She carefully studied the old farmhouse. "Are you ready?" her dad asked. Jasmine only shrugged. She had talked with her "G", as the kind lady had referred to herself, a few times on the phone, but at the age of eight, she had never actually met her grandma. It seemed that work, school, or illness had kept her away.

Jasmine's parents had told her stories about her "G" and that she had met her when she was only a few months old, but in Jasmine's mind this was the first time. She exited the car and was greeted by a petite, black-haired lady, standing in the doorway. Her smile looked familiar. It seemed to be a combination of her own and the warm smile that her dad seldom showed, but that warmed her heart, over and over.

Her "G" had scooped her up. "Come on in here, Jasmine." Jasmine felt a bit nervous, but she walked into the house with her grandmother's arms still around her. I bet you are tired of sitting. "How long have you had my beautiful granddaughter cooped up in that car?" asked her "G".
Jasmine's dad replied, "It has been a while."

"Come on, honey. There is so much that I want to show you." her grandma cooed. Jasmine followed her grandmother through the house. It seemed that they exited one doorway, only to enter another. "Here is a surprise for you," her grandma stated. Looking down, Jasmine saw the most beautiful locket. She picked it up, nervously. "I have been saving this for you. It was your great granny's...my mom's." Jasmine pulled it closer for a better view.

"Let me put it on you, you beautiful girl."

4. How are the themes in these passages related?

Ⓐ Both girls have negative feelings about a new situation that they are being made to do. Both of their experiences turned out to be positive.

Ⓑ Both girls have negative feelings about something they are being made to do. Their experiences turn out to be worse than planned.

Ⓒ Both girls are excited to try something new.

Ⓓ Both girls are meeting someone new for the first time.

Question 5 and 6 are based on the passages below.

Read BOTH passages, and answer the questions that follow.

Passage 1: Cell Phones in the Classroom

A familiar ringtone sounds in the classroom directing everyone's attention to a shy student in the back row. Several years ago, this would have seemed a bit strange, but not today. A recent study showed that one in three third-grade students have a cell phone. With so many students having access to technology devices, a lot of talks have gone into deciding whether to use them as learning tools or to ban them from the classroom.

Let's think about cell phones' role as learning tools. Annie needs a calculator but forgot hers. She takes out her cell phone and can use the calculator app on the phone. Just across the room, Johnny is trying to spell the word "similar," so he uses the dictionary app on his phone to find the correct spelling. Mitchell, has completed all of his work early, so he decides to use the multiplication app on his phone to review multiplication facts in a fun and interactive way. These devices are causing teachers and other school officials to see that cell phones give students access to resources that actually save schools money.

While cell phones may sound great, not every school district is ready to lift the cell phone ban. There are still those that have major concerns. One concern is what to do about students who do not have a cell phone. Another worry is how to make sure students are using the phone as a learning tool instead of texting and social media. Additional concerns arise with how to address when a phone is broken or stolen while at school. Certainly, the list of problems that some schools have goes on and on.

The answer isn't clear for schools across the United States. Some schools are starting to lift the cell phone ban, but others are keeping it in place. As students pack backpacks with cell phones, the discussion of having them in the classroom will certainly continue.

Passage 2: Always Worked Fine Before

I hear a lot of talk about allowing cell phones in the classroom. Why? There is nothing wrong with the way things are now. If you allow cell phones in classrooms, you are asking for trouble.

Cell phones may distract students to off-task behaviors. Students may tell you that they are playing learning games, but how do you know that they are not sending texts? Students may skip doing their assignments so that they can hurry and play learning games. Cell phones will make classrooms noisier. If everyone gets messages, plays games, or receives phone calls, think about how noisy class-rooms will be.

We really do not need cell phones in our classrooms. It seems to me that our classrooms are functioning correctly as they are right now. They are helping prepare me and other students for the future.

5. According to Passage 1, What is the BIGGEST reason that schools are considering allowing the use of cell phones?

Ⓐ Schools are running out of money.
Ⓑ Cell phones are great educational tools.
Ⓒ Cell phones could help with the constant stream of school emergencies.
Ⓓ Parents are forcing schools to allow their kids to have access to their phones.

6. How are these passages different?

Ⓐ One passage is talking about both sides of the cell phone argument. The second passage is talking only about why cell phones are needed in the classroom.
Ⓑ The first passage is talking about both sides of the cell phone argument. The second passage is talking only about why cell phones are NOT needed in the classroom.
Ⓒ Both passages are too similar to pick out a difference.
Ⓓ One passage argues that cell phones cost too much money. The other passage argues that cell phones are too noisy.

Question 7 is based on the passage below.

The Olympic games have endured for over 100 years. They remain a passion for fans, athletes, and trainers all over the world. While the love of this worldwide event is well-known, many changes have occurred since 1896.

In 1896, the Olympic games had 42 events and 245 competitors. These games were hosted in Athens, Greece. Only 14 nations were represented in the Olympic games. In Greece, A little over one hundred years ago, women were not allowed to participate in the Olympic games. The most successful athlete from the 1896 games was a German wrestler and gymnast named Carl Schumann. Schumann won 4 gold medals.

The 2008 Olympic Games showed how much a century can change things. Over 200 nations were represented in Beijing, China. There were over 10,000 males and females who competed for their chance at gold. A total of over 300 events were completed. The most successful athlete from the 2008 games was American swimmer Michael Phelps. Phelps earned 8 gold medals in the 2008 Olympics. This was a new record for the most gold medals won during a single Olympics event. The 2008 Olympic games marked an end for two popular events: baseball and softball.

While a lot has changed about the Olympic games, some have remained the same. The games are still held every four years. The International Sports Federation Rules continue to apply to the event. The gold, silver, and bronze medals are given today, just as they were 116 years ago in Athens, Greece.

7. Which of the following would be a major change to the present day Olympic games?

Ⓐ Changing the Olympic Games to be in the same location EVERY year
Ⓑ Adding new events
Ⓒ Getting rid of some outdated events
Ⓓ Adding new countries to those that already participate in the Olympic Games

Question 8 is based on the passages below.

From McGuffey's <u>Second Eclectic Reader</u>

1. There are three kinds of bees: workers, drones, and queens.
2. Bees live in a house that is called a hive.
3. Only one queen can live in each hive. If she is lost or dead, the other bees will stop their work.
4. They are very wise and busy little creatures. They all join together to build cells of wax for their honey.
5. Each bee takes its proper place, and does its own work. Some go out and gather honey from the flowers; others stay at home and work inside the hive.
6. The cells which they build, are all one shape and size, and there are no spaces between them.
7. The cells are not round, but have six sides.
8. Have you ever looked into a glass hive to see the bees at work? They are always busy.
9. The drones do not work. Every year before winter, all of the drones are driven from the hive or killed. The reason the drones are driven from the hive or killed is because they did not help make the honey.
10. It is not quite safe for children to handle bees because they have stingers. Bees use their stingers as a great defensive tool.

8. Based on this paragraph, how is the queen bee different from the other bees in the hive?

Ⓐ The queen bee is much smaller than the other bees.
Ⓑ The queen bee works harder than the other bees.
Ⓒ There are more worker bees than there are queen bees.
Ⓓ The queen bee lives in the hive while the other bees live outside of the hive.

Question 9 and 10 are based on the story below.

Brandon lived with his mother at one end of the forest. His school was at the other end of the forest. Every day he had to go through the forest to get to school and the forest was very scary.

One day he told his mother that he felt very scared to cross that forest.

His mother said, "Don't be scared" "Your brother lives in the forest. Whenever you get scared, you can always call him. He won't answer you but he will see that no harm comes to you."

Brandon said, "Why did you not tell me about my brother earlier? What is his name?"

Mother said, "His name is Courage. Whenever you get frightened, call his name, and he will silently follow you to school and see that you come back home safely."

The next day Brandon was happy to get ready for school. He was not scared as he went through the forest on the way to school. That day, while coming home from school, he got scared when he heard the sounds of animals. He then remembered his mother's words that his brother would protect him whenever he was frightened.

Brandon called out "Courage, Courage" with full confidence. Suddenly he began to feel better. He began to feel brave. He again called out, "Courage!, Courage!" He thought that his brother was silently following him, he began to sing softly and then loudly. He realized that he was not frightened after all. He crossed the forest confidently with courage.

The only thing we need to have is confidence and courage in ourselves to move ahead.

9. How do Brandon's feelings about the forest change from the beginning of the story to the end of the story?

   Ⓐ Brandon is scared of the forest at the beginning of the story but because he finds courage he is not scared of the forest at the end of the story.
   Ⓑ Brandon's feelings about the forest are the same in the beginning and end of the story.
   Ⓒ Brandon loves the forest in the beginning of the story but becomes afraid of the forest at the end of the story.
   Ⓓ Brandon actually lives in the city and only dreams of the forest.

10. How does Brandon change as the story moves along?

   Ⓐ Brandon becomes less brave.
   Ⓑ Brandon becomes more afraid.
   Ⓒ Brandon becomes less afraid.
   Ⓓ Brandon becomes more and more lost in the forest.

Question 11 and 12 are based on the passage below.

The New Year Celebrations in Different Countries

In the United States, the New Year begins every January 1st. On the night before, most people celebrate the coming of the New Year right before and when the clock strikes 12:00 am. People generally make what is called "New Year's Resolutions". In doing so, they choose something that they want to change or make better in their lives. Some may decide to lose weight, save money, get along better with others, or even to quit a bad habit. The resolution is supposed to be kept and followed all during the year. It is a kind of promise a person makes to themselves. People tend to break self-made promises early on in the year.

Chinese New Year

The Chinese New Year, commonly called the Spring Festival in China is celebrated at the changing of the traditional lunisolar calendar"-Chinese calendar. The Chinese celebrate beginning on the first new moon, between what we in the United States know as January 21 and February 20. The Chinese start their celebrations on the evening before and continue to celebrate through until around the 15th day of their first calendar month. The Chinese New Year is centuries old and began as a time to honor ancestors and people of high ranking political and religious statuses. Many of the customs of Chinese New Year continue to be followed not only in China, other Chinese influenced countries, but in the United States, as well. These include the annual family dinner, the complete house cleaning to ward off evil and welcome good, and the many parades, brightly decorated costumes, and wall hangings.

The Indian New Year

Ugadi is the official name given to the festival celebrated as the New Year in India. The name, Ugadi, means the beginning of a new age. It is celebrated on the first day of the Hindu month, Chaitra, thus marking the beginning of spring. It is thought that the Lord Brahma began creation on this day according to Hindu culture. The celebration is highlighted by the serving of magnificent meals. The festival is also known for the cleaning of houses, and wearing of new clothes. In the Indian calendar, each year has a name. There are 60 names and the names are repeated every 60 years.

11. What ways are the celebrations in China and India similar to one another? Circle the correct answer choice

Ⓐ The celebrations occur at different times and have no similarities.
Ⓑ In both China and India, houses are cleaned and expansive meals are served.
Ⓒ The calendars seem to be similar to one another.
Ⓓ None of the above.

12. **Which fact stands out to be unique regarding one of the celebrations and historical information given? Circle the correct answer choice.**

Ⓐ China has been celebrating for centuries.

Ⓑ The United States starts celebrating the night before the New Year.

Ⓒ The fact that in India they have 60 different names for each New Year and it repeats itself after 60 years.

Ⓓ China and India celebrate at different times of the year.

Question 13 is based on the passage below.

Thomas Jefferson (Founding Father) and Benjamin Franklin (Politician)

Thomas Jefferson, Founding Father and Third President of the United States of America. Apr 13, 1743 - Jul 04, 1826

Thomas Jefferson is known as one of the Founding Fathers of the United States. He helped the Americans to realize they needed to separate from Great Britain (England) and form a new nation. He was the main author of the Declaration of Independence. Before becoming President of the United States in 1800, he was the Vice President under John Adams.

He was born and educated in Virginia. After graduating from college, he became a lawyer. He helped to increase the new United States shipping trade as President. He also organized the Louisiana Purchase which gave the United States more land as its own. He served two terms as President and is considered one of the greatest Presidents of the United States.

Benjamin Franklin- Politician, Author and Inventor Jan 17, 1706 - Apr 17, 1790

Benjamin Franklin was also considered one of the Founding Fathers of the United States of America. He was a well-known author. Many of his writings caused great uproar when the colonies were having such political differences with England (Great Britain). In fact, some people said he was a revolutionary because his literary works helped the people in fighting to leave (separate from) England and become their own country . He is noted for his many inventions, as well. His major inventions were that of electricity, the lightning rod, and a cooking stove. Benjamin Franklin was a former speaker of the Pennsylvania House of Representatives.

His writings include Poor Richard's Almanack. He was focused on improving one's one behavior and even wrote a list of 13 virtues that he tried to improve on throughout his life. He wrote these at the early age of 20.

They are as follows: 1. Temperance, 2. Silence, 3. Order, 4. Resolution, 5. Frugality, 6. Industry, 7. Sincerity, 8. Justice, 9. Moderation, 10. Cleanliness, 11. Tranquility, 12. Chastity, and 13. Humility. Franklin was an excellent reader, but did not graduate from any well- known school or college. He was as some would say, self- educated. His family did not have the money to send him to school.

13. Now reread both passages, look at the Venn diagram and Match the characteristics that are only for "Jefferson", "Franklin" under the respective space provided and the common characters of both under the "Like" space.

Use these detailed characteristics to complete your diagram.

1. Founding Father
2. President of the United States
3. Inventor of electricity, lightning rod, cooking stove
4. Politician
5. Author
6. Lived in the 1700s
7. Helped the colonists in breaking away from England
8. Well remembered in US History
9. Attended college
10. Unable to attend college, but well educated
11. Known to have helped the US acquire the Louisiana Purchase
12. Wrote Poor Richard's Almanack.

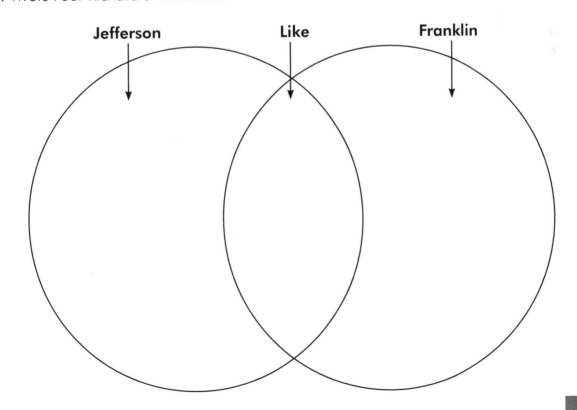

Chapter 2

Lesson 11: Setting the Scene

You can scan the QR code given below or use the URL to access additional EdSearch resources including videos and mobile apps related to *Setting the Scene*.

Search

Setting the Scene

URL	QR Code
http://www.lumoslearning.com/a/rl39	

Question 1-4 are based on the story below.

Brandon lived with his mother at one end of the forest. His school was at the other end of the forest. Every day he had to go through the forest to get to school and the forest was very scary.

One day he told his mother that he felt very scared to cross that forest.

His mother said, "Don't be scared" "Your brother lives in the forest. Whenever you get scared, you can always call him. He won't answer you but he will see that no harm comes to you."

Brandon said, "Why did you not tell me about my brother earlier? What is his name?"

Mother said, "His name is Courage. Whenever you get frightened, call his name, and he will silently follow you to school and see that you come back home safely."

The next day Brandon was happy to get ready for school. He was not scared as he went through the forest on the way to school. That day, while coming home from school, he got scared when he heard the sounds of animals. He then remembered his mother's words that his brother would protect him whenever he was frightened.

Brandon called out "Courage, Courage" with full confidence. Suddenly he began to feel better. He began to feel brave. He again called out, "Courage!, Courage!" He thought that his brother was silently following him, he began to sing softly and then loudly. He realized that he was not frightened after all. He crossed the forest confidently with courage.

The only thing we need to have is confidence and courage in ourselves to move ahead.

1. Where did Brandon live?

[ ]

2. In what setting does Brandon find his courage?

Ⓐ the forest
Ⓑ his house
Ⓒ school
Ⓓ his friend's house

3. Which is a likely setting for this story?

Ⓐ a jungle
Ⓑ a zoo
Ⓒ a forest
Ⓓ on an African safari

4. What does the setting in a story mean? Circle the correct answer choice.

Ⓐ the main person in the story
Ⓑ the time and place where the story happens
Ⓒ the message in the story
Ⓓ the end of the story

Question 5 is based on the story below.

An astronomer used to go out every night to observe stars. Often, he would be seen with a telescope in one hand and a notebook in the other. One evening, while he wandered through the suburbs with his attention fixed on the sky, he accidentally fell into a deep uncovered well. He cried out loudly for help. As he waited to be rescued, he moaned and howled about his sores and bruises. His neighbor was passing by and happened to hear his wailing and weeping. He quickly helped him out of the well. After he came to know how the accident happened, this is what he said to the astronomer: "Hark you old fellow, why in striving to pry into heaven, do you not manage to see what is on earth?"

5. Part A

Where does this paragraph take place?

Ⓐ in the astronomer's home
Ⓑ in a planetarium
Ⓒ outdoors at night
Ⓓ outdoors during the day

Part B

How might this story be different if it was set during the day?

Ⓐ The astronomer's neighbor would be able to hear him better during the day.
Ⓑ The astronomer would not have been looking at the stars in the sky, and would have been paying attention to where he was going.
Ⓒ The astronomer would be able to see the stars more clearly during the day.
Ⓓ The astronomer would have been asleep during the day.

Question 6 is based on the poem below.

Camels are bumpy,
Their backs are all lumpy,
Giraffes are long- legged and meek:
Bears are so growl,
Hyenas are howly,
Dolphins are slippery and sleek.

Kangaroos have a pocket,
But no way to lock it,
Their babies can look out and peep,
But monkeys are funny
I wish I had money,
Enough to buy one and keep.

6. Where does this poem most likely take place?

 Ⓐ at an amusement park
 Ⓑ at a veterinarian's office
 Ⓒ at the zoo
 Ⓓ in the forest

Question 7 is based on the story below.

My First Trip to the Beach

About three weeks ago, Jeremiah's parents surprised him with some news. They were taking him to the beach. He was excited and couldn't wait to tell all of his friends at school.

Soon enough, Friday afternoon arrived. Jeremiah, his sister, his parents, and his nanny all loaded into the car, and set out for the long drive to Destin, Florida. Listening to DVD's grew old rather quickly. A nap was sure to allow Jeremiah to get closer to Florida without growing bored from the ride.

When he awoke from his nap, it was time to stop for dinner. He exited the car, excited to stretch his legs. "Come on, Jeremiah," exclaimed his nanny. He was glad that she had been able to come to the beach. This was also going to be her first time seeing the ocean.

After a quick meal at a fast-food restaurant, the family piled back into the car.

The family arrived at their condo, almost too tired to enjoy the peaceful sound of the ocean. As Jeremiah headed to bed, he knew that the beach would be his to explore in a few hours. He stretched out his small frame across the twin-sized bed and soon fell asleep. He awoke a few hours later, hearing his dad outside on the balcony.

When Jeremiah finally saw the view in the daylight, he was in awe. Beautiful green waters lay off in the distance. They seemed to go on and on, as far as his eyes could see. The sand reminded him of snow.

"Wanna go for a walk?" asked his dad.

Jeremiah smiled, "Yes!" Running back inside, he threw his shoes on. His dad said that he didn't want to try to wear those in the soft, grainy sand. He dressed, and then off they went.

"What's this?" asked Jeremiah, pointing to a loose mound of sand.
"This is a sand dune, it keeps the buildings safe," his dad replied.

"Oh, okay…" Jeremiah and his dad walked along the ocean's edge. There were few words spoken, but the looks on their faces expressed feelings of happiness, as they walked along the beautiful water's edge.

7. Which of the following BEST describes the family's vacation destination?

Ⓐ   the beach
Ⓑ   Destin, Florida
Ⓒ   across state lines
Ⓓ   somewhere with a lot of water

Question 8 is based on the passage below.

Directions: Read the following play. Then answer the question that follows.
BROCK: (Brock enters the stage.) What a great day it is.
TERRY: (Snarls) What's good about it?
BROCK: (Laughs) I found something outside on the playground.
TERRY: (Rolls eyes).
MRS. ADAMS: (Walks over). Good morning, boys.
BROCK AND TERRY: Good morning.
MRS. ADAMS: (MOTIONS). Sit down, boys.
TERRY: (Pushes Brock.)
BROCK: Why did you do that? (In a rather loud voice).
TERRY: (Throws hands into the air and pushes Brock again).
MRS. ADAMS: (Runs over). Boys, is this how we want to start the week off?
TERRY: (Sighs.) But, Brock says it is a great day, and…
MRS. ADAMS: (Looks confused). You are upset, just because Brock is happy?
TERRY: (Shakes head no).
BROCK: I don't know what's wrong with him.
TERRY: (Reaches into his pocket.) My mom gave me twenty dollars to pay for my lunch bill, but I can't find it. She is going to be really mad.
BROCK: (Smiles)
MRS. ADAMS: When did you last have the money?
BROCK: (Reaches into his pocket.) Remember that I told you I found something?

TERRY: (Nods).
BROCK: (Hands money to Terry). I found this outside. I bet you dropped it.
TERRY: (Hugs Brock).

8. Where is the setting for this play?

Ⓐ inside of a classroom
Ⓑ outside on the playground
Ⓒ at Terry's house
Ⓓ at the park

Question 9 is based on the story below.

Jasmine nervously left the car. She and her parents had been riding for what seemed like days, but after ten hours, they were finally here. She carefully studied the old farmhouse. "Are you ready?" her dad asked. Jasmine only shrugged. She had talked with her "G", as the kind lady had referred to herself, a few times on the phone, but at the age of eight, she had never actually met her grandma. It seemed that work, school, or illness had kept her away.

Jasmine's parents had told her stories about her "G" and that she had met her when she was only a few months old, but in Jasmine's mind this was the first time. She exited the car and was greeted by a petite, black-haired lady, standing in the doorway. Her smile looked familiar. It seemed to be a combination of her own and the warm smile that her dad seldom showed, but that warmed her heart, over and over.

Her "G" had scooped her up. "Come on in here, Jasmine." Jasmine felt a bit nervous, but she walked into the house with her grandmother's arms still around her. I bet you are tired of sitting. "How long have you had my beautiful granddaughter cooped up in that car?" asked her "G".

Jasmine's dad replied, "It has been a while."
"Come on, honey. There is so much that I want to show you." her grandma cooed. Jasmine followed her grandmother through the house. It seemed that they exited one doorway, only to enter another. "Here is a surprise for you," her grandma stated. Looking down, Jasmine saw the most beautiful locket. She picked it up, nervously. "I have been saving this for you. It was your great granny's...my mom's." Jasmine pulled it closer for a better view.
"Let me put it on you, you beautiful girl."

9. Which of the following BEST describes Jasmine's location in this story?

Ⓐ At her home
Ⓑ At her daddy's house
Ⓒ At her friend's house
Ⓓ At her G's house

End of Reading: Literature

Answer Key and Detailed Explanations

Chapter 2: Reading: Literature

Lesson 1: The Question Session

Question No.	Answer	Detailed Explanations
1	C	Margaret is Amy's mother. The story's opening two lines, "Margaret was a simple lady who lived with her husband Robert. They had a daughter named Amy," explains the relationship between Margaret and Amy. Since Margaret is a lady and her daughter is Amy that makes Margaret her mother.
2	D	Rebecca is the one who slipped on the narrow bridge as she was crossing it. The beginning of paragraph 4 provides this answer for the reader.
3	C	Robert and Margaret went along with the girls because both destinations were across the river. The girls were going to school and Robert and Margaret were going to buy groceries.
4	B	The elephant's skin has too many folds. This is the reason it looks wrinkly. This answer is found in paragraph 5 when the swans describe the elephant's skin.
5	B	Line 2 of stanza 1 answers the question of where is the camel's hump. It is on the back.
6	C	Giraffe is the correct answer because line three of the first stanza describes the giraffe as long-legged.
7 Part A		The first paragraph of the poem tells us that the Dolphins are slippery and sleek. From this, we can understand that the Dolphins live underwater, and skin texture makes them slippery. The body shape is sleek and helps to move underwater with ease.
7 Part B		As stated in the poem dolphins are slippery and sleek. One can draw the conclusion that dolphins are slippery because of being in the water and the texture of their skin is smooth.

Question 8:

Animals	Has Hump	Has Pocket	Slippery	Long legged
Kangaroo		✓		
Camel	✓			
Giraffe				✓
Dolphins			✓	

Question No.	Answer	Detailed Explanations
9	C	Before the operation the lady could not see clearly. This is found in the second sentence of the selection.

Question No.	Answer	Detailed Explanations
10		"Confidence and Courage" is the best title for this selection because it describes what the story is about. A young boy must find the confidence and courage to travel through a forest that scares him. This is a sample title given. Other relevant titles may be suitably graded by teacher / parent.
11	The Neurosurgeon	The neurosurgeon is the character who saved Andrew's life. He performed the brain operation, free of charge, that was needed to save Andrew's life.
12	C	Tess' parents were worried because Andrew was sick and they did not have the money needed for his treatment. This answer is found in the opening paragraph of this selection.

Lesson 2: Tell Me Again

Question No.	Answer	Detailed Explanations
1	B	A baby elephant trumpeted loudly. This loud sound woke the monkey. This exact answer is found in the text.
2	A	The swans laughed at the elephant because they thought he was ugly due to his odd appearance. The description the swans use, "long nose, ears like fans, and big wrinkly skin," can cause the reader to draw this conclusion. The elephant also responds by saying, "Why am I so ugly?"
3	C	The bear was frightened of the herd of elephants is the reason that the bear ran away. The author writes, "A herd of wrinkled elephants came charging up. Seeing the herd the frightened bear ran away." The word frightened is used in the text to describe the bear.
4	C	Brandon's mother states in the story, "Don't be scared. Your brother lives in the forest." Therefore the answer to the question is brother.
5	A	The author is arguing with her brother. This can be determined from the first line of stanza one.
6	A	The only answer choice supported by the text is Robert milked the cows each morning. This is found towards the end of paragraph one.
7	A	A narrow bridge is the correct answer because in paragraph 3 the author explains that the girls had to cross a river by crossing over a narrow bridge to get to school.
8	B	Madison was whistling as she came into the gym because she knew her chances of making the team were good. The last paragraph explains this by stating, "she had worked hard and practiced every day."
9	D	The character traits, optimistic and hardworking, are best in describing Madison according to her actions in this reading selection. For example, in paragraph 1 she is optimistic by saying she knows she lacks experience but she makes up for that with effort and attitude. In paragraph 2, Madison discussed how hardworking she would be if she made the team. Also, her parents could see how hardworking she was because Madison continued to practice throughout the story until the day of tryouts.
10	B	Fall is the correct season because in paragraph four the author explains that summer faded into fall. No other season is mentioned and then tryout day arrives.

Question No.	Answer	Detailed Explanations
11	C B, D, A	C. Maggie didn't know if she could go to the party on Sunday if she didn't get all of her chores done before then. B. Maggie asked her brother to explain what her mom had told her. D. Maggie's brother helps her to understand what prioritizing means. A. Maggie finally understands what she needs to do.
12	1. F 2. D 3. B 4. A 5. C 6. E	The sequence of events. 1. Mr. Clark was going to have a celebration for the class after their unit on bears. 2. The girls were excited. 3. His sister, LaTasha, laughed at him. 4. Tyrone decided to take Beary to school. 5. Mr. Clark had decorated the room in bears, including his own "Buddy" on his desk. 6. Tyrone had a great day at the celebration.
13	B	The son goes to town and is wanting to learn more about he Princess. He wants her for his bride. Answer B is correct. The other answers are not found.
14		Students must write an answer that includes the farmer asked Dame Fortune to grant him 3 wishes.
15		Students are to illustrate, visualize their thoughts on this poem. Accept all reasonable drawings that depict the poem.

Lesson 3: Caring Characters & Life Lessons

Question No.	Answer	Detailed Explanations
1	B	The only saying that matches the actions of the thirsty crow is, "where there's a will, there's a way." The crow wanted the drink so he came up with a way in which to get to the water that at first was unreachable.
2	D	The message taught in this story is that miracles can happen when one has faith. The other three choices don't support a lesson. They are just mere thoughts. Tess, one of the main characters in the story, believed that her money could buy the miracle that her father spoke of. She acts on her faith and goes to buy the miracle.
3	D	Answer D, "persistence is more likely to get you what you want rather than doing nothing at all," is the best answer for the moral of this story. Tess explains her situation to the neurosurgeon after deciding she can buy the miracle. The other choices are not morals. Tess being eight years old is just a fact. The other two choices do not explain anything about what happens in the story.
4 Part A	A	"He who hesitates is lost," is the moral for fable A. Although the gazelle could swim, she hesitated on the bank of the river, not wanting to jump in. While she debated, the lion overtook her, and she became his dinner. Had she not hesitated, she would have been saved.
4 Part B	B	"Look before you leap," is the moral for fable B. Without looking, gazelle jumped into the water where a crocodile was waiting, and she became his dinner. Her life would have been saved, otherwise.
5	D	"To be well known is not always to be admired," is the best choice for the moral to end this selection. Everyone in the story knew of the dog's habit of biting and went in the other direction when they heard its bell. This means the characters knew the dog but they also didn't like his actions. Therefore, he was not admired by others but was well known.
6	A	"Liars are not believed, even when they tell the truth" is the best choice. The villagers had been fooled once or twice by the boy's lie, and they were not going to be fooled again. Unfortunately for the boy this time the wolf really did appear.
7	B	"Too many cooks spoil the broth," is the moral for fable A since it describes what happens when too many cooks try to prepare the same dish without correct communication. Instead of sharing the preparation they each just added salt without discussing it with the other chefs.

Question No.	Answer	Detailed Explanations
8	A	"Many hands make light work," is the best moral choice for fable B because it describes how the work of all the cooks makes the preparation of the soup successful.
9	B	The moral of this poem is about spring and how it brings about new life and new happenings to the world around us. This is evidenced through the examples the author uses of bud covered trees, new born critters, kites soaring in the sky, and games at the park. These are all examples of nature coming alive or events people are involved in during the spring season.
10		Three miles long and a quarter mile wide. This is the only answer to show how small the island is. It is found in the last sentence of the first paragraph.
11		Answers may vary, but should include the house or piazza, the gardens, the college. These details help you to picture or visualize the story.
12	A	The poem clearly states they are building ships using things they find and that one friend got hurt. A is the correct answer. B and C are not correct as it is not ships everywhere and they are not in the actual sea but on stairs.

Lesson 4: Calling All Characters

Question No.	Answer	Detailed Explanations
1 Part A	C	Amy ignored her fear and jumped into the river because saving her friends was more important than being afraid. This answer is found in paragraph 4.
1 Part B	A	The answer to this question is located in paragraph 5. Robert jumped into the river to save the girls who had fallen or jumped in.
2	A	The action above that demonstrated the elephant was happy was that he danced. This is found in the text in paragraph 3. The author describes the elephant dancing happily.
3	B	The best answer choice for this question is that the little elephant wanted to be like the other elephants because he admired them for being strong. He saw how the other elephants frightened away the bear.
4	B	The answer to this question is that the doctor did not want the lady to see him stealing her things. The other choices do not explain the doctor's motives for why he would ask the lady to close her eyes during treatments.
5	C	Brandon began to feel brave because he followed his mother's instructions and called out to "Courage". This was just a verbal way for him to remind himself he had nothing to fear. What one believes helps in how one feels.
6	C	The monster was terrible to look at, frightening, strong, and large. The passage does not describe the monster as gentle. Everyone was frightened by it. Although the monster says he was good and kind inside and turned evil after people treated him badly, there is evidence in the passage to say he is gentle. Option C is the correct answer choice.
7	B	B is the correct answer choice that best describes Jeremiah. He was not familiar with the beach. The author used the sentence, "this was going to be her first view of the ocean, too." Jeremiah also says, "What's this?" when he sees a sand dune. This tells the audience that Jeremiah is not familiar with items typically seen on the beach.
8	C	The best answer choice to describe Xavier's mom is C, "open." She allows her son to play with a child that she knows has been in trouble. She also allows the boy to spend the night. These things demonstrate that Xavier's mom is open to her son having a new friendship with someone of uncertainty.

Question No.	Answer	Detailed Explanations
9	A	Paragraph two provides the details needed to answer this question. Xavier explained about Danny getting into trouble and losing recess but Xavier never did. Therefore the best answer for how Xavier and Danny are different is A, "Danny often gets in trouble while Xavier follows the rules."
10	C	Based on the story, you can determine that Maggie's problem is how to get everything done that she needs and wants to do.
11		Check each students sentences, the following are examples of possible answers. 1. Maggie will make her list of Need to or Have to do. 2. Maggie will make a list of want to do. 3. Maggie will do the Need to or Have to do list first, so she can get to the want to do things
12		The sentence should reference that Beary meant so much to Tyrone because his grandfather bought it for him at his birth, or that his grandfather had passed away and Beary reminded him of his grandpa.

Lesson 5: A Chain of Events

Question No.	Answer	Detailed Explanations
1	B	"When the little elephant saw the bear he was frightened and trumpeted loudly." This line from the text shows how the event of the bear coming caused the elephant to trumpet loudly. Therefore the best answer choice is B.
2	C	Answer choice C is correct. "The girls fell into the river," can be found in the text to support what happened after Rebecca grabbed Ingrid on the bridge.
3	B	The correct order of this selection should be choice B because it gives the events in the order they happened.
4	B	The line, "Oh, come along! We can't go on all night" supports that the brothers apologized to each other.
5	B	Mitchell completed all his assignments prior to opening the multiplication app on his cell phone. This answer choice is B. This is found in paragraph 2.
6	B	The correct answer is B. The reader can draw the conclusion that Danny being friends with Xavier caused him to get into less trouble. This is supported with the mother's words in paragraph 10.
7	B	The only event that happened from the list above is B. Xavier's mother bought Danny new pajamas. This is found in paragraph 9.
8	D	Answer D, "the doctor returned everything he had stolen," shows what happened last in the story and therefore would go last in the flow chart showing the chain of events in sequential order.
9	D	The answer to this question is D because it is the event that happened first in the text. The astronomer went for a walk and that began the rest of the chain of events listed above.
10	B	Emily seeing the wildlife that she had never seen before causes her to change her mind about the camping trip. This is answer choice B. She did listen to her MP3 player but this did not cause her to change her mind. The other two choices did not happen in the story.
11	Summarize	The passage states it is his most favorite technique- summarize.
12	C	Answer A is not found as a fact or detail in the story. Although Mr Clark might like celebrations, answer B is not the best answer. It states in the story that he is giving the celebration as a culmination of the unit and to tie in the unit with the students' real life, so answer C is the best choice.

Question No.	Answer	Detailed Explanations
13	A	A is the correct answer choice. It is clear that the characters emotions are shown by the phrase "bystanders cheered along with Sarah, Blaire and Cody".
14		Mrs. Jo and Mrs. Meg The sentence should include that the ladies are talking and they reference Mr. Laurence's legacy to improve everything around the area.
15	B	Chart shows some improvement in taking responsibilities.

Lesson 6: Figurative Language Expressions

Question No.	Answer	Detailed Explanations
1	C	"Can't go on" means one cannot continue. This phrase refers to when a person or thing can no longer continue doing something. This answer choice is C.
2	A	Answer choice A is the best meaning for the phrase, "we fell out." This means the siblings had a disagreement. The context clue of a quarrel helps the reader determine the meaning of this phrase.
3	D	Answer choice D is the correct meaning for "charging up." It means rushed forward to attack. This can be determined by the use of words such as crashing and stamping. These actions would happen when something is moving forward quickly.
4	B	The phrase, "made of money," refers to a wealthy person. The author refers to buying cars and a boat which helps one draw the conclusion that grandfather is rich.
5	C	In this sentence, "take a hike" does not literally mean to go for a walk. It refers to being told to go away, so someone can be left alone. The answer choice C is correct.
6	C	Fair and square is a phrase that means honestly without cheating or help. The word "but" allows the reader to know it means the opposite of cheated used at the beginning of the sentence.
7	C	Answer choice C is correct. "You're toast" in this sentence refers to being in trouble. The reader knows that a person cannot actually be toast. Also knowing that something bad happened helps draw the conclusion of someone getting in trouble for their actions.
8	D	"Dig my heels in," is a phrase often used to describe a stubborn person who does not want to be told what to do, and if they are told what to do they often refuse. The answer choice is D. The context clue, "I hate to be told what to do," helps the reader figure out this meaning.
9	C	Answer choice C is the correct one. Staying calm means about the same as "kept his cool." This can be concluded by the batter calmly hitting a home run.
10	B	"Cloud over your head," refers to what is making you feel a certain way. In this story it means sad. This can be found in the opening paragraph of the text when Antonio's mom noticed his sad face. Choice B is correct.

Question No.	Answer	Detailed Explanations
11	A, B & C	All of the answer choices are correct based on the passage.
12	cloth	Detail found in the passage, 4th paragraph
13	natural	Detail found in the passage, 1st and last paragraph.

14

Definition	Magic Tricks for reading
Infer	F. Use the clues in reading to figure out what is really going on.
Prior Knowledge	**A. Use what you already know to learn more.**
Summarize	**B. Tell what's important in a sentence or two.**
Visualize	**E. Make pictures or movies in your mind about the story.**
Question	**C. Ask yourself what is the author trying to tell me?**
Reread	**D. Read the story or passage again.**

15

Definition	Vocabulary
NASA	C. government agency in charge of space exploration
Launch vehicle	**G. powerful rocket used to launch space craft or satellite**
Aeronautics	**B. the science of space craft operation**
Astronaut	**H. a person who operates spacecraft or works in space, from US**
Space shuttle	**F. a reusable space craft, takes off like a rocket, lands like a plane**
Orbit	**I. path of a spacecraft or heavenly body as it goes around a planet**
Johnson Space Center	**A. headquarters of US manned spacecraft projects and location of Mission Control**
Kennedy Space Center	**D. launch facility in Cape Canaveral, FL**
Space Station	**E. orbiting space craft designed for occupancy for long period of time**

Lesson 7: Parts of a Whole

Question No.	Answer	Detailed Explanations
1	A	The correct answer is choice A because the parts of the poem are often referred to as stanzas. These parts are not sentences, so they cannot be paragraphs or passages.
2	A	The first answer choice, A, is the line from the story that tells where the astronomer lived, the suburbs. Choices B and C are events from the story but not settings.
3	C	The bold parts of this selection are called headings. These headings tell the reader what the paragraph following them is about.
4	B	The text says, "his dad said that he really didn't want to try to wear those in the soft grainy sand." This means that Jeremiah's dad advised him not to wear shoes. This is why Jeremiah did NOT wear shoes to the beach.
5	B	Near the end of the selection dad says, "the sand dunes to keep the property safe." Answer choice B goes along with this text.
6	C	This answer cannot literally be found in the text. However, answer choice C can be figured out by the reader since the family is on a trip and traveling to get to the beach sooner.
7	A	The only logical answer is A, because the other three choices did not happen in the story.
8	B	Answer choice B is correct and is the only choice that be found in the text. His diary entry did not prove any of the selection choices but letter B.
9	A	The correct choice is A. Terry acts mean toward Brock because he lost his $20.00 and cannot pay his lunch bill. The other three choices are not true according to the play.
10	D	The only answer choice that can be proven from the text is D. Therefore, this has to be the answer. Jasmine's G explained she had been saving the locket for her.
11 Part A	He died	The story states he died.
11 Part B		He died because he no longer had Good Luck watching over him. The story states that Good Luck no longer could help him.
12		Students are to write the rhyming pattern used by the poet. It needs to include the fact that every 2 lines rhyme together.
13		The details show that Alice is in a house. Students sentence needs to state that the setting is in a house of some kind.

Question No.	Answer	Detailed Explanations
14	C	The first sentence in the excerpt states it is an island. C is correct.
15	B	Answer choice B is correct. These are the rhyming patterns in the poem. Other answers are not showing rhyming patterns.

Lesson 8: Who's Talking Now?

Question No.	Answer	Detailed Explanations
1	C	"I" is the narrator of the poem. The pronoun "I" is used throughout the poem. The other choices are images in the poem that are referred to by name.
2	C	A narrator is telling the story. The reader knows this because Pearl's name is used, not "I." This means Pearl did not tell the story. A bus driver and Pearl's mother are not mentioned in the story.

Question 3

	Yes	No
The man	○	●
The goose	○	●
A narrator, outside of the story	●	○
The golden eggs	○	●

You can tell it is someone telling the story, the narrator or someone outside of the story. The other options are characters in the story.

Question No.	Answer	Detailed Explanations
4	C	This story is told in 3rd person with someone outside the story. The use of Emily's name is an example of 3rd person. Emily's dad and brother are mentioned in the story so they are not telling the story.
5	A	Answer choice A is correct. This is a diary entry which usually means it is written in the first person. The entry also uses the pronoun "I" which refers to the first person point of view.
6	D	The point of view for this story is first person by Ann. The reader can determine this by seeing Xavier and Danny's names used and then the pronoun I used in reference to Xavier's mom Ann.
7	A	This text is from the student's point of view (first person). Each thought or feeling starts with the pronoun I.
8	A	Someone outside the story is telling the story. The text does not use pronouns such as I, me, or we which would mean a character in the story was telling it.
9	B	Choice B is correct because if the spider had told the story the reader would hear spider's thoughts and feelings. The spider would not have changed the events if it were telling the story.
10	C	The narrator is not in the story. We know this because there is no reference to "I." The characters are referred to by name.

Question No.	Answer	Detailed Explanations
11		Allow 4 related answers. These do not have to be from the selection if they are feasible and understood by the teacher. Some ideas could include forming a water conservation club, limiting water usage around the home, watering lawns less, picking up liter, using less water to bathe and wash dishes- all listed in the passage.
12	B	Answer A is a good idea, but does not show that you are eating healthy. Answer B is a good way to see what you eat. Answer C is not related to good health. Answer D is not correct, as answer B does show a way to check what you eat. Answer B is the best choice.
13 Part A		Accept all reasonable answers
13 Part B		Each ingredient the student lists should be a cooking ingredient and should include either vegetables, meat, seasoning, flour, cornmeal, etc. Be sure they list 4 ingredients.
14		Some ideas may include on the positive side that no weapons would come to school, and that the school hallways would be safer and have order to them. For negative effects it might include that the cost to parents is too high or that students' privacy would be violated. Solutions could include finding out what other schools are doing, having an assembly to go over reasons why the school decided to change the rules, allowing special needs or small frame students to bring carts, or to try a week without backpacks and carts vs a week with backpacks and carts.

Lesson 9: I Can See It Now

Question No.	Answer	Detailed Explanations
1	C	Pizza is the most popular item on the lunch menu at Curbside School. This can be determined because pizza has the tallest bar graph.
2	D	Numbers, answer choice D is the correct answer. Numbers would allow the reader to see the exact number of students who like the different foods. This would help to determine which food is liked almost as much as spaghetti.
3	A	Hamburgers is the correct answer to what food item is the second favorite. This is represented by the bar graph because hamburgers have the second highest bar.
4	C	The lunch ladies should serve pizza in order to make the kids happy. The bar graph shows pizza as their favorite lunch item with the highest bar.
5	E	Mac and Cheese should be the one item that the lunch ladies drop from the menu if given the opportunity. The bar graph shows Mac and Cheese is the least favorite lunch item with the shortest bar.
6	B	I think this story will be a fantasy. The mood will be mysterious. I can tell this because there is a spaceship in the picture and spaceships are intriguing.
7	B	I think this story will be a narrative. The mood will be happy. I can tell this because the two dogs look like they are having a good time. They are smiling.
8	C	I think this story will be a narrative. The mood will be serious. I can tell this because the girl in the picture is concentrating very hard on her work.
9	C	I think this story will be a fantasy narrative. The mood will be scary. I can tell this because the dragon looks large and destructive because he is breathing fire.
10	A	The logos above represent the Olympic games. The rings on the logos are the Olympic trademark.
11	D	The lowest number of likes and the highest dislikes for books to read was books on history. So answer D is the correct choice.
12		In any order, California, Oregon, Washington, Hawaii, Alaska. These are the five states that have the Pacific Ocean as one or more borders.

Question No.	Answer	Detailed Explanations

13

Texas, Louisiana, Mississippi, Alabama, Florida.
These are the five states that have the Gulf of Mexico as borders.

14

	Monday	Tuesday	Wednes-day	Thurs-day	Friday	Saturday	Sunday	Totals
Playing Video Games	4 hours	4 hours	3 hours	3 hours	2 hours	3 hours	3 hours	**22 hours**
Doing Home-work	30 min	30 min	1 hour	1 hour	1 hour	none	none	**4 hours**
Doing Chores	15 min	15 min	45 min	45 min	45 min	2 hours	1 hour	**5 hours 45 min**
Going to Bed On Time	Not done	Not done	Not done	Done	Not done	Done	Done	**Went to be on time 3 days**

Students must add up the time for each activity, then add the number of days that he did go to bed on time.

Lesson 10: Alike and Different

Question No.	Answer	Detailed Explanations
1	B	"He looks different than the other animals" is correct. Throughout the opening of the text, the author gives a physical description of the elephant.
2	A	A is correct. When the little elephant expressed wanting to be like the big elephants they told him he was already like them.
3	D	According to the last part of the text, the neighbor questions the astronomer as to why he is not seeing things on earth but paying attention to things in heaven. Therefore, choice D is the best answer.
4	A	Answer choice A is best in comparing how the theme of both stories are similar. Emily did not want to go on the family vacation but as the trip progresses she realizes her first impression of the trip was wrong and that the outdoors can be fun. Jasmine is worried about meeting her "G" but realizes that meeting someone for the first time can still be fun even when you are nervous.
5	B	"Cell phones are great educational tools" as proven in paragraph two of the text.
6	B	Answer option B is the correct answer. Passage one provides the reader with reasons why cell phones should be allowed in the classroom as well as arguments for why cell phones should NOT be allowed in the classroom. However, the second passage is ONLY about the reasons that cell phones should NOT be allowed in classrooms.
7	A	The only answer choice that would make the greatest change to the Olympics is Option A: changing the Olympic Games to the same location every year. The other three choices have already occurred.
8	C	"There are more worker bees than there are queen bees" is correct, according to number 3.
9	A	A is correct. The closing of paragraph 1 states that Brandon was scared crossing the forest while later in the text his mother explains that his brother is in the forest and will protect him.
10	C	"Brandon becomes less afraid" is correct. The opening paragraph describes Brandon as being scared of the forest. Near the end of the text, Brandon realizes he was not frightened at all.

Question No.	Answer	Detailed Explanations
11	B	The articles do not show answer A. Answer B does note the similarities between China and India. Answer C does not, nor does D. Answer B is the only correct answer.
12	C	Answer a is noted, but does not stand out as unique. Answer B is also noted, but not unique. Answer C is a unique fact. Answer D is not unique either. Therefore, the best answer is C.
13		1. Founding Father 2. President of the United States 3. Inventor of electricity, lightning rod, cooking stove 4. Politician 5. Author 6. Lived in the 1700s 7. Helped the colonists in breaking away from England 8. Well remembered in US History 9. Attended college 10. Unable to attend college, but well educated 11. Known to have helped the US acquire the Louisiana Purchase 12. Wrote Poor Richard's Almanack.

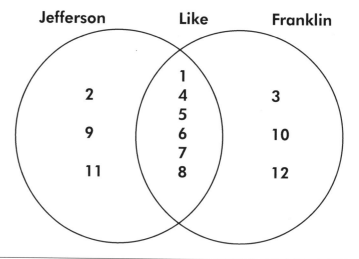

Lesson 11: Setting the Scene

Question No.	Answer	Detailed Explanations
1	at the end of the forest	Brandon lives at the end of the forest. This answer is located in the opening sentence of the story.
2	A	The first answer choice is correct. Brandon finds his courage in the setting of the forest. This line is found near the end of the reading selection. "He crossed the forest confidently with courage."
3	C	Answer choice three is the best answer for this question. The likely setting of this story is a forest since the author explains that Brandon and his mother live on the end of a forest and later that Brandon gets his confidence and courage as he travels through the forest.
4	B	The answer choice B is correct. A setting is the location and time of the story.
5 Part A	C	The correct answer to this question is the third choice, outdoors at night. The reader can determine this by the opening line in which the author writes, "the astronomer used to go out every night to observe the stars." Since stars are seen at night this tells the time of day which is night. The word "out" refers to going outside in order to observe the stars.
5 Part B	B	The second answer choice is correct. This is the logical choice for how the story would have been different if it had taken place during the day. The astronomer would have seen the uncovered well if it was during the day. The other three answer choices do not really make sense.
6	C	The correct choice for this question is the 3rd answer. The type of animals being discussed in the poem would more than likely be found in a zoo. An amusement park has rides, not wild animals. A veterinarian usually would not be treating these type of animals in a medical office. Animals such as monkeys, kangaroos, camels, etc. are not typically found in the forest. Therefore, the only logical answer is a zoo.
7	B	The second answer choice is the best answer because it provides the exact destination where the family vacationed. In the reading this answer is provided in paragraph two and sentence one.
8	A	The first choice is the correct answer. The setting of this story is inside the classroom. The reader can determine this because the kids just came in from the playground and they are referring to their teacher as Mrs. Adams.

Question No.	Answer	Detailed Explanations
9	D	Answer choice D is the correct answer. The author describes Jasmine leaving the car, looking at the old farmhouse, and that her G scooped her up and told her to come on into her home. This allows the reader to know that Jasmine traveled somewhere other than her home or her daddy's home. There is no mention of a friend in the story.

Chapter 3 - Reading Informational Text

The objective of the Reading Informational Text standards is to ensure that the student is able to read and comprehend informational texts (history/social studies, science, and technical texts) related to Grade 3.

To help students master the necessary skills, information to help the student understand the concepts related to the standard is given. Along with this, we encourage the student to go through the resources available online on EdSearch to gain an in depth understanding of these concepts. The EdSearch page for each lesson can be accessed with the help of the URL or the QR code provided.

A small map is provided after each passage or text in which the student can enter the details as understood from the literary text. Doing this will help the student to refer to key points that help in answering the questions with ease.

Chapter 3

Lesson 1: Explicitly Comprehension

Let us understand the concept with an example.

Explicitly: definitely and clearly expressed.

The Water Cycle

The water cycle is a cycle. After it rains, you may see lots of water puddles on the ground. Then the sun comes out and the puddles disappear. Did you know the sun will then change the water on the ground into a gas called "water vapor"? This part of the water cycle is called evaporation (liquid changed to a gas). As the water vapor rises into the air, it sticks with pieces of dust. The air gets cooler and the vapor changes back into liquid (water). This is called condensation. The condensation collects and forms clouds. When there is too much water for the clouds to hold, precipitation falls back to earth as rain, snow, sleet or hail. This cycle continues again and again. Evaporation, condensation, and precipitation are the processes involved in the water cycle.

Here are some questions and answers you might write to show that you understand the text. Included in your answers are words and phrases that are explicitly (definitely and clearly expressed) in the text.

1. When something is called a "cycle", what does it mean?

It means that there is more than one event taking place and these events will repeat themselves over and over again in the same order.

2. What events make up the water cycle?

Rain, puddles, sunshine, evaporation of puddles into water vapor, rising of water vapor into the air, clouds formed by water vapor sticking to dust, and rain, snow, sleet or hail falling from the clouds.

3. What happens to rainwater in puddles during evaporation?

The puddles disappear because the water in the puddles is heated by the sun until it becomes a gas called water vapor, which you cannot see.

4. What is the last event in the water cycle and what causes it to occur?

The last event in the water cycle is the return of water to earth as rain, snow, sleet or hail. It occurs when clouds collect more water from condensation than they can hold.

You can scan the QR code given below or use the URL to access additional EdSearch resources including videos and mobile apps related to *Explicitly Comprehension.*

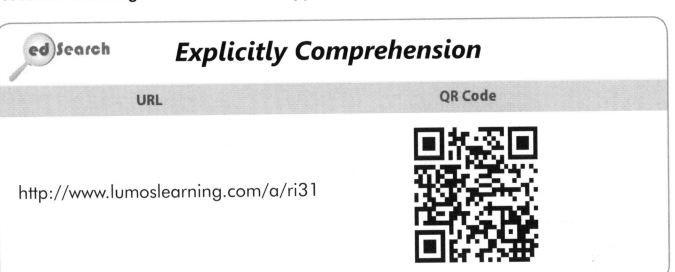

ed Search **Explicitly Comprehension**	
URL	**QR Code**
http://www.lumoslearning.com/a/ri31	

Question 1-3 are based on the passage below.

The Blues

The Blues is a genre of music that can be directly traced to the "Deep South". The Blues were influenced by a mixture of traditional African music and Southern spirituals. The bedrock of the Blues is set in the Mississippi Delta, where many of the most influential Blues musicians were born. Many of these musicians are self-taught artists. This genre of music has influenced other music genres such as Rock and Roll, Rap, and Country.

One of the most famous Mississippi Delta Blues artists was a man named Robert Johnson. His ability to play the guitar has spawned numerous stories of his ability to play the guitar so well. No matter what story you choose to believe, it is undeniable that Mr. Johnson inspired many future artists with his unique playing style. So the next time you hear your favorite song, ask yourself if you believe that the Blues had some influence on that song.

1. According to the passage where was Robert Johnson from?

Ⓐ The passage does not state specifically where Robert Johnson was from.
Ⓑ Robert Johnson was from Chicago.
Ⓒ The passage states that Robert Johnson was from the Mississippi Delta.
Ⓓ Robert Johnson was from Africa.

2. Where did the Blues begin?

Ⓐ The Blues began in Africa.
Ⓑ The passage states that the Blues began in the Deep South.
Ⓒ The Blues began in Europe according to the passage.
Ⓓ The Blues began in the Northern states of the U.S.

3. What type of music does the passage say that the Blues has influenced?

Ⓐ The passage does not say that the blues have influenced any other type of music.
Ⓑ The passage states that the Blues have influenced Rock and Roll, Rap, and Country.
Ⓒ The passage says that the Blues have only influenced classical music.
Ⓓ The passage says that the Blues have only influenced guitar players.

Question 14 is based on the passage below.

THE WATER CYCLE

The water cycle is a cycle that repeats itself over and over again. After it rains, you may see a lot of water puddles on the ground. Then the sun comes out and the puddles disappear. Did you know the sun will then change the water on the ground into a gas called "water vapor"? This part of the water cycle is called evaporation (liquid changed to a gas). As the water vapor rises into the air, it sticks with pieces of dust. The air gets cooler and the vapor changes back into liquid (water). This is called condensation. The condensation collects and forms clouds. When there is too much water for the clouds to hold, the cloud bursts and precipitation falls back to earth as rain, snow, sleet, or hail. This cycle continues again and again. Evaporation, condensation, and precipitation are the processes involved in the water cycle.

4. According to the passage what does evaporation mean?

Ⓐ   The air gets cooler and the vapor changes back to liquid.
Ⓑ   The liquid changes to a gas.
Ⓒ   The condensation collects and forms clouds.
Ⓓ   The gas changes to liquid.

Question 5-9 are based on the passage below.

Good manners can be seen at home, at school, on the playground, and at the dining table where we eat our meals. A well-mannered person is polite and gentle when he talks.
Everyone likes a person who is polite and well-mannered. Good manners are always liked by everyone and bring good rewards.

All that is right pleases everyone. Therefore, we should do what is right always. We should always remember to do what is right.

All that is wrong displeases everyone. Therefore, we should not do what is wrong. We will be rewarded for our good actions.

A boy or girl who constantly comes late for work cannot be depended upon. People do not give him or her any important work for they do not know whether he/she will come on time or not. A person who is always late loses friends.

All of us make mistakes. When we make a mistake, we do not like to be punished for it. We like to be forgiven. Therefore, we too should forgive the mistakes of others. Forgiveness is a great virtue.

It is easy to make a mistake, but it is not easy to forget that mistake. If we make some mistake, we should feel sorry for it. We should also apologize to the person whom we have hurt.

We should not cheat on an examination. Cheating always does more harm than good. We should not keep bad company.

5. What title best shows what this selection is MOSTLY about?

Ⓐ Good Virtues
Ⓑ Stealing
Ⓒ Late Coming
Ⓓ Examinations

6. Why does everyone like a person who is good-mannered?

Ⓐ Because he answers rudely.
Ⓑ Because he talks out of turn.
Ⓒ Because he is polite and gentle.
Ⓓ Because he shouts at everyone.

7. According to this selection, what pleases others?

Ⓐ Doing what is right.
Ⓑ Telling lies.
Ⓒ Being stubborn.
Ⓓ Talking ill of others.

8. Why is 'late coming' a bad habit?

Ⓐ Because late comers will not do any work.
Ⓑ Because it is good to come late.
Ⓒ Because late comers cannot be depended upon.
Ⓓ Because late comers go late.

9. According to the selection, do we like anyone to punish us for our mistakes? Why?

Ⓐ No, we like to be forgiven.
Ⓑ We like to get punished.
Ⓒ We never get punished.
Ⓓ We do not like to be forgiven.

Question 10 is based on the paragraph below.

Pearl reached in her pocket for the coins, but she could not feel them. Desperately, she pulled everything out of her pocket. She found a chocolate wrapper, a bus pass, her student ID card, lipstick, mascara, and her cell phone. There were no coins!

10. Which items in Pearl's pocket shows the reader she is a teenager, not a young child?

Ⓐ The makeup
Ⓑ The bus pass
Ⓒ The student ID
Ⓓ All of the above

Question 11-14 are based on the passage below.

States in the US

Look at the map. Then read the list of states in ABC order. Note that the states of Hawaii and Alaska are not shown in the correct location. The reason for this is simple. Alaska is located on the end of Canada far above Washington to the left. One side of Alaska is located on the Pacific Ocean. It is not connected to the rest of the US. The state of Hawaii is a group of islands located in the Pacific Ocean and again is not adjoined to the US. Thus it, too, would not fit correctly on this map. The Pacific Ocean is on the left of the map in blue, the Gulf of Mexico is on the bottom in blue and flows into the Atlantic Ocean on the right in blue.

Carefully review all that you read, and see before answering the questions below.

The Fifty States in ABC Order:

Alabama, Alaska, Arizona, Arkansas, California,
Colorado, Connecticut
Delaware, Florida, Georgia, Hawaii, Idaho, Illinois,
Indiana
Iowa, Kansas, Kentucky, Louisiana, Maine,
Maryland, Massachusetts, Michigan.
Minnesota, Mississippi, Missouri, Montana,
Nebraska, Nevada,
New Hampshire, New Jersey, New Mexico, New York,
North Carolina, North Dakota, Ohio,
Oklahoma, Oregon, Pennsylvania, Rhode Island,
South Carolina,
South Dakota, Tennessee, Texas,
Utah, Vermont, Virginia, Washington, West Virginia,
Wisconsin, Wyoming.

After reviewing the facts given, the map and the list of states in ABC order, answer the questions.

11. Where is Hawaii located?

12. Where is Alaska located?

13. How many states begin with the letter T?

14. Which letters in the alphabet are not used for state names? List them.

Question 15 is based on the passage below.

Playing Video Games

Scotty loves to play video games! I mean he plays every chance he gets. He even plays when he should be doing his homework, chores or going to bed! It has gotten so bad that his parents are considering a punishment to teach him a lesson.

Scotty doesn't understand why they are upset with him and is trying to figure out what he can do so that he doesn't get his video game machine taken away. He has asked his friends for their ideas on the subject, too. He even asked his counselor at school. Scotty has been seeing her since his grades started dropping. The counselor told him it is very simple, give up the game playing on his own and get back to doing homework, chores, and going to bed on time.

To Scotty, the ideas his counselor told him are good, but he is very reluctant to do it. So one of his friends, Hailey, has offered to help. She is going to make him a chart of time spent on playing games compared to time spent on his responsibilities. He agrees to give it a try.

15. Who should Scotty share his chart with? Circle the correct answer choice.

Ⓐ His counselor
Ⓑ His parents
Ⓒ His friend, Hailey
Ⓓ All of the above

Chapter 3

Lesson 2: The Main Idea Arena

Main idea: the most important idea (or ideas) in a text. Sometimes called the theme of the text. The main idea can be the purpose of the author in writing the text (for example, an attempt to persuade you to agree with the author's opinion), or just to entertain you (for example, telling a funny story). Supporting statements: text that explains or adds more detail to the main idea (for instance, giving examples).

Let us understand the concept with an example.

School Uniforms: A Good Idea
By Emily Adams

I think school uniforms would be good for all schools, because they can cause changes that make a school better. How? By stopping kids from judging other kids by the clothes they wore. Also, by making a good impression about the school because all students would be wearing nice looking uniforms. Judging people by the clothes they wear would stop for sure if uniforms were required in the school. Let's say someone wore an outfit that was different from the clothes most kids wore. If the clothes were very fashionable and expensive, some kids would be jealous, or if the clothes were "not cool," some kids would think they were inferior. Some kids are criticized for being sloppy in the way they wear their clothes – shirts not tucked in, pants that sag below the waist or prewashed jeans with rips in them. Uniforms would prevent this appearance.

It would be better if kids judged each other by who they were, not by what they wore. If kids were all wearing the same uniform, there would not be a reason to judge anyone based on their clothing. But what if kids wanted to personalize their uniforms so they could look a little different? The school's dress code could allow different accessories. For example, if a student liked glitter, she could add a glittery bow or a cute belt. Or an athlete could wear a button or belt with a team logo.

To sum it all up, uniforms are the best choice for the school because they eliminate kids judging each other by what they wear, and they create a nice, similar look for all kids attending that school.

Determine the main idea of a text.
The main idea of this text is to give a positive opinion about school uniforms.

Recount the key details and explain how they support the main idea.
By stopping kids from judging other kids by the clothes they wore. Also, by making a good impression about the school because all students would be wearing nice looking uniforms. It would encourage kids to judge each other by who they were, not by what they wore.

You can scan the QR code given below or use the URL to access additional EdSearch resources including videos and mobile apps related to *The Main Idea Arena*.

 **The Main Idea Arena**

URL	QR Code
http://www.lumoslearning.com/a/ri32	

Question 1 and 2 are based on the passage below.

After reading the passage, enter the details in the map below. This will help you to answer the questions that follow.

Everything in nature follows a pattern. Circles, lines, spirals, and angles are repeated to make a design or a pattern. Patterns in nature are not just pretty adornments. They serve a purpose that has helped nature survive and flourish.

Have you ever taken a close look at a beehive? Well, not too close or you might get stung! The natural pattern in beehives is so perfect that it seems to be computer designed. The hives are made up of layers and layers of cells. Each cell has six perfectly equal sides or hexagons. Why would bees build six-sided cells, instead of round, or box shaped ones? The reason is that the bee is a genius at geometry and architecture! Six-sided cells use up every bit of space and allow bees to get the maximum area for storing honey. Also, hexagons use the least honeycomb wax because all six sides are identical in length. The bees don't waste space, material, or effort. Aren't they smart insects?

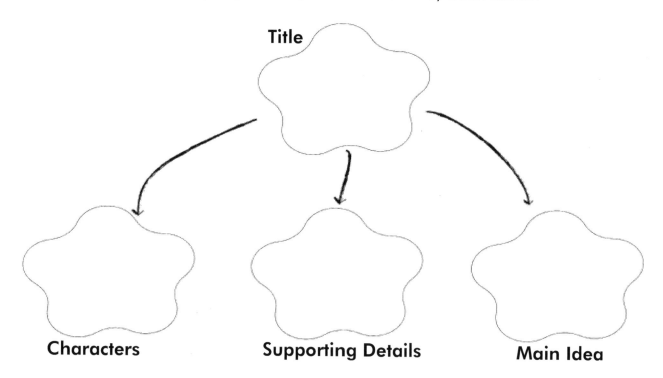

1. What is the main idea of the selection?

- (A) Beehives have a disorganized pattern.
- (B) Every cell in the beehive has a different shape.
- (C) Every cell in the beehive has five sides.
- (D) Everything in nature follows a pattern.

2. What is the above passage telling us?

Ⓐ It's introducing the reader to patterns.
Ⓑ It tells us how bees makes use of patterns.
Ⓒ It tells us how patterns are used only by people.
Ⓓ It tells us how bees have limited intelligence.

Question 3 and 4 are based on the passage below.

After reading the passage, enter the details in the map below. This will help you to answer the questions that follow.

A robot is a device that can do tasks that are difficult or impossible for human beings. A robot does not have to be shaped like a person; robots can be shaped like animals or machines. Law enforcement agencies have robots that can go into dangerous areas, which might cause injury to individuals and thereby help in maintaining law and order with ease. Medical facilities have microscopic robot cameras that go into areas of the human body, robot cameras bloodstreams, that are too small for a doctor to see. Military units have robotic devices such as drone airplanes that can deliver bombs without risk to the soldiers who are operating the planes. Robots are also being sent into outer space to explore areas that are too dangerous for humans to visit.

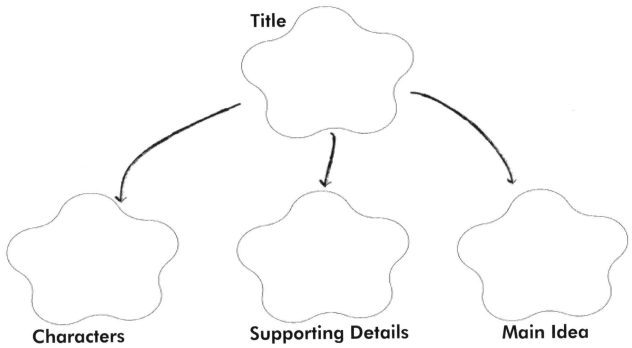

3. What is the main idea in this passage?

Ⓐ Robots can be shaped like animals or machines.
Ⓑ A robot is a device that can do tasks that would be difficult or impossible for human beings.
Ⓒ Law enforcement, agencies have robots that can go into dangerous areas where a person could be injured.
Ⓓ A robot does not have to be shaped like a person.

4. Which sentence in the passage gives a detail that does not support the main idea?

Ⓐ A robot does not have to be shaped like a person; robots can be shaped like animals or machines.

Ⓑ Military units use robotic devices such as drone airplanes that can deliver bombs without risk to the soldiers who are operating the planes.

Ⓒ Robots are being sent into outer space to explore areas that would be dangerous for humans to visit.

Ⓓ Law enforcement, agencies have robots that can go into dangerous areas where a person might be injured.

5. Which sentence in the paragraph is its main idea?

1. The thermometer read -15. 2. The edges of Jeremy's ears were stinging with cold. 3. He wished he had put on two pairs of socks. 4. His forehead was numb. 5. He couldn't feel his fingers any longer. 6. This was the coldest day he had ever lived through.

Ⓐ Sentence 2.
Ⓑ Sentence 5.
Ⓒ Sentence 6.
Ⓓ Sentence 1.

6. Which sentence in the paragraph shows its main idea?

1. All of Jennifer's favorites were on the table. 2. There was corn on the cob. 3. There were mashed potatoes with gravy, and fried chicken. 4. There was frosty lemonade to drink. 5. There were strawberries with whipped cream for dessert.

Ⓐ Sentence 1.
Ⓑ Sentence 2.
Ⓒ Sentence 4.
Ⓓ Sentence 5.

7. Which sentence in the paragraph shows its main idea?

1. Joe was as surprised as anyone when he won the race. 2. He hadn't done nearly enough conditioning. 3. He hadn't eaten a good breakfast that morning. 4. He hadn't gotten enough sleep last night 5. The other runners were very fast. 6. In spite of all those problems, Joe was the fastest guy on the track and he left all the other runners behind.

Ⓐ Sentence 4.
Ⓑ Sentence 2.
Ⓒ Sentence 5.
Ⓓ Sentence 6.

8. Which sentence in the paragraph shows its main idea?

1. The gifts were wonderful. 2. The guests were courteous and cheerful. 3. The food was delicious. 4. The decorations were beautiful. 5. It was a perfect party in every way.

   Ⓐ Sentence 1.
   Ⓑ Sentence 3.
   Ⓒ Sentence 2.
   Ⓓ Sentence 5.

9. Which sentence in the paragraph shows its main idea?

1. Karen had never had such a miserable day. 2. She was seasick as the tiny tourist boat pulled out to sea. 3. She wished she had waited back on shore. 4. It was cold on the boat and she hadn't brought a jacket. 5. She didn't know any of the other passengers, and no one seemed to want to talk to her.

   Ⓐ Sentence 1.
   Ⓑ Sentence 2.
   Ⓒ Sentence 3.
   Ⓓ Sentence 5.

10. What sentence is the main idea of this paragraph?

1. For one thing, he never answered the phone when the citizens called to ask him questions. 2. For another thing, he was rude to them when they tried to get his attention. 3. For another thing, he was getting richer every day, as the townspeople became poorer. 4. In short, he was the worst mayor the little town had ever seen.

   Ⓐ Sentence 1
   Ⓑ Sentence 2
   Ⓒ Sentence 3
   Ⓓ Sentence 4

Question 11 is based on the passage below.

What do you see?

Have you ever laid down on your back in a green field on a bright sunny day and gazed up at the clouds? I do it all the time when I get a chance. It can be so much fun to see what you can see in a fluffy cloud or groups of clouds. Look at one that has a thin long end, several little ends coming down in the middle and a much bigger other end…What do you see? It might be a dog. Yes, look, there are the ears on top! It could even be a lion with the larger end opening up like its mouth.

Then start to find many clouds. How many different animals or plants or even people can you locate?

See how they are similar or different in both size and formation.

Try doing this with a group of friends and the possibilities are endless. This kind of activity can help to stimulate your brain better than any video game or TV show! Take a sketch pad or drawing tablet with you. You will be surprised at how easy it can be to draw these! Have one of your buddies close their eyes. Describe the cloud you are looking at. Next have your friend open up their eyes and find the cloud in the sky that you described. Keep a record of who can tell which cloud was the right one. But, be careful, clouds can change their formations sometimes rather quickly!

Before answering the questions, try rereading the passage to get a better understanding of the author's message.

Hint: The author is describing an event and things that you might try to do.

11. Which sentence best summarizes the above selection? Select the right answer choice by circling it.

Ⓐ Clouds are everywhere.
Ⓑ Watching clouds is better than playing video games.
Ⓒ Watching clouds by yourself or with friends can be enjoyable, fun and can stimulate your brain.
Ⓓ You can describe clouds to other people.

Question 12 is based on the passage below.

Who says guys only cook on the grill

My grandma, mom and sister always do the cooking in the kitchen at our house. It is very good indeed, do not get me wrong. Sometimes, however, I would like to cook on the stove, too! Dad says that guys do the grilling on the bbq pit outside. Why can't we cook inside, too?

So one day I asked Dad, "Dad, what would you like for supper tonight?" He replied, "Gee, Howard, I would really love hamburger steak with onions, but your mom doesn't want to cook that."

I announced, "Please, let me try to cook it!" Mom and Dad looked at each other and nodded yes.

I was so elated! First thing I did was ask Mom if she had everything we needed. She said she had no idea what we needed. So I looked on our computer under recipes and found several. I began to read off the ingredients. Some she had already and some she said we do not use. I decided to combine a couple of recipes and make my own. Here it is!

Ingredients for the hamburger steak patties:

1 to 1 ½ lbs of hamburger meat- preferably the ground chuck

3-4 tablespoons of cooking oil, we use canola

1 large egg

2/3 cups of really fine chopped onions

1 teaspoon of Worchester sauce- spicy sauce if you would rather

A pinch of salt

A pinch of garlic powder

A pinch of black pepper
About 1/3-1/2 cup of all-purpose flour- use that to coat the patties to brown

Now, the gravy:

Instead of making homemade gravy, Dad and I decided I could use the package of onion gravy mix- I used 2 packages!

A half of an onion sliced real thin, long slices!

A little more Worchester sauce for flavor- a splash or two

Directions:

Take the ingredients for the hamburger steak patties and mix them together- do not add the flour. Form large patties, it will probably make at least 5-6. Flatten as much as you can, but not too thin. Now pat the flour on each side of the patties. In a very large frying pan or skillet, heat your cooking oil until it starts to bubble just a bit. Now place the patties in the oil and cook on each side for about 4-5 minutes until brown. Remove them from the frying pan. Lay aside, but keep warm. (Warning, do not try to flatten your patties, as it will cause them to fall apart. One of mine did fall apart.)

While the pan is still hot and on, add the thinly sliced onions. Let them cook until they start to turn a little brown. Now, lower the flame and add the gravy mix according to the package. Turn the flame back up and let it come to a low boil. Be sure to use a spoon or ladle and stir the gravy while it is cooking.

Let the gravy mix cook on low for about 5 minutes. Add more water a little at a time if it thickens too fast. Now take the patties and add them to the gravy mix. Cover with a lid and cook for no more than 20 minutes on low.

Enjoy! We did! Yes, now my grandma, mom and sister let me cook inside any time I want to try a new recipe! Who says guys only cook on the grill?

12. Read the steps given below. Arrange it in the correct sequence of the recipe.

> **A.** Remove the patties and set aside but keep them warm.
> **B.** Mix the hamburger steak patty ingredients without the flour and make patties.
> **C.** Cook the patties in the onion and onion gravy mix for about 20 minutes.
> **D.** Now add the onion gravy mix according to the package directions.
> **E.** Cover patties with flour and cook about 5 minutes until brown on each side.
> **F.** Take the thinly sliced onions, add them to the pan and cook a little.

Question 13 is based on the passage below.

Monarch Butterflies- The King of Butterflies

The Monarch butterfly travels very far each fall. Millions of monarch butterflies leave the Great Lakes and New York areas and fly to Mexico. It takes what is called the fourth generation cycle for this to happen. This means that the first three generations do not make it to Mexico. Some scientists believe they do this to get away from the cold weather. Mexico has reserved and dedicated mountain regions as preserved lands for the species. The butterflies stay in Mexico until the next summer. Then they travel back to the Great Lakes and New York area where they lay eggs, and then die. The life cycle of the monarch butterfly that goes to Mexico is about eight to nine months after becoming an adult. Butterflies have what is considered to be four life cycle stages. The female monarch lights on milkweed leaves to begin the process. The mother chooses the milkweed so that the caterpillar can eat off of the leaves. The first stage is eggs being laid, the larvae comes next-caterpillar, and then is the pupa stage- the chrysalis and finally the adult. The caterpillar is grown in around 2 weeks. He then finds a stem to attach itself so it can go through the process of metamorphosis. During this stage of major changes, he stays inside the pupa and does not come out until he is a full grown butterfly.

Once the monarch emerges it is so beautiful that it is often called the King of Butterflies!

13. How long do adult monarch butterflies usually live once they are adults and travel many miles? Circle the correct option.

Ⓐ They usually live to be about ten months old.
Ⓑ They usually live to be about eight to nine months old.
Ⓒ They die within 10 days after being laid as eggs.
Ⓓ None of the above.

Question 14 is based on the passage below.

Fishing Industries Along the Gulf Coast

If you live in the area of the United States known as the Southern Gulf Coast, along the Gulf of Mexico, you live in Texas, Louisiana, Mississippi, Alabama or Florida. The Gulf Coast has been called the Fishing Capital of the United States by many people. From Brownsville to the Florida Keys, fisherman go out into the gulf waters in their boats to make a living off of the fish, shrimp, crab, and other seafood they catch.

Trawler is the name usually given when talking about the shrimp and fish boats that go out into the Gulf of Mexico along the established waters to bring in catches. These boats that go out in the gulf are generally about 70' long or longer and most all are refrigerated and steel hull boats now. The refrigeration helps the boat captain to stay out for extended periods of time, ranging anywhere from 3 to about 14 days. Before refrigeration was common on trawlers, the boats would have to go in to a port to dock and get more ice or come back to their home port frequently. Steel hull trawlers are much sturdier than the old wooden hull boats that could be easily damaged by storms, hitting sunken boats or other objects.

 Boats or trawlers have a bunk house (sleeping quarters), galley (kitchen), bathroom, and a wheel-house. The trawlers are equipped with high tech radios and equipment in the wheelhouse to help the crew find areas of fish and shrimp. Thus little time is wasted in putting their nets down and dragging the bottom of the gulf to find the seafood they need to bring in.

The people working on a trawler are most often referred to as the crew. The crew consists of the captain (sometimes the owner, sometimes not- whose job it is to run the boat, steer, and make sure all the crew are working), the deck hands (deck hands help to keep the nets in order, repair as needed while out at sea, dropping nets in the water and hauling them in), headers (people head the shrimp as the nets are hauled in, clean fish, and store the catch.), and usually a separate man, the cook, whose only job is to keep the boat clean, and keep the crew well fed. Although some women do work on the boats, more often than not, the boat crew is all male.

The fishing industry is vital to the economy on the Southern Gulf Coast. It is estimated that in the entire US, this industry employs over 1.6 million people. On the Gulf Coast alone, the industry brings in over 22.6 billion dollars to aid the economy.

14. Write a sentence of your own explaining the benefit of refrigeration as related to the fishing industry. Use facts from the passage to help you.

Question 15 is based on the passage below.

Hobbies are Good for the Mind and Body

Many people enjoy hobbies. They can range from designing arts and crafts to singing in a choir. Hobbies improve self-esteem, physical well-being and can increase your academic gains, as well.

Arts and crafts have been known to enable you to gain higher fine motor skills while creating unique works of art. Learning how to work slowly and taking time to complete projects can help you to learn self- control, and develop patience. Some forms of arts and crafts include drawing, painting, building model cars, model airplanes, jewelry making, and leather work. There are many arts and craft stores where you can find your interests.

Sports have always been great hobbies for the young and old. Team and individual sports include football, baseball, soccer, swimming, tennis, wrestling and more. Quite often you join a sport to be with friends, learn to develop physical strength, or to enjoy what you like doing most. Communities generally have organizations to help parents and their children find the best sport for them.

Another form of hobby includes collecting. You can start collecting sports cards, and comic books at an early age. Doll collections, kept in pristine condition over the years can even be a financial plus when you get older. Your parents and relatives can help you start your collection if you ask them to give you collectible items you want for birthday presents or other occasions.

Did you know that even the performing arts are considered a hobby? Joining a ballet class, drama club, tap and gymnastics, theatre or choir, can be your hobby. Again these types of hobbies help develop physical and emotional skills to improve your health and well-being.

15. **Which is NOT the best way to summarize the selection about hobbies? Circle the correct answer choice.**

   Ⓐ Hobbies help you physically, emotionally, and can improve your life.
   Ⓑ Hobbies can be fun and help you get along with others.
   Ⓒ Hobbies include many things that people like to do.
   Ⓓ Hobbies take a lot of time and can be expensive to do.

Chapter 3

Lesson 3: Cause and Effect

Publisher's Notes: to correctly answer the requirement of the standard to "Describe the relationship between a series of ...events, ...ideas, ...concepts or steps", each of the events, ideas, concepts or steps has to be related to the other events, ideas, concepts or steps in the text.

Examples:

1. Series of historical events: the American Revolution happened because the British government passed some laws that the American colonists did not agree with and could not vote on.

2. Scientific ideas or concepts: the recognition that climate change was taking place and that it had harmful effects came about because of events such as glaciers shrinking in size and an increase in carbon dioxide in the air. See "Your assignment" on this page for more details about the relationship between scientific ideas and concepts and climate change.

3. Steps in technical procedures: before takeoff, an airline pilot and copilot must follow a checklist of procedures to make sure all of the systems on the airplane are working, before they take off.

Time sequence: the period of time taken for a series of events, ideas, concepts or steps to happen or be performed, from the beginning time to the ending time.

Cause and effect: describe the cause (British taxation, increase in the earth's average surface temperature, pre-takeoff procedures) and effect (American Revolution, melting of glaciers, a safe flight).

Your assignment: You have been assigned to read the following article, and then to follow the instructions in the standard above.

Scientists tell us that changes in our climate are happening. Average temperatures around the world are getting higher. The planet's average surface temperature has risen about 2.0 degrees Fahrenheit since the late 19th century. The warmest year on record was 2016; eight months were the warmest on record. The number of warm days in a year has increased while the number of cold days has decreased. This is called global warming.

Because of the rise in temperature, the ice cap in Greenland lost 281 gigatons of ice from 2002 through 2016. Here and in Antarctica melting ice caps are causing sea levels to rise 8" in the last 100 years; glaciers are shrinking; ocean water temperatures are rising. Carbon dioxide levels in the air have risen from an average of 300 ppm (parts per million) to 400 ppm, the highest levels ever. Carbon dioxide forms a blanket above the earth that traps heat, an additional contributor to global warming.

Studies by scientists point out that global warming is having bad effects on humans, animals and plants. Carbon dioxide reduces air quality and it is not healthy for humans and animals to breathe. Water is essential for living creatures; without enough water, they die. Global warming decreases the amount of water on the planet. Some creatures cannot adapt quickly to changes in climates and will die, and those that migrate can be forced to change their migration patterns.

Why is this happening? Ninety seven percent of global scientists think this is happening because of things we humans are doing. Our use of fuels from fossils, such as oil and coal, are major causes, and our manufacturing activities are another cause.

The author says that global warming is happening. The author shows data proving that global temperatures have been rising, that a major ice cap is melting and that carbon dioxide levels in the atmosphere have increased, all of which are results of global warming.

The author says that scientific studies show that global warming is having bad effects on humans, animals and plants. The author supports this statement by presenting these effects, such as a reduction (decrease) in air quality, reduction in water supplies, inability (not able to do something) of some creatures to adapt to changes in climate and disruption (change) of migration patterns.

Your assignment: Describe the relationship between the series of historical events that caused climate change and what effect climate change has had on the earth.

This is an example of what you might write

Over a period of many years, average temperatures for countries on planet Earth have been rising. This has been called global warming. Global warming is affecting planet Earth in many ways. The supply of fresh water on the planet is decreasing. Glaciers are melting. Sea levels are rising and there is more carbon dioxide in the air than ever before. This increase in carbon dioxide is not healthy for humans and animals to breathe.

You can scan the QR code given below or use the URL to access additional EdSearch resources including videos and mobile apps related to *Cause and Effect*.

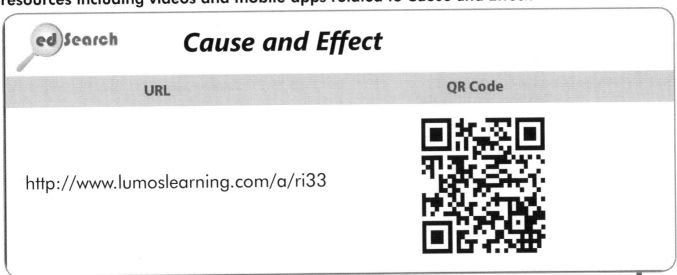

URL	QR Code
http://www.lumoslearning.com/a/ri33	

Question 1 is based on the passage below.

The Bluegrass State

There is one state with water, wildlife, and mountains. Does this sound too good to be true? Well, it isn't all of these natural features are in The Bluegrass State. Kentucky is home to wonderful lakes that offer fun water activities. These are some of the reasons that people visit Kentucky.

The Bluegrass State has a lot to offer for those looking for fun in the water. Cumberland Falls is a huge waterfall. It has been nicknamed "the Niagara of the South". If you are looking to do more than just see the water, a visit to beautiful Lake Cumberland might be a good stop for you. Here you can enjoy boating, fishing, or jet skiing.

Maybe, you are more of a wildlife person. Many people love hunting in the western part of the state. Natural wildlife can be found throughout the area. There are excursions in the Daniel Boone National Forest that are great also.

If this does not sound like fun to you, then you might like to learn more about Kentucky's horses. You can visit one of the race tracks or horse farms. Visitors from all over the world have visited Churchill Downs. Their horses race in the Kentucky Derby. Several other races that can be attended throughout the year. Other locations that allow you to enjoy Kentucky's best thoroughbreds include the Kentucky Horse Park and Keeneland.

Kentucky's tourism doesn't stop there. Guests can visit Mammoth Cave and the home of Abraham Lincoln. Certainly, the Bluegrass State is filled with features that keep people visiting this beautiful state.

1. **Which of the following probably happened BEFORE tourists started visiting Kentucky to see the exciting race horses?**

   Ⓐ Churchill Downs was built.
   Ⓑ Lake Cumberland was developed.
   Ⓒ The Daniel Boone National Forest was named.
   Ⓓ The owners of Keeneland invited guests from all around the world.

Question 2 is based on the passage below.

Amelia Earhart

Amelia Earhart was born on July 24, 1897. She lived with her grandparents until the age of 12 when she and her sister went to live with their parents in 1909. Amelia's plans were to attend college, but when she came across four wounded World War I soldiers, she decided that she wanted to become a nurse. Her dedication to helping people led her from nursing to work as a social worker. While she worked as a social worker, she often spent her free time teaching immigrant children how to speak English.

Her most noteworthy journey began in 1920 when she took a ten-minute plane ride that completely changed her life. She decided to focus on earning a pilot's license. She challenged herself with a variety of jobs to earn the $1,000 needed for flying lessons to fulfill her dream.

Amelia Earhart proceeded to excel as a pilot. She received a medal from President Herbert Hoover in 1932 for her solo flight across the Atlantic. She did not stop there. Earhart was the first female to fly from Hawaii to California.

Amelia Earhart's contribution to history ended on July 2, 1937, when a frantic message was received by the U. S. Coast Guard. The message was from Earhart stating that she and the plane were in trouble. The plane went down, and no one has ever seen Earhart again. Her devotion to creating change remains a legacy. This legacy emphasizes how setting dreams and achieving goals can be done through hard work and determination.

2. Which sentence indicates why Earhart never went to college?

Ⓐ
Ⓑ She lived with her grandparents until the age of 12 when she and her sister went to live with their parents in 1909.

Amelia's plans were to attend college, but when she came across four wounded World War I
Ⓒ soldiers, she decided that she wanted to become a nurse.

Her dedication to helping people led her from nursing to work as a social worker, where she
Ⓓ spent her free time teaching immigrant children the English language.

Her most noteworthy journey began in 1920 when she took a ten-minute plane ride that forever changed her life.

Question 3 is based on the passage below.

Cell Phones in the Classroom

A familiar ringtone sounds in the classroom directing everyone's attention to a shy student in the back row. Several years ago, this would have seemed a bit strange, but not today. A recent study showed that one in three third-grade students have a cell phone. With so many students having access to technology devices, a lot of talks have gone into deciding whether to use them as learning tools or to ban them from the classroom.

Let's think about cell phones' role as learning tools. Annie needs a calculator but forgot hers. She takes out her cell phone and can use the calculator app on the phone. Just across the room, Johnny is trying to spell the word "similar," so he uses the dictionary app on his phone to find the correct spelling. Mitchell, has completed all of his work early, so he decides to use the multiplication app on his phone to review multiplication facts in a fun and interactive way. These devices are causing teachers and other school officials to see that cell phones give students access to resources that actually save schools money.

While cell phones may sound great, not every school district is ready to lift the cell phone ban. There are still those that have major concerns. One concern is what to do about students who do not have a cell phone. Another worry is how to make sure students are using the phone as a learning tool instead of texting and social media. Additional concerns arise with how to address when a phone is broken or stolen while at school. Certainly, the list of problems that some schools have goes on and on.

The answer isn't clear for schools across the United States. Some schools are starting to lift the cell phone ban, but others are keeping it in place. As students pack backpacks with cell phones, the discussion of having them in the classroom will certainly continue.

3. What does the author state would be a positive effect of allowing students to have cell phones in the classroom?

Ⓐ Students could access learning apps to assist in learning.
Ⓑ Students could stay in touch with their family and friends throughout the school by texting.
Ⓒ Students could stay connected through social media.
Ⓓ The school would have to buy students a new phone if their phone was broken or stolen while at school.

Question 4-6 are based on the passage below.

THE WATER CYCLE

The water cycle is a cycle that repeats itself over and over again. After it rains, you may see lots of water puddles on the ground. Then the sun comes out and the puddles disappear. Did you know the sun will then change the water on the ground into a gas called "water vapor"? This part of the water cycle is called evaporation (liquid changed to a gas). As the water vapor rises into the air, it sticks with pieces of dust. The air gets cooler and the vapor changes back into liquid (water). This is called condensation. The condensation collects and forms clouds. When there is too much water for the clouds to hold, precipitation falls back to earth as rain, snow, sleet, or hail. This cycle continues again and again. Evaporation, condensation, and precipitation are the processes involved in the water cycle.

4. What stage in the water cycle is complete when the water falls back to the ground?

Ⓐ precipitation
Ⓑ condensation
Ⓒ evaporation
Ⓓ perspiration

5. Choose the sentence that BEST explains what happens during evaporation.

Ⓐ The hot sun beats down on the earth and changes the water to water vapor.
Ⓑ The water is turned into liquid.
Ⓒ The water is formed into sleet, rain, snow, or hail.
Ⓓ Water does not evaporate.

6. Which of the following activities shows the results of condensation?

- Ⓐ The rain begins to beat heavily on the roof.
- Ⓑ Jimmy's birthday party is at 1:00. He keeps looking at the sky, watching it become filled with black, dark clouds.
- Ⓒ The hot sun makes playing outside very hard.
- Ⓓ The snow falls, turning everything into a perfect white blanket.

Question 7 is based on the passage below.

Over the past 100 years, the Olympic games have endured. They remain a passion for fans, athletes, and trainers all over the world. While the love for this worldwide event is well-known, many changes have occurred since 1896.

In 1896, the Olympic games had 42 events and 245 competitors. These games were hosted in Athens, Greece. Only 14 nations were represented in those Olympic games. While only a little over one hundred years ago, women were not allowed to participate in the Olympic games. The most successful athlete from the 1896 games was a German wrestler/gymnast named Carl Schumann. Schumann won 4 gold medals.

The 2008 Olympic Games showed just how much a century can change things. Over 200 nations were represented in Beijing, China. There were over 10,000 males and females who competed for their chance at gold. A total of over 300 events were completed. Meanwhile, the most successful athlete from the 2008 games was American swimmer Michael Phelps. Phelps earned 8 gold medals in the 2008 Olympics. This was a new record for the most gold medals won during a single Olympic game. The 2008 Olympic games also marked an end for two popular events: baseball and softball. While a lot has changed about the Olympic games, some things remain the same. The games are still held every four years. Additionally, the International Sports Federation Rules apply to the event. There are gold, silver, and bronze medals given today, just as they were 116 years ago in Athens, Greece.

7. Which of the following events MOST LIKELY contributed to the grand success of the Olympics as it is today?

- Ⓐ The original Olympics were held in Greece the 1800s.
- Ⓑ The 2008 Olympic games
- Ⓒ Phelps victorious performance in 2008, earning him 8 gold medals.
- Ⓓ The first American-hosted Olympic games in 1904.

Question 8 and 9 are based on the passage below.

The Asteroid Belt

It's shaped like a doughnut, made from lumps of rock, and looks like a pattern of floating rocks moving in a circle. This strange sounding object is the Asteroid Belt. The Asteroid Belt was formed from lumps of rock left over after other planets formed. Yes, it is shaped like a doughnut and can be found between the orbits of Mars and Jupiter. The Asteroid Belt has two layers. The inner layer has asteroids made of metals. The outer layer has rocky asteroids.

When you look at the Asteroid Belt it looks like floating rocks moving in a circle. Scientists say that there are millions of asteroids in this belt. It may sound pretty funny, but scientists say that there is still a lot of empty space. As you have probably already guessed, the Asteroid Belt is pretty big. It is actually 215 million miles wide. Jupiter keeps the asteroids inside the belt and prevents them from hitting the planets in space. Jupiter's gravity is what holds the asteroids in place.

The chunks of rock inside of the belt were named asteroid, meaning star and rock. The first asteroids seen in the belt were named after gods and heroes. The first largest asteroid found was named Ceres after a Roman goddess. Ceres was discovered on January 1, 1801. It is the size of Texas, and is it called a dwarf planet. Before an asteroid is named, a group of people check to make sure it is not an inappropriate name. Now that most Roman hero names have been used up, scientists are using the name of the astrophysicist to name an asteroid. A lot of information remains unknown about the extremely real Asteroid Belt.

8. Which of the following DID NOT happen before the naming of the Asteroid Belt?

Ⓐ Mars was formed.
Ⓑ Mercury was formed.
Ⓒ Ceres was identified and named.
Ⓓ Venus was formed.

9. What happened BEFORE the Asteroid Belt formed?

Ⓐ The asteroid Ceres was named.
Ⓑ The names of the Roman gods and goddesses were all used up.
Ⓒ An asteroid the size of Texas was identified.
Ⓓ The Earth was made

Question 10 is based on the passage below.

"Inventions have long since reached their limit." This was said by Julius Sextus Frontinus in AD 10. The Romans had invented aqueducts that could carry water for miles from lakes and rivers to dry places. Their engineers built roads that were so well-made that some of them still exist today. Their bridges spanned large distances. Frontinus decided that they had invented everything that could possibly be invented.

The patent office reviews new inventions to make sure that inventors are protected from those who might steal or copy their designs. The same statement made by Frontinus was later made by Charles H. Duell, who worked in the U.S. patent office in 1899. Telegraphs, phonographs, and steam engines had been invented. Mr. Duell became famous when he said, "Everything that can be invented has already been invented."

10. **Why have the statements by Frontinus and Duell both become famous? Circle the correct answer choice.**

Ⓐ The statements are famous because they are similar.
Ⓑ The statements are famous because they are different.
Ⓒ The statements are famous because they are correct.
Ⓓ The statements are famous because they are wrong.

Question 11 is based on the passage below.

In 218 B.C., Romans ruled most of the world that they knew about. They felt protected by the Alps – high, snow-covered mountains to the east and north of them that enemies would find very difficult to cross. Then Hannibal came from Carthage, in what is now North Africa, with 9000 infantrymen – soldiers on foot – and something even more surprising: elephants. Hannibal had crossed the Alps with 37 elephants – creatures so terrifying that the Romans, who had never seen such animals, were thrown into a panic.

11. Based on what you know in this passage, what do you predict happened next?

Chapter 3

Lesson 4: Educational Expressions

This standard asks you the reader to "Determine the meaning" of words or phrases in written text. If you don't know the meaning of a word or phrase, you have to either look it up in a dictionary or thesaurus (contains other words that mean the same thing) or figure it out by reading the other words in the text. But sometimes a word or phrase can have different meanings, so you have to decide what the author of the text wanted the meaning to be.

Here are some examples of words and phrases and ways to figure out their meanings without using a dictionary or thesaurus.

1. Many animals in the wild eat other animals. These animals are called **carnivores**. Examples of carnivores are dogs, lions and bears.

What does carnivore mean?
The best clue for figuring out what carnivore means is the sentence "Many animals in the wild eat other animals." The word actually means an animal that eats flesh. Flesh is the soft material between the skin and the skeleton of an animal, and that is what a carnivore eats (it does not eat an animal's bones). In today's world, many animals do not live in the wild, such as dogs that are pets or animals in zoos, and they are fed pet or animal food made by humans. Still, they are called carnivores.

2. Because her country was at war, Marta's family decided to leave their country and move to the United States. They were called **immigrants**.

What does immigrant mean?
The best clue for figuring out what immigrant means is the sentence "Marta's family decided to leave their country and move to the United States." An immigrant is someone who moves from their country to another country. They usually have to qualify under certain rules in order to be accepted legally by the country they want to move to, and may be able to become legal citizens of that country.

3. What would be a logical (reasonable) **setting** for a story about the Plymouth colonists and Wampanoag Indians sharing an autumn harvest feast that is acknowledged today as one of the first Thanksgiving celebrations in the colonies?

What does setting mean?
Stories are about people, places and/or things (or events).

You probably know that people in a story are known as characters. Events in a story are about things that happen. So that leaves one other word: places. The setting of a story is the location where the story takes place. It is also the time period in which the story takes place. In this case, a logical setting is the place where Pilgrims founded the colony of Plymouth, which was in the colony of Massachusetts. The time period is the 1600's, 1621 being the year this feast took place.

You can scan the QR code given below or use the URL to access additional EdSearch resources including videos and mobile apps related to *Educational Expressions.*

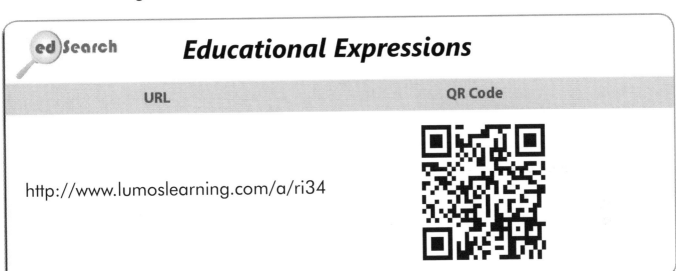

1. What does carnivore mean in this paragraph?

Many animals in the wild eat other animals. These animals are called carnivores. Carnivores include lions, tigers, and bears.

Ⓐ A plant eating animal
Ⓑ An animal that eats plants and animals
Ⓒ A meat eating animal
Ⓓ An animal that eats dead

2. What is evaporation?

Clouds in the sky are able to produce rain. They get their water through evaporation. The sun heats the water in rivers, lakes, and even puddles, turning it into a vapor. Clouds are produced when lots of this vapor comes together.

Ⓐ Water turning into rain.
Ⓑ Clouds making rain.
Ⓒ Water heating up and turning into a vapor.
Ⓓ Water being absorbed by clouds.

3. What does the underlined word mean?

The world's population is growing every day! Thousands of babies are born each day, adding to the number of people on Earth.

Ⓐ number of babies
Ⓑ number of countries
Ⓒ number of days
Ⓓ number of people

4. What is the meaning of the underlined word?

My cousin Hans lives in Germany. He is a German citizen.

Ⓐ person
Ⓑ country
Ⓒ A person living in a particular country
Ⓓ visitor to a particular country

5. What is the meaning of the underlined word?

Because her country was at war, Marta's family decided to move to the United States. She and her family are <u>immigrants</u>.

Ⓐ people who move from a country
Ⓑ people who move to another country
Ⓒ people who are at war
Ⓓ people who are forced out of a country

6. What is the meaning of the underlined word?

I read an interesting story online today. The <u>setting</u> of the story is Mexico in 1870.

Ⓐ sitting
Ⓑ people in the story
Ⓒ the time and place the story occurred
Ⓓ cover of a book

7. What must the students do to come up with the sum?

My math teacher wrote five numbers on the board and asked the class to figure out the sum of the numbers.

Ⓐ subtract the numbers
Ⓑ add the numbers
Ⓒ divide the numbers
Ⓓ multiply the numbers

8. What is your teacher asking you to write?

After reading a book to the class, your teacher asks you to write a summary of the story.

Ⓐ A sentence about the main character.
Ⓑ The title of the book.
Ⓒ A few sentences describing what the story is about.
Ⓓ Your own story that is similar to the story she read.

Question 9 and 10 are based on the passage below.

Over the past 100 years, the Olympic games have endured. They remain a passion for fans, athletes, and trainers all over the world. While the love for this worldwide event is well-known, many changes have occurred since 1896.

In 1896, the Olympic games had 42 events and 245 competitors. These games were hosted in Athens, Greece. Only 14 nations were represented in those Olympic games. While only a little over one hundred years ago, women were not allowed to participate in the Olympic games. The most successful athlete from the 1896 games was a German wrestler/gymnast named Carl Schumann. Schumann won 4 gold medals.

The 2008 Olympic Games showed just how much a century can change things. Over 200 nations were represented in Beijing, China. There were over 10,000 males and females that competed for their chance at gold. A total of over 300 events were completed. Meanwhile, the most successful athlete from the 2008 games was American swimmer Michael Phelps. Phelps earned 8 gold medals in the 2008 Olympics. This was a new record for the most gold medals won during a single Olympic game. The 2008 Olympic games also marked an end for two popular events: baseball and softball.

While a lot has changed about the Olympic games, some things remain the same. The games are still held every four years. Additionally, the International Sports Federation Rules apply to the event. There are gold, silver, and bronze medals given today, just as they were 116 years ago in Athens, Greece.

9. What does the underlined word in the following sentence from the passage above MOST LIKELY mean?

While a lot has changed about the Olympic games, some things <u>remain</u> the same.

    Ⓐ   change over time
    Ⓑ   stay the same
    Ⓒ   left over
    Ⓓ   new and exciting

10. What does the underlined word in the following sentence from the passage above MOST LIKELY mean?

The 2008 Olympic games showed just how much a <u>century</u> can change things.

    Ⓐ   one year
    Ⓑ   five years
    Ⓒ   ten years
    Ⓓ   one hundred years

Question 11 is based on the passage below.

Simple Machines

Most of us don't go through our daily lives thinking about all the simple machines that we use, but they are everywhere. Without things like the lever, the wheel and axle, the pulley, the inclined plane, the wedge, and the screw, our lives would be much more complicated. Although simple machines have few parts, their function is to help maximize human strength and motion by using less force. As a result, there are six simple machines that make our lives easier.

Simple machines were created to make everyday tasks faster and less frustrating. Just think about how hard it would be to raise a flag without a pulley or how difficult loading a lawnmower on a trailer would be without the assistance of an inclined plane. Simple machines make jobs lighter.

Did you know that simple machines are used for fun activities too? Teeter-totters that allows children to move smoothly up and down use simple machines. Or picture the wheel and axle movement of your parents' steering wheel as you ride to and from the baseball field, the park, or a friend's birthday party.

These simple machines are also used to make some careers and <u>basic</u> tasks easier. An artist's job is made easier through the use of a wedge and chisel. They are able to use these simple machines when sculpting an image out of wood or clay. Additionally, a construction work might use a simple machine called a lever to drive nails into wood. Yes, to us this would be known as a hammer, but levers are nothing more than tools that aid in lifting or moving loads. A screw is an inclined plane that is wrapped around a pole to help hold objects together. This can be seen during the motion of turning a key in a lock.

The world around us uses these simple machines everywhere. Our lives are overflowing with uses for them. Next time, you walk through your home or enjoy a day at the park, take a moment to notice just how much these simple machines help us in our daily.

11. What does the underlined word in the following sentence from the passage MOST LIKELY mean? Circle the correct answer choice.

   These simple machines are also used to make some careers and <u>basic</u> tasks easier

   Ⓐ extra
   Ⓑ main
   Ⓒ really hard
   Ⓓ boring

Question 12 is based on the passage below.

Amelia Earhart

Amelia Earhart was born on July 24, 1897. From that point forward, she was focused on earning a pilot's license. Holding on to that dream, she challenged herself with a variety of jobs to earn the $1,000 needed for flying lessons.

Soaring to new heights, Earhart proceeded to excel as a pilot. She received a medal from President Herbert Hoover in 1932 for her solo flight across the Atlantic. Meanwhile, she did not stop there. Earhart was the first female to fly from Hawaii to California.

Earhart's contribution to history ended on July 2, 1937 when a frantic message was received by the U. S. Coast Guard. Meanwhile, her devotion to creating change remains a <u>legacy</u>. This legacy emphasizes how setting dreams and achieving goals can be done through hard work and determination.

12. What does the underlined word in the following sentence from the passage MOST LIKELY mean? Circle the correct answer choice.

> **Meanwhile, her devotion to creating change remains a <u>legacy</u>.**

Ⓐ plan
Ⓑ wisdom
Ⓒ gift
Ⓓ problems

Question 13 is based on the passage below.

Cell Phones in the Classroom

A familiar ringtone sounds out in the classroom directing everyone's attention to a shy student in the back row. Several years ago, this would have seemed a bit strange, but not today. A recent study showed that every one in three, third-grade students, has a cell phone. With so many students having access to these technology devices, a lot of talk has gone into whether to use them as learning tools or keep them banned from the classroom.

Let's think about their role as learning tools. Annie needs a calculator but forgot hers. She takes out her cell phone and can use the calculator app on the phone. Just across the room, Johnny is trying to spell the word "similar" so he uses the dictionary app on his phone to find the correct spelling. Another student in the class, Mitchell, has completed all of his work early, so he decides to use the multiplication app on his phone to review his multiplication facts in a fun and interactive way. These and other apps are making teachers and other school officials to see that cell phones do give students access to many resources that could actually save schools money.

While cell phones may sound great, not everyone is ready to lift the cell phone ban. There are still those that have major concerns. One concern is what to do about students that do not have a cell phone. Another worry is how to make sure students are using the phone as a learning tool instead of texting and social media. Additional concerns arise with how to address when a phone is broken or stolen while at school. Certainly, the list of problems that some schools have goes on and on.

The answer isn't clear for schools across the United States. Some schools are starting to lift the cell phone ban, but others are keeping it in place. As more and more backpacks get armed with cell phones, the discussion of having them in the classroom will certainly continue.

13. What does the underlined word in the following sentence from the passage MOST LIKELY mean? Circle the correct answer choice.

These and other apps are making teachers and other school officials to see that cell phones do give students <u>access</u> to many resources that could actually save schools money.

Ⓐ money
Ⓑ a waste of time
Ⓒ a block
Ⓓ a connection

Chapter 3

Lesson 5: Special Text parts

You can practice hyperlink searching, keyword searching and related concepts with the help of the example below

Junk Food

These days junk food is very popular. Junk food is used to describe cheap food containing high levels of <u>calories</u> from <u>sugar</u> or <u>fat</u> with little fiber, protein, vitamins or minerals. Junk food can also refer to high protein food like meat prepared with saturated fat, which some believe may be unhealthy. Some fast-food restaurants (restaurants that prepare and serve food very quickly to the customer, usually without waiters or waitresses) supply food considered to be junk food. Despite being labeled as "junk", such foods usually do not pose any immediate health concerns and are generally safe when integrated into a well-balanced diet. However, concerns about the negative health effects resulting from the consumption of a junk food-heavy diet, especially obesity, have resulted in public health awareness campaigns, and restrictions on advertising and sale in several countries.

Assignment: Your teacher has asked you to read this article and explain what tools you would use to get more information about junk food.

You might write this:

I would click on the highlighted words "calories", "sugar" and "fat" with my computer mouse, because these words are in blue and underlined text. This means there is a link to more information about the subject. I would also go the internet and use a search engine like Google to search for information using key words like junk food, calories, sugar, fat, saturated fat, good nutrition and any other key words I could think of.

You can scan the QR code given below or use the URL to access additional EdSearch resources including videos and mobile apps related to *Special Text parts*.

ed)Search

Special Text parts

URL	QR Code
http://www.lumoslearning.com/a/ri35	

Question 1 and 2 are based on the passage below.

From McGuffey's Second Eclectic Reader

1. There are three kinds of bees: workers, drones, and queens.
2. Bees live in a house that is called a hive.
3. Only one queen can live in each hive. If she is lost or dead, the other bees will stop their work.
4. They are very wise and busy little creatures. They all join together to build cells of wax for their honey.
5.   Each bee takes its proper place, and does its own work. Some go out and gather honey from the flowers; others stay at home and work inside the hive.
6. The cells which they build are all one shape and size, and there are no spaces between them.
7. The cells are not round, but have six sides.
8. Have you ever looked into a glass hive to see the bees at work? They are always busy.
9. The drones do not work. Every year before winter, all of the drones are driven from the hive or killed. The reason the drones are driven from the hive or killed is because they did not help make the honey.
10. It is not safe for children to handle bees because they have stingers. Bees use their stingers as a great defensive tool.

1. How does the author of this selection help the reader easily locate information?

Ⓐ By using a title
Ⓑ By using headers
Ⓒ By numbering the sentences
Ⓓ By organizing the sentences

2. Which sentence tells the reader about the jobs bees perform?

Ⓐ Sentence 3
Ⓑ Sentence 4
Ⓒ Sentence 6
Ⓓ Sentence 9

Question 3 and 4 are based on the passage below.

With junk food becoming increasingly popular, and families being on the go more than ever, kids and their parents need to know how to make healthier food choices. It is important that children learn to make healthy food choices from an early age. If children learn to make these choices, it not only makes them healthy, but also it keeps them in shape.

Staying in shape is one way of saying that someone makes wise decisions about eating, exercising and maintaining a healthy weight. Staying in shape not only helps your body to work well, but helps you feel better too. Who doesn't want to feel well to enjoy fun activities with others?

While parents are responsible for making wise choices too, there are many ways that kids can step up to the plate and take charge. Let's start by talking about the types of foods that kids should eat. Sure, there are special occasions when a treat is in store, but fruits and vegetables should be a part of your daily food habits, not cake and ice cream. Your body needs a variety of healthy foods. By giving your body a lot of different foods, it will be able to get the nutrients that it needs. Don't be afraid to try new foods. You may not like everything that you try, but by trying new things, you will find more foods that you like. Throughout each day, try to eat five servings of fruits and vegetables. Hopefully, out of the five you will be able to find two fruits and three vegetables to enjoy.

Now that we have looked at some wise food choices, let's take a look at what you should be drinking. Water and milk are always the best choices. There is nothing that quenches your thirst like a cold glass of water. Now, you may have often wonder why schools serve cartons of milk. The truth is, milk is needed to help build strong bones because it contains calcium. Kids younger than 9 years old should drink 2 cups of milk per day. If milk isn't your favorite thing to drink, there are other ways to get the calcium that your body needs.

Some great dairy alternatives that introduce calcium into your diet are cheddar cheese and yogurt. You may be wondering if milk and water should be your only drink choices, and the answer is no. You can choose juice drinks that are 100% pure. This means that they are not loaded down with sugar. Many sodas, juice cocktails, and fruit punches have extraordinary amounts of sugar. Along with choosing the right foods and drinks, try to stay in shape with exercise.

It is important to try to find a way to be active for at least one hour daily. This might include playing basketball, riding a bike, or swimming. Now sometimes the weather won't allow you to enjoy these outdoor activities, so choose to get physical indoors by turning on some music that you enjoy and dancing to the beat. Other ideas include going bowling or turning your living room into a studio for "Simon Says" where you get to follow and give commands, such as: "Simon Says do 10 jumping jacks...." Just remember the idea is to get up and get active.

Staying fit doesn't have to be hard. It simply requires making wise choices. Try to make fruits, vegetables, milk, water, and exercise a part of your daily routine! You will feel great, and your body will thank you by giving you lots of energy to do the things that you most enjoy.

3. If the author of this passage wanted the reader to do additional research, what key word would BEST help them in their Internet search?

Ⓐ Jumping Jacks
Ⓑ Ways to Stay Healthy
Ⓒ Drinking Milk and Water
Ⓓ The Food Group

4. What type of picture WOULD NOT help to make the information in this passage clearer?

- Ⓐ The Food Pyramid
- Ⓑ A chart showing types of exercise for kids
- Ⓒ A chart showing fruits and vegetables
- Ⓓ Favorite junk foods

Question 5 is based on the passage below.

Good Manners Can Help You

Good manners can be seen at home, at school, on the playground, and at the dining table where we eat our meals. A well mannered person is polite and gentle when talking.

Everyone likes a person who is polite and good mannered. Good manners are always liked by everyone and after can bring good rewards.

Therefore, we should always remember to do what is right.

All that is wrong displeases everyone. Therefore, we should not do what is wrong. Often, we will be rewarded for our good actions.

Children who consistently come late to school are not dependable. It is difficult to provide important work for them. These children could even lose some friends.

All of us make mistakes. When we make a mistake, we do not like to be punished. We like to be forgiven. Therefore, we, too, should forgive the mistakes of others. Forgiveness is a great virtue.

It is easy to make a mistake, but it is not easy to forget that mistake. When we make a mistake, we should feel sorry about it. We also apologize to the person whom we have hurt.

We should not cheat on an examination. Cheating always does more harm than good. We can choose out friends wisely.

5. What part of this selection gives the reader a clue to know what they will be reading about?

- Ⓐ the second sentence
- Ⓑ the header
- Ⓒ the title
- Ⓓ the italics

Question 6 and 7 are based on the passage below.

The Amazon Rainforest

The Amazon Rainforest is full of life. It has sounds of all kinds, water rushing and falling, and animals communicating. It's a busy place where animals are looking for food, trying to survive, and looking to expand their families. The Amazon Rainforest in South America, has one tiny animal that is almost completely camouflaged from the rest of the animals, except for one small body part: its bright red eyes!

This animal is known as the Red-Eyed Tree Frog. It lives deep in the tall trees in the Amazon. It resides mostly in South America, it can also be found in Central America and parts of Mexico.

Many bright colors decorate the body of the adult Red-Eyed Tree frog. Its main color is green, with a mixture of yellow, orange, and blue on its belly. The frog can change its colors based on its feelings or needs; the color often changes from green to reddish-brown. Its toes have suction cups that help the Red-Eyed Tree Frog attach itself to the environment. The suction cups give the frog traction to stand firm on wet leaves. Its legs are built better for climbing than for swimming, and it is almost never on the ground. It keeps jumping around steadily pace from tree to tree.

The physical properties of the Red-Eyed Tree Frog also makes it different, and helps it survive. Unlike most humans, or even other animals, the male frog is actually smaller than the female. Male frogs only reach around two inches in length while the females can grow to be three inches. The RedEyed Tree Frog is also a carnivore. The tree frog eats grasshoppers, moths, and other insects. However, it eats smaller frogs, too! It is known to eat almost anything that can fit in its mouth.

Many people find it fascinating to know that the red eyes are not just for looks; they help the frogs survive. In fact, the red eyes scare other animals easily and help these frogs escape from their predators. With their greenish color skin, they tend to blend in with their surroundings. When they sleep, they are virtually invisible. However, if other animals see them and try to attack, the Red-Eyed Tree Frog will open its wide, red eyes, and the predators, which usually consist of snakes, birds, or bats, will scurry away. In many cases, the predators may also be stunned into stillness at the sight of the red eyes, long enough for the frog to escape.

The Red-Eyed Tree frog is a unique animal that is able to protect itself even though it is very small. With deadly predators and a dangerous environment surrounding it, the frog relies on camouflage, and its bright red eyes to scare off unwanted guests and enemies.

6. What would be a better title for this selection?

Ⓐ The Amazing Red-Eyed Tree Frog
Ⓑ The Animals of the Amazon Rainforest
Ⓒ Where to Find the Amazon Rainforest
Ⓓ The Endangered Amazon Rainforest

7. What text feature would help the reader better understand the third paragraph in this selection?

    Ⓐ A map of the Amazon rainforest
    Ⓑ A diagram of the tree frog
    Ⓒ A photograph of the tree frog
    Ⓓ An illustration of where the tree frog lives

Question 8 and 9 are based on the passage below.

Matter is everything that surrounds you on a daily basis. There are five primary states of matter. Matter is made of atoms and molecules, mass, and takes up any amount of space. There are five states that matter can be found in: solid, liquid, gas, plasma, and Bose-Einstein condensate; but, the main states are solid, gas, and liquid. It is possible for matter to move from one state to another. One example of this is water. In its liquid form, we can put water in a cup and drink it. Water can also be found in a solid form which is ice, or in a gas form which is fog.

8. What would be an appropriate heading title for this section of text?

    Ⓐ Matter
    Ⓑ Space
    Ⓒ Atoms
    Ⓓ Objects

9. Which of the following could be included to improve the information provided in this passage?

    Ⓐ a picture of space
    Ⓑ a picture of water as a solid, liquid, and a gas
    Ⓒ a picture of rain
    Ⓓ a diagram of an atom

10. This poem is meant to be read out loud. Why does the author use apostrophes (') in this selection?

from McGuffey's Second Eclectic Reader
blos'soms drear'y wea'ry pinks smell'ing toil'ing
lev'ies buzz fra'grant this'tle weeds scent
treas'ure yel'low mead'ow tax sum'mer clo'ver
cloud'y dai'sy daf'fo dil lies columbine humming

    Ⓐ To show the reader how to pronounce the words
    Ⓑ To show the reader where the syllables divide in the words
    Ⓒ To show the reader the meaning of each word
    Ⓓ To show the reader how loudly to read the selection

Chapter 3

Lesson 6: What Did You Already Know?

Let us understand the concept with an example.

Assignment: Read the text below. Figure out what the author's point of view (opinion) is. Then write your own point of view that is different from the author's.

Publisher's Note: when you write from your point of view, you can either put your name in as the author and/or you can use the pronoun "I" when giving your opinion. In the article below, the author made statements but did not use "I". She was writing directly to the reader, so she used the pronoun "you".

Why Allowing Smartphones and Tablets in Classrooms is a Bad Idea?

Allowing each student to use his/her smartphone or tablet in the classroom gives away too much freedom with too little oversight. There are students who will not handle that freedom well; bright students may complete the assignment quickly, and struggling students may become discouraged. In either case, they will have the means to access games or social media such as Facebook or Twitter using their smartphones or tablets and either waste class time by not moving on to another assignment or not give the necessary attention to their assignment. And how do you prevent this from happening? Are you going to have the school install spyware that tracks what each student is doing on the computer, turning the teacher into a spy and enforcer and not a teacher?

It is easier for a teacher to monitor each student's work by walking around glancing at the screens of the school's computer system than trying to see what is displayed on the smaller screens on a smartphone or tablet. It is better that students use the school computer system when at school.

There are enough school computers for most students, but for those who have to wait, a teacher can assign other non-computer related tasks. Also, each student has a study period during which he/she can use a school computer.

In summary, requiring students to use the school computer system at school while allowing access to the school system from outside the school, will give them all the flexibility they need, while allowing teachers to do the necessary supervision and control over their students' work in school.

This is what you might write to give the opposite opinion on this subject.

I think it is a good idea for a school to allow students to bring their smartphones or tablets to school. The school will have to make a rule that students can only use their smartphones and tablets to do school work. Also, when a teacher is actually teaching new lessons, the smartphones and tablets must be turned off. Anyone breaking these rules will be punished.

When a teacher makes an assignment that students must work on in class, students will be working on their own at different speeds and will complete their assignments at different times. Students who finish the assignment quickly can then move on to another assignment online without interrupting the teacher or distracting other students. Also, we eliminate the problem of students sitting idle waiting for a computer to become available. This happens a lot since the school has not purchased enough computers to allow everyone in the class to be on one all at the same time.

If students are allowed to use their smartphones and tablets as I am suggesting, the teacher will have more free time to help students who have questions. Best of all, the teacher can access online each student's progress with the assignment, either when she is in class, or after class, or after school, from inside or outside the school. And, if a student is absent, the teacher can quickly send homework assignments electronically to the student, eliminating the time spent arranging for a parent or another student to pick up and deliver the assignment.

In summary, I think allowing students to bring their smartphones and tablets to school will allow more work to get done and allow the teacher more time to help students that need it. But, there are rules that need to be made and enforced.

You can scan the QR code given below or use the URL to access additional EdSearch resources including videos and mobile apps related to *What Did You Already Know?*.

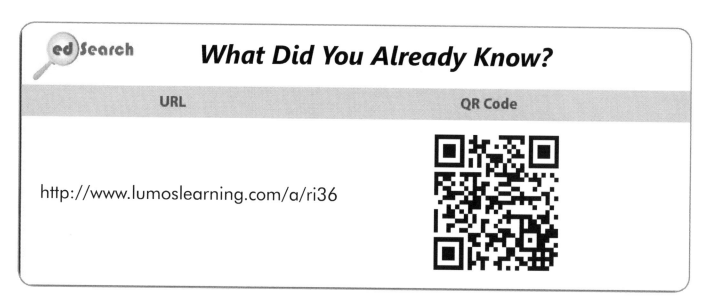

ed Search — **What Did You Already Know?**

URL	QR Code
http://www.lumoslearning.com/a/ri36	

Question 1 is based on the passage below.

Everything in nature follows a pattern. Circles, lines, spirals, and angles are repeated to make a design or a pattern. Patterns in nature are not just pretty adornments. They serve a purpose that has helped nature survive and flourish.

Have you ever taken a close look at a beehive? Well, not too close or you might get stung! The natural pattern in beehives is so perfect that it seems to be computer designed. The hives are made up of layers and layers of cells. Each cell has six perfectly equal sides or hexagons. Why would bees build six-sided cells, instead of round, or box shaped ones? The reason is that the bee is a genius at geometry and architecture! Six-sided cells use up every bit of space and allow bees to get the maximum area for storing honey. Also, Hexagons use the least honeycomb wax because all six sides are identical in length. The bees don't waste space, material, or effort. Aren't they smart insects?

1. Where might a reader use the information about hexagons from this passage?

    Ⓐ When solving a math problem on algebra.
    Ⓑ When writing a math paper on geometric properties of a hexagon.
    Ⓒ When building your home.
    Ⓓ None of the above.

Question 2 is based on the passage below.

What is the most poisonous creature on Earth? Many people guess that the answer would be a snake, a jellyfish, a scorpion, or a spider. Actually, most scientists agree that the most venomous animal is a harmless-looking small golden frog, called "teribilis." The golden frog is so toxic that even touching it can be dangerous to humans. A single frog contains enough poison to kill 20,000 mice or ten people.

2. What should you do if you see a teribilis? Write your answer in the box below

>

Question 3 is based on the passage below.

The Bluegrass State

There is one state with water, wildlife, and mountains. Does this sound too good to be true? Well, it isn't all of these natural features are in The Bluegrass State. These are some of the reasons that people visit Kentucky. Kentucky is home to wonderful lakes that offer fun water activities.

Cumberland Falls is a huge waterfall. It has been nicknamed "the Niagara of the South". If you are looking to do more than just see the water, a visit to beautiful Lake Cumberland might be a good stop for you. Here you can enjoy boating, fishing, or jet skiing. The Bluegrass State has a lot to offer for those looking for fun in the water.

Maybe, you are more of a wildlife person. Many people love hunting in the western part of the state. Natural wildlife can be found throughout the area. There are excursions in the Daniel Boone National Forest that are great also.

If this does not sound like fun to you, then you might like to learn more about Kentucky's horses. You can visit one of the race tracks or horse farms. Visitors from all over the world have visited Churchill Downs. Their horses race in the Kentucky Derby. Several other races that can be attended throughout the year. Other locations that allow you to enjoy Kentucky's best thoroughbreds include the Kentucky Horse Park and Keeneland.

Kentucky's tourism doesn't stop there. Guests can visit Mammoth Cave and the home of Abraham Lincoln. Certainly, the Bluegrass State is filled with features that keep people visiting this beautiful.

3. Based on the author's description of Kentucky, what type of person might NOT enjoy visiting Kentucky?

Ⓒ a hiker
Ⓓ a horse lover
Ⓔ a person who loves shopping
Ⓕ a camper

Question 4 is based on the passage below.

The ostrich is the largest bird in the world, but it cannot fly. Its legs are so strong and long that it can travel faster by running. Ostriches use their wings to help them gather speed when they start to run. They also use them as brakes when they are turning and stopping.

Ostriches have been known to run at a rate of 96 km an hour. This is faster than horses can run, and as fast as most people drive a car. These huge birds stand as tall as a horse and sometimes weigh as much as 135 kg. In Africa, their home continent, they are often seen with large animals. The zebra, which is also a fast runner, seems to be one of their favorite companions.

Each ostrich egg weighs as much as two dozen chicken eggs. Ostrich eggs are delicious to eat and are often used as food in Africa. The shells also are made into cups and ornaments.

4. What does the author of this article assume the reader knows before reading the passage?

Ⓒ What an ostrich looks like
Ⓓ What horses look like
Ⓔ How heavy chicken eggs are
Ⓕ Where ostriches live

214

Question 5 is based on the passage below.

Amelia Earhart was born on July 24, 1897. She lived with her grandparents until the age of 12 when she and her sister went to live with their parents in 1909. Amelia's plans were to attend college, but when she came across four wounded World War I soldiers, she decided that she wanted to become a nurse. Her dedication to helping people led her from nursing to work as a social worker. While she worked as a social worker, she often spent her free time teaching immigrant children how to speak English.

Her most noteworthy journey began in 1920 when she took a ten-minute plane ride that completely changed her life. She decided to focus on earning a pilot's license. She challenged herself with a variety of jobs to earn the $1,000 needed for flying lessons to fulfill her dream.

Amelia Earhart proceeded to excel as a pilot. She received a medal from President Herbert Hoover in 1932 for her solo flight across the Atlantic. She did not stop there. Earhart was the first female to fly from Hawaii to California.

Amelia Earhart's contribution to history ended on July 2, 1937, when a frantic message was received by the U. S. Coast Guard. The message was from Earhart stating that she and the plane were in trouble. The plane went down, and no one has ever seen Earhart again. Her devotion to creating change remains a legacy. This legacy emphasizes how setting dreams and achieving goals can be done through hard work and determination.

5. How might some readers disagree with the author's opinion in this passage?

- Ⓐ Some might believe that Earhart was not a pilot.
- Ⓑ Some might disagree with Earhart's choice to not attend college.
- Ⓒ Some readers might think that Earhart DID NOT leave a legacy behind.
- Ⓓ Some readers might think that Earhart did not live during World War II.

Question 6 is based on the passage below.

Cell Phones in the Classroom

A familiar ringtone sounds in the classroom directing everyone's attention to a shy student in the back row. Several years ago, this would have seemed a bit strange, but not today. A recent study showed that one in three third-grade students have a cell phone. With so many students having access to technology devices, a lot of talks have gone into deciding whether to use them as learning tools or to ban them from the classroom.

Let's think about cell phones' role as learning tools. Annie needs a calculator but forgot hers. She takes out her cell phone and can use the calculator app on the phone. Just across the room, Johnny is trying to spell the word "similar," so he uses the dictionary app on his phone to find the correct spelling. Mitchell, has completed all of his work early, so he decides to use the multiplication app on his phone to review multiplication facts in a fun and interactive way. These devices are causing teachers and other school officials to see that cell phones give students access to resources that actually save schools money.

While cell phones may sound great, not every school district is ready to lift the cell phone ban. There are still those that have major concerns. One concern is what to do about students who do not have a cell phone. Another worry is how to make sure students are using the phone as a learning tool instead of texting and social media. Additional concerns arise with how to address when a phone is broken or stolen while at school. Certainly, the list of problems that some schools have goes on and on.

The answer isn't clear for schools across the United States. Some schools are starting to lift the cell phone ban, but others are keeping it in place. As students pack backpacks with cell phones, the discussion of having them in the classroom will certainly continue.

6. If a parent responded to this passage by saying that their child was spending too much time texting in class, what is their point of view regarding this author's passage?

Ⓐ They agree with him entirely.
Ⓑ The parent dislikes the author.
Ⓒ They think that cell phones should be banned from the classroom.
Ⓓ They think that parents should be able to make this choice, not schools.

Question 7 is based on the passage below.

The Asteroid Belt

It's shaped like a doughnut, made from lumps of rock, and looks like a pattern of floating rocks moving in a circle. This strange sounding object is the Asteroid Belt. The Asteroid Belt was formed from lumps of rock left over after other planets formed. Yes, it is shaped like a doughnut and can be found between the orbits of Mars and Jupiter. The Asteroid Belt has two layers. The inner layer has asteroids made of metals. The outer layer has rocky asteroids.

When you look at the Asteroid Belt it looks like floating rocks moving in a circle. Scientists say that there are millions of asteroids in this belt. It may sound pretty funny, but scientists say that there is still a lot of empty space. As you have probably already guessed, the Asteroid Belt is pretty big. It is actually 215 million miles wide. Jupiter keeps the asteroids inside the belt and prevents them from hitting the planets in space. Jupiter's gravity is what holds the asteroids in place.

The chunks of rock inside of the belt were named asteroid, meaning star and rock. The first asteroids seen in the belt were named after gods and heroes. The first largest asteroid found was named Ceres after a Roman goddess. Ceres was discovered on January 1, 1801. It is the size of Texas, and is it called a dwarf planet. Before an asteroid is named, a group of people check to make sure it is not an inappropriate name. Now that most Roman hero names have been used up, scientists are using the name of the astrophysicist to name an asteroid. A lot of information remains unknown about the extremely real Asteroid Belt.

7. How might someone most successfully disagree with the author of this passage?

Ⓐ A reader might think that the world does not date back millions of years.
Ⓑ The reader might argue that there are no other planets besides Earth.
Ⓒ The reader might believe that there are no such things as asteroids.
Ⓓ The reader might believe that the Earth is an asteroid.

Question 8 is based on the poem below.

From McGuffey's Second Eclectic Reader "Yes, we're busy night and day,

As o'er the earth we take our way.
We are bearers of the rain
To the grasses, and flowers, and grain;
We guard you from the sun's bright rays,
In the sultry summer days."

8. What is most likely the "we" described in this poem?

Ⓐ birds
Ⓑ trees
Ⓒ clouds
Ⓓ rivers

Question 9 and 10 are based on the passage below.

Let the Adventure Begin...

There is nothing better than hopping in the car or on a plane and setting off for an adventure. Adults and children alike love exploring new places. Now, sometimes this desire for adventure can leave parents and kids disagreeing about where to go. Let's take a look at some places that are sure to make everyone happy.

Who wouldn't love spending some time at the Grand Canyon? This type of trip may take some planning, but it is sure to be worth it. Families can enjoy looking at the Grand Canyon from a glass-bottom observation deck that extends about 70 feet over the West Rim of the Canyon. Did I also mention that you will be 4,000 feet above the Colorado River?

Another hot spot for families to visit is the Redwood National Park in California. Now, looking at the ancient, skyscraper high sequoias is quite breath-taking, but leave some excitement for the cool aquatic life that can be experienced in this area. There are underwater creatures such as orange and purple ochre sea stars and green anemones that can be explored during one of the free summer tide pool tours available at the Redwood National Park.

If geographically, you desire a location closer to the East Coast, consider checking out Monticello in Virginia. Here, families can enjoy viewing Thomas Jefferson's estate. There is even the Griffin Discovery Room where everything can be touched. That's right – everything! Kids can enjoy touching replicas of Jefferson's most prized possessions, including his alcove bed and his polygraph machine. There are also clothes that were modeled after the third President's sense of style for kids to try on and role play in.

Don't worry if you are the northern part of the country, your family might enjoy the Craters of the Moon National Monument in Preserve. This Idaho attraction is "the only official weird park" in the country. There is a jagged, black landscape that was molded by volcanic eruptions that date back 15,000 years ago. There is even a 618-square mile lava field. You won't find another one of those in the United States.

Sure, the discussion of great places to visit could go on, but don't you have somewhere to go? Pack your bags and start discovering some of nature's beauty that awaits you all across the United States.

9. Which of the following people would DISAGREE with the information provided by the author of this passage? Circle the correct answer choice.

Ⓐ A person who has visited all seven continents
Ⓑ Someone that only enjoys traveling to locations close to their home
Ⓒ Someone that hates traveling
Ⓓ Someone that only enjoys historical tourist attractions

10. Which of the following statements is a FACT?

Ⓐ Idaho has the only official weird park in the United States.
Ⓑ Monticello, Virginia has beautiful scenery.
Ⓒ If you love history, you will love visiting Jefferson's home.
Ⓓ The Grand Canyon is the most beautiful sight in the United States.

Question 11 is based on the passage below.

PATTY AND THE SQUIRREL
from McGuffey's Second Eclectic Reader

1. Little Patty lives in a log house near a great forest. She has no sisters, and her big brothers are away all day helping their father.

2. But Patty is never lonely; for, though the nearest house is miles away, she has many little friends. There are two squirrels that live in the woods that are her friends.

3. How did Patty teach them to be so tame? Patty came to the woods often, and was always so quiet

and gentle that the squirrels soon found they need not be afraid of her.

4. She brought her bread and milk to eat under the trees, and was sure to leave crumbs for the squirrels.

5. When they came near, she sat very still and watched them. So, little by little, she made them her friends, till, at last, they would sit on her shoulder, and eat from her hand.

6. Patty even helps the squirrels build their summer and winter homes. Their summer homes are made of leaves, and sticks, and moss. Their winter homes are found in hollow old trees.

7. Patty helps the squirrels and the squirrels help Patty not be lonely.

11. What do you think caused Patty to befriend the squirrels?

Chapter 3

Lesson 7: Informational Illustrations

Publisher's Note: the following is an example of how to use this standard when it is assigned to you. The illustration uses a table (but it could have used a chart or graph).

In this example, the teacher lists questions that the student is to answer, and a correct answer shows that the student understands the illustration and the text. If there were not questions given, then the student could either make up questions based on the illustration or explain the meaning of the illustration.

The computer technology teacher in the Deep Canyon school district did a survey of all students in grades 3 through 6 to find out the percentage of time students spend using computer software for three kinds of applications: school work, social media and computer-based games. The results of the survey are shown in the table below.

Percentage of Time Students In The Deep Canyon School District Spend Using Computing Software				
Grade	School Work %	Social Media (Ex. Facebook, Twitter, You Tube, Email) %	Computer based Games %	%
3	15	70	5	100
4	30	60	10	100
5	40	50	10	100
6	50	35	15	100

The students were asked to answer the following questions using the information in the table:

1. The students in which grade spent the most time doing school work?
2. Did time spent using the computer for social media increase, stay the same, or decrease from grade 3 to grade 6?
3. The students in which grade spent the most time playing computer-based games?

Your assignment: Your teacher has asked you to use the information in the table to answer the three questions, and to explain how the information in the table helped you.

Here is an example of what you might write to finish this assignment.

It was easy to answer the first question. All I had to do was look down the School Work column and find the largest number, which was 50%, and look at the first column to see which grade matched the 50%. It was Grade 6. To answer the second question, I looked down the Social Media column and noticed that the numbers in each row were getting smaller, so it was easy to see that social media usage decreased from grades 3 to 6. To answer the third question, I looked down the Computer-based Games column and found the largest number opposite Grade 6, which was the grade spending the largest percentage of time playing computer-based games. The table format was a big help.

You can scan the QR code given below or use the URL to access additional EdSearch resources including videos and mobile apps related to *Informational Illustrations*

Read the following sentence and view the map to answer the question 1 and 2.

 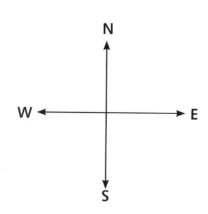

Elizabeth recently moved to Riverville. She is having a hard time finding her way around town.

1. What direction will Elizabeth have to travel in order to get to Mill Street?

Ⓐ South
Ⓑ East
Ⓒ North
Ⓓ There is not a Mill Street listed on this map.

2. If Elizabeth leaves River Street walking west what streets will she travel to get to the school?

Ⓐ Main, Oak, Pine, Maple, School
Ⓑ River, Hill, Grove, School
Ⓒ River, Maple, School
Ⓓ River, Maple, Lemon, Pine

Read the following information about our solar system. Use the illustration to help in answering the questions 3-5.

There are eight named planets in our solar system. The planets orbit the sun at their own pace. Mercury takes 87.969 days to make a complete trip around the sun. Neptune makes the longest journey around the sun. It takes this planet 60,190 days to make a trip around the sun. Neptune is the farthest planet from the sun; this is the reason for the extended travel time. Despite the placement of the planets each one has to orbit the sun.

Orbiting Times around the Sun

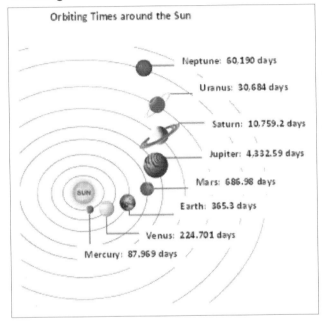

Orbiting Times around the Sun

Neptune: 60,190 days

Uranus: 30,684 days

Saturn: 10,759.2 days

Jupiter: 4,332.59 days

Mars: 686.98 days

Earth: 365.3 days

Venus: 224.701 days

Mercury: 87.969 days

3. Which planets take fewer days than Earth to orbit the sun?

Ⓐ Mars, Jupiter, Saturn, Uranus, Neptune
Ⓑ Earth takes the fewest days to orbit the sun.
Ⓒ Venus and Mercury
Ⓓ Neptune and Uranus

4. From the passage and the illustration, what would be the climate difference between Mars and Uranus?

Ⓐ Mars' climate is colder than Uranus.
Ⓑ Uranus' climate is warmer than Mars.
Ⓒ There is no difference in the two planets' climates.
Ⓓ Mars' climate is warmer than Uranus.

5. From the passage and the illustration, what would be the climate difference between Neptune and Jupiter?

Read the following passage about primates and use the illustration to assist you in answering the question 7.

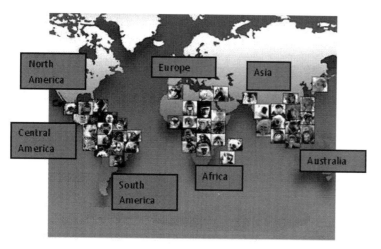

Primates

There are more than 300 species of primates identified by scientists. There are three major categories of primates. These three categories are: apes, monkeys, and prosimians. Apes are generally larger than the other two categories of primates. The smallest primate is a pygmy mouse lemur and the largest is a gorilla. Apes, monkeys, and prosimians can be found on the continents of Africa and Asia. Additionally, some species of monkeys can be found in the wild in Central and South America.

6. After reading the story and viewing the map, where can you find primates in the wild?

- Ⓐ North America, Central America, South America, Europe, Asia, Africa, and Australia
- Ⓑ Central and South America only
- Ⓒ Primates are found on every continent in the wild.
- Ⓓ Central America, South America, Africa, and Asia

Question 7 is based on the passage below.

Primates

There are three basic categories of primates. These three categories are apes, monkeys, and prosimians. There are distinct differences in apes, monkeys, and prosimians. For instance, each primate has a unique nose shape. Apes have hook shaped noses that are dry, monkeys have flat noses that are dry, and prosimians have dog-like snouts that are always wet. Additionally, they are dissimilar in the number of species that have been identified. Scientists have acknowledged that there are approximately 23 species of apes, hundreds of species of monkeys, and about 50 species of prosimians. Further, differences in the three categories of primates are the lifespan of each. Apes can live to be sixty years old, whereas prosimians generally only live to be nineteen. Monkeys have been known to live up to thirty years. A final contrast is when the different primates are most active. Apes and monkeys are more active during the day while prosimians are more active at night. As you can see these three categories of primates have distinct differences

Types of Primates	Apes	Monkeys	Prosimians
Nose	Hook Shaped and Dry	Flat Nosed and Dry	Dog-like Snout and Wet
Number of Species	23	Hundreds	50
Lifespan	Up to 60 years	Up to 30 years	Up to 19 years
Time of Activity	Diurnal (during the day)	Diurnal (during the day)	Nocturnal (at night)

7. Part A

Which two facts do apes and monkeys have in common?

Ⓐ They both have dry noses and are active during the day.
Ⓑ They have the same number of identified species.
Ⓒ There are no similarities between monkeys and apes.
Ⓓ They have similar lifespans and their noses are the same shape.

Part B

What is one of the differences between the prosimians and monkeys?

Ⓐ There are no noted differences between prosimians and monkeys.
Ⓑ They are both larger than most apes.
Ⓒ Monkeys have hundreds of species that have been identified and there are only eighty species of prosimians identified.
Ⓓ Prosimians have a lifespan of only nineteen years and monkeys can live up to thirty years.

Question 9 and 10 are based on the passage below.

Ice cream has become a popular treat for many Americans.

The United States of America consumes more ice cream in one year than any other country. The average American eats forty-eight pints of ice cream a year. The most common flavor is vanilla. July has been deemed National Ice Cream Month in the United States. Since Americans love ice cream so much it might be important to examine the history of ice cream in the U.S.

Ice cream was first introduced in the United States in the 1700s. Only the wealthy could afford to buy it. The first widely seen advertisement for ice cream was circulated in 1777. The ice cream industry began in Boston in 1851. The ice cream sundae was created in 1874. The first ice cream cone was in 1904 at the St. Louis World's Fair.

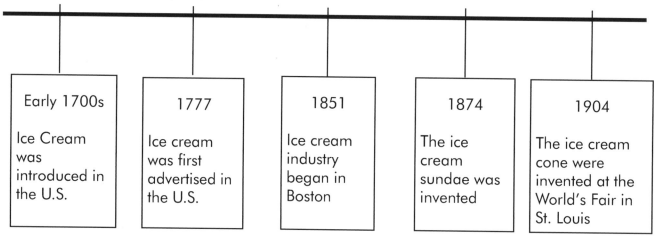

Early 1700s	1777	1851	1874	1904
Ice Cream was introduced in the U.S.	Ice cream was first advertised in the U.S.	Ice cream industry began in Boston	The ice cream sundae was invented	The ice cream cone were invented at the World's Fair in St. Louis

8. In which year was ice cream first advertised in the United States? Circle the correct answer choice.

Ⓐ 1904
Ⓑ 1851
Ⓒ Early 1700s
Ⓓ 1777

9. What two ice cream events occurred during the 1800s?

Ⓐ Ice cream was introduced in America and the ice cone was invented.
Ⓑ The ice cream sundae and the ice cream cone were invented.
Ⓒ The ice cream industry began in Boston and the first ice cream sundae was invented.
Ⓓ Ice cream was introduced in the U.S. and it was first advertised.

Lesson 8: Connect the Dots

Let us understand the concept with an example.

<u>Example 1</u>: Cause/effect. This example shows a logical connection between a cause and its effects.

Scientists tell us that changes in our climate are happening. Average temperatures around the world are getting higher. The Earth's average surface temperature has risen about 2.0 degrees Fahrenheit since the late 19th century.

Cause: Ninety seven percent of global scientists think this is happening because of things we humans are doing. Our use of fuels from fossils, such as oil and coal, are major causes, and our manufacturing activities are another cause.

Effects: Global warming is responsible for the following effects on planet Earth:

- The warmest year on record was 2016.
- The ice cap in Greenland lost 281 gigatons of ice from 2002 through 2016.
- Melting ice caps have caused sea levels to rise 8" in the last 100 years.
- Ocean water temperatures are rising.
- Carbon dioxide levels in the air have risen from an average of 300 ppm (parts per million) to 400 ppm, the highest levels ever. Carbon dioxide forms a blanket above the earth that traps heat, an additional contributor to global warming.

<u>Example 2</u>: This example shows a logical connection between steps (in a recipe) that must be completed in sequence (in order).

Did you know that you can make homemade chocolate chip cookies? All you need to do is gather up the needed ingredients and follow the steps in the recipe below to make them.

Recipe

1. Gather the needed ingredients. They are: 1 1/2 cups of all-purpose flour, 3/4 tsp. baking soda, ½ tsp. baking powder, ½ tsp. salt, 2/3 cup granulated sugar, 2/3 cup firmly packed dark brown sugar, 1 egg, 1 ½ tsp. vanilla extract and 2 cups of semi-sweet chocolate chips and white chocolate chips.
2. Preheat the oven to 375° and grease the cookie sheet.
3. Combine flour, baking soda, baking powder and salt in a medium bowl and set it to the side till later.
4. Mix the butter and sugars together in a large bowl until the mixture is light and fluffy. This should take about 5 minutes to complete.

5. Mix in the egg and vanilla.

6. Retrieve the medium bowl that you set aside earlier, and dump it into the large bowl. Mix this together thoroughly. Finally add the white and chocolate chips to the mixture, and stir until completely mixed in.

7. Drop tablespoons of cookie dough mix onto a cookie sheet leaving a 2 inch space between each dropping, and put the cookie sheets into the oven.

8. Bake for 10 minutes or until golden brown, take the cookie sheets out of the oven, and let cool for 5 to 10 minutes.

Example 3: Comparison. This example makes a logical connection between two choices about how to reach a destination by comparing the choices.

An elderly couple wants to travel from New York to Florida. They no longer drive, so there are only two choices: to fly or take a train. Flying is cheaper and faster, but the taxi they will use must deal with heavy traffic, so they will have to leave home much earlier than being driven to the train station. They will have to lug their luggage to and through security, and then be squeezed into the middle and window seats on a crowded airplane. Also, fog is expected which will likely delay their departure. Once they arrive, they will have to take a taxi to the house and wait several hours until their son and his wife come home from work.

While the train trip takes longer, the seats are much roomier and the train car is much quieter. There is no security check, and the fog will not delay their departure. Also, they will arrive after their son and wife return from work, so they can pick them up.

You can scan the QR code given below or use the URL to access additional EdSearch resources including videos and mobile apps related to Connect the Dots.

ed Search

Connect the Dots

URL	QR Code
http://www.lumoslearning.com/a/ri38	

Question 1 is based on the passage below.

The ostrich is the largest bird in the world, but it cannot fly. Its legs are so strong and long that it can travel faster by running. Ostriches use their wings to help them gather speed when they start to run. They also use them as brakes when they are turning and stopping.

Ostriches have been known to run at a rate of 96 km an hour. This is faster than horses can run, and as fast as most people drive a car. These huge birds stand as tall as a horse and sometimes weigh as much as 135 kg. In Africa, their home continent, they are often seen with large animals. The zebra, which is also a fast runner, seems to be one of their favorite companions.

Each ostrich egg weighs as much as two dozen chicken eggs. Ostrich eggs are delicious to eat and are often used as food in Africa. The shells also are made into cups and ornaments.

1. What is the author's opinion of the ostrich?

   Ⓐ   The author does not find it interesting.
   Ⓑ   The author finds the ostrich extraordinary.
   Ⓒ   The author likes ostrich eggs.
   Ⓓ   The author likes zebras.

Questions 2-6 is based on the passage below.

Everything in nature follows a pattern. Circles, lines, spirals, and angles are repeated to make a pattern. Patterns in nature are not just pretty adornments. They serve a purpose that has helped nature survive and flourish. Have you ever taken a close look at a beehive? (Well, not too close or you might get stung!) The natural pattern in beehives is so perfect that it seems to be computer designed. The hives are made up of layers and layers of cells. Each cell has six perfectly equal sides. Why would bees build hexagonal cells, why not circular or box-shaped ones? The bee is a genius at geometry and architecture! Six-sided cells allow bees to get maximum space for storing honey. Hexagons also use the least building material because all six sides are common to other cells. The bees don't waste space, material or effort. Aren't they smart insects?

2. Based on the selection, what is likely to happen to you if you go near a beehive?

   Ⓐ   You will be stung.
   Ⓑ   You will eat honey.
   Ⓒ   You will be worried.
   Ⓓ   You will get hurt.

3. What can you conclude after reading this passage?

   Ⓐ   Hexagon shaped buildings use more building materials.
   Ⓑ   Bees are very smart insects.
   Ⓒ   Nothing in nature follows a pattern.
   Ⓓ   Bees are lazy.

4. Based on this passage, which of the following statements is true?

Ⓐ The above passage can be used to write a paper on nature and bees.
Ⓑ The above passage can be referred to while writing a paper on hornets.
Ⓒ The above passage can be used while writing a paper on spiders.
Ⓓ The above passage can be used while writing a paper on how not to waste space.

5. Where might a reader use the information about hexagons from this passage?

Ⓐ When solving a math problem on algebra.
Ⓑ When writing a math paper on geometric properties of a hexagon.
Ⓒ When building your home.
Ⓓ None of the above.

6. Why does the author ask, "Have you ever taken a close look at a beehive"?

Ⓐ The author wants to know whether you have seen a beehive.
Ⓑ The author likes the beehives.
Ⓒ The author wants to introduce us to beehives and the way they look.
Ⓓ The author does not like the look of the beehives.

Question 7 is based on the passage below.

THE BEE from McGuffey's Second Eclectic Reader

1. There are three kinds of bees: workers, drones, and queens.
2. Bees live in a house that is called a hive.
3. Only one queen can live in each hive. If she is lost or dead, the other bees will stop their work.
4. They are very wise and busy little creatures. They all join together to build cells of wax for their honey.
5. Each bee takes its proper place, and does its own work. Some go out and gather honey from the flowers; others stay at home and work inside the hive.
6. The cells which they build are all of one shape and size, and no room is left between them.
7. The cells are not round, but have six sides.
8. Have you ever looked into a glass hive to see the bees while at work? They are always busy.
9. The drones do not work. Every year before winter, all the drones are driven from the hive or killed. The reason the drones are driven from the hive or killed is because they did not help make the honey.
10. It is not safe for children to handle bees because they have stingers. Bees use their stingers as a great defensive tool.

7. Based on this selection, what are you LEAST likely to see a worker bee doing?

Ⓐ Building a six-sided hive
Ⓑ Gathering honey from a flower
Ⓒ Sitting still
Ⓓ Stinging a child who is holding it

8. Which of the following types of writing will Annie be completing?

Annie is writing a speech about the effects of second-hand tobacco smoke. She is going to present this to the members of the city council at their monthly meeting.

Ⓐ An opinion piece
Ⓑ An autobiography piece
Ⓒ A narrative piece
Ⓓ A poetry reading

9. Which of the following types of writing did Jose compose?

Jose wrote an interesting passage about the similarities and differences between flies and mosquitos.

Ⓐ An opinion piece
Ⓑ An informational piece
Ⓒ A narrative piece
Ⓓ A fictional short story

10. Which type of writing is Michael using to complete the PowerPoint?

Michael just returned from the Dominican Republic. He is creating a Powerpoint presentation about his exciting trip to share with the class, it is complete with pictures and descriptions.

Ⓐ An opinion piece
Ⓑ An informational piece
Ⓒ A narrative piece
Ⓓ A fictional short story

Question 11 and 12 are based on the passage below.

With junk food becoming increasingly popular and families being on the go more than ever, kids and their parents need to know how to make healthier choices. It is important that children learn to make healthy choices from an early age. If children learn to make these choices it not only makes them healthy but also it keeps them in shape.

Staying in shape is one way of saying that someone makes wise decisions about what they eat, have active exercise routines, and is able to stay at a healthy weight. Staying in shape not only helps your body to work well, but you will feel better too. Who doesn't want to feel well enough to enjoy fun activities with the people around us?

While parents are responsible for making wise choices too, there are many ways that kids can step up to the plate and take charge. Let's start by talking about the types of foods that kids should eat. Sure, there are special occasions when a treat is in store, but fruits and vegetables should be a part of your daily foods, not cake and ice cream. Your body needs a variety of healthy foods. By giving your body a lot of different foods, it will be able to get the nutrients that it needs. Don't be afraid to try new foods. You may not like everything that you try, but by trying new things, you will find more and more foods that you do like. Throughout each day, try to eat five servings of fruits and vegetables. Hopefully, out of those five you will be able to find two fruits and three vegetables to enjoy.

Now, that we have looked at some wise food choices, let's take a look at what you should be drinking. Water and milk are always the best choices. There is nothing that quenches your thirst like a cold glass of water. Now, you may have often wondered why schools offer up cartons of milk. Truth is, milk is needed to help build strong bones because it contains calcium. Kids younger than 9 years old should drink 2 cups of milk per day. If milk isn't your favorite thing to drink there are other ways to get the calcium that your body needs. Some great alternatives to introduce calcium into your diet is cheddar cheese and yogurt.

You may be wondering if milk and water should be your only drink choices, and the answer is no. Choose juice drinks that are 100% pure. This means that they are not loaded down with sugars the way that sodas, juice cocktails, and fruit punches are. Choosing to drink and eat right is one step towards staying in shape, but you also need to get exercise!

It is important to try to find a way to be active for at least one hour daily. This might include playing basketball, riding a bike, or swimming. Now sometimes the weather won't allow you to enjoy these outdoor activities, so choose to get physical indoors by turning on some music that you enjoy and dancing to the beat. Other ideas include going bowling or turning your living room into a studio for "Simon Says" where you get to follow and give commands, such as: "Simon Says do 10 jumping jacks...." Just remember the idea is get up and get active.

Staying fit doesn't have to be hard. It simply requires making wise choices. Make fruits, vegetables, milk, water, and exercise a part of your daily routine! You will feel great, and your body will thank you by giving you lots of energy to do the things that you most enjoy.

11. What was the author's purpose for including facts in this passage?

12. Which of the following organizational techniques BEST describes how the author wrote this passage? Choose the correct answer by circling it.

Ⓐ In the order that things happened
Ⓑ Showing causes and effects for making healthy lifestyle choices
Ⓒ Telling the events that created someone's opinion about junk food
Ⓓ Telling memories from the author's life about his experiences with food

Question 13 and 14 are based on the passage below.

It's the Twenty-First Century

With new times comes change. Allowing cell phones in classrooms is one type of change that I am talking about. So many kids have them, so why not let them be used for something good?

If we were allowed to use cell phones in class, we wouldn't have to always be waiting for the computer lab to open up. We can use our cell phones to do research.

Our teachers love showing us cool learning tools, but we never get to use them during the school day. Sometimes we forget about them before we go home. If we have our cell phones right there in class, we can use them then and not forget about what we are being shown.

Cell phones can also replace planners. They can allow us to keep track of important due dates for assignments, the days tests are scheduled, and other important reminders. Students lose their assignment books, but they will keep up with their cell phones.

I hope that I have shown you why having cell phones in the classroom is a great idea. This resource can benefit all of us. Let's lift that cell phone ban. After all, it is the twenty-first century.

13. What was the author's reason for writing this piece? Circle the correct answer choice.

Ⓐ To state an opinion
Ⓑ To narrate a memory
Ⓒ To inform about the history of cell phones
Ⓓ To entertain the reader with a fictional story

14. Why does the author MOST LIKELY end the first paragraph with a question? Circle the correct answer choice.

Ⓐ He wants the reader to stop what they are doing and go research the answer.
Ⓑ He wants to make the reader pause and think.
Ⓒ He wants to make sure that all readers agree with his opinion.
Ⓓ He wants to take up space with one extra sentence.

Lesson 9: Compare and Contrast Important Points & Key Details

Compare: describe similarities between the two texts in important points and key details.
Contrast: describe the differences between the two texts in important points and key details.

Let us understand the concept with an example.

How to Plan to Present a Theater Play

Here are two different texts on the subject of planning a live theater play.

Text 1: I am Emily, a third-grade student. Every year my grade is allowed to put on a show for all the kids in our school. I am so excited! I have been asked to help our theater teacher plan for the play. There are so many things to think about. Here is what I think needs to be done.

First, what kind of show will it be? A comedy, where the actors say and do goofy things to make the audience laugh? Or a drama, where everything is serious? Could it have singing and dancing - a musical comedy or musical drama?

I think a musical would be best. So many of my friends sing in our school chorus, and several take dancing lessons. We would need to ask the kids to buy special dance shoes. We would have to order sheet music for them. We would have to order costumes. We will have to schedule auditions and re-hearsals when kids are available to attend them. But that should not be a problem, since basketball will be over and softball will not have started. And, some of my friends, who do not want to memorize songs or dance steps, can still help by working backstage with props, the curtain, sound and lighting. Oh and I can't wait to see my name in the playbill! Oops, can't forget to write up a playbill.

Text 2: I am Mr. Jones, the theater arts teacher. Every year my theater students are allowed to put on a show. I have to decide what kind of show my students are best at performing: an original variety show, or an existing comedy or drama? With singing and dancing, or only with spoken dialogue (conversations)? Because time is limited, it has to be an existing show, not an original creation. Because so many students have had dance and singing lessons, and audiences enjoy comedy, I think a musical comedy will be best.

Next, I have to decide which musical comedy to choose. And how much will the script cost? I want to have a large cast, so many students can have a part onstage or backstage. And an orchestra, which will allow even more students to participate. I will need scenery, which I will have to build, and props which I will have to buy or borrow. And costumes which I will have to find talented parents to make them or money to buy them. Sheet music for each singer and for the orchestra. I will have plan for microphones and lighting, and find students who will run the audio and lights and move the curtains and scenery and props. I will have to schedule auditions and rehearsals. And I need to design the playbill and be sure I include everyone! And all this within the budget I have been given by the principal. I am glad to have Emily helping me. Lots to do – time to get started.

Compare and contrast.

Both Emily and Mr. Jones thought about some of the same tasks needed to plan the play. For example, both chose a musical comedy as the best kind of play. They also knew to include sheet music, costumes, a backstage crew and a playbill.

Mr. Jones also thought of some other tasks. He had concerns about performing the play within a budget, including the costs of the scripts and how to get the costumes made or rented. He thought about the scenery needed, and the need for the orchestra, instead of recorded music. He also realized he would have to give training specific to the play for the students handling lighting, sound, props and scenery.

You can scan the QR code given below or use the URL to access additional EdSearch resources including videos and mobile apps related to *Compare and Contrast Important Points & Key Details*.

 **Compare and Contrast Important Points & Key Details**

URL	QR Code
http://www.lumoslearning.com/a/ri39	

Questions 1-3 are based on the passage below.

Louisiana

It has been said that the state of Louisiana is a melting pot of people. Many different ethnic groups have settled into pockets of this great state. Not only are there Vietnamese, Spanish, and Europeans, but there are also two unique ethnic groups. These two groups are the Cajuns and the Creoles. The Cajuns are the French Canadians that moved down from Canada to Southern Louisiana. They fled Canada because of a British imposed rule that attempted to force all Canadians to accept the King's Protestant religion. Most of the French Canadians who moved to Louisiana were Catholics. When the Cajuns arrived in Louisiana they were accepted and allowed to practice any religion. As the Cajuns became more settled in Louisiana their customs and heritage began to impact the current populations' way of life. The Cajuns impact is still seen today throughout Louisiana.

Louisiana

The state of Louisiana has a mix of people from many different backgrounds. Many ethnic groups have settled into different parts of the state. There are people from Vietnam, Canada, and European countries that call this great state home. Additionally, there are two groups that moved into Louisiana many years ago. These two groups are the Creoles and Cajuns. It can be said these two groups of people have a blended set of backgrounds.

The Creoles are defined as any person who was born in New Orleans that has French or Spanish family roots. This includes anyone that comes from Africa, the Caribbean, France, or any Spanish country. The Creoles, like the Cajuns, have had a huge impact on the Louisiana lifestyle. Many of their traditions have contributed to Louisiana's unique art, music, and cooking. New Orleans is truly a different place to live and visit thanks to the Cajuns and the Creoles.

1. **From the two passages, which of the following answer choices explain a similarity between the Cajuns and the Creoles?**

   Ⓐ Cajuns and Creoles both moved to Louisiana from Canada.
   Ⓑ Both Cajuns and Creoles fled to Louisiana because they were Catholic and were not allowed to practice their religion in their home countries.
   Ⓒ All Cajuns and Creoles came from Spanish speaking countries.
   Ⓓ Both Cajuns and Creoles have impacted the Louisiana lifestyle.

2. **Which of the following answer choices accurately describe a difference in the two passages?**

   Ⓐ Cajuns fled Canada because they were not allowed to practice the Catholic religion.
   Creoles are people who live in New Orleans and are from French or Spanish family roots.
   Ⓑ Cajuns only live in New Orleans and Creoles live in only Southern Louisiana.
   Ⓒ There are no differences between Cajuns and Creoles because they are the same people.
   Ⓓ Cajuns are mainly from Africa while, Creoles are from Canada.

3. Which of the following answer choices accurately describe a key detail of these passages?

(A) A key point of these passages is that Louisiana offers many different types of food.

(B) A key point of these passages is that a lot of people have moved from Canada to Louisiana.

(C) A key point of these passages is that Cajuns and Creoles have impacted the Louisiana way of life.

(D) A key point of these passages is that you should visit Louisiana on your next vacation.

Question 4 and 5 are based on the passage below.

Cell Phones in the Classroom

A familiar ringtone sounds in the classroom directing everyone's attention to a shy student in the back row. Several years ago, this would have seemed a bit strange, but not today. A recent study showed that one in three third-grade students have a cell phone. With so many students having access to technology devices, a lot of talks have gone into deciding whether to use them as learning tools or to ban them from the classroom.

Let's think about cell phones' role as learning tools. Annie needs a calculator but forgot hers. She takes out her cell phone and can use the calculator app on the phone. Just across the room, Johnny is trying to spell the word "similar," so he uses the dictionary app on his phone to find the correct spelling. Mitchell, has completed all of his work early, so he decides to use the multiplication app on his phone to review multiplication facts in a fun and interactive way. These devices are causing teachers and other school officials to see that cell phones give students access to resources that actually save schools money.

While cell phones may sound great, not every school district is ready to lift the cell phone ban. There are still those that have major concerns. One concern is what to do about students who do not have a cell phone. Another worry is how to make sure students are using the phone as a learning tool instead of texting and social media. Additional concerns arise with how to address when a phone is broken or stolen while at school. Certainly, the list of problems that some schools have goes on and on.

The answer isn't clear for schools across the United States. Some schools are starting to lift the cell phone ban, but others are keeping it in place. As students pack backpacks with cell phones, the discussion of having them in the classroom will certainly continue.

Always Worked Fine Before

I hear all of this talk about allowing cell phones in the classroom. Why? There is nothing wrong with the way things are now. If you allow cell phones in our classrooms, you are asking for trouble.

Cell phones encourage students to get off task. Students may tell you that they are playing learning games, but how do you know they are not sending texts? Also, they may skip doing their assignments just so they can hurry and play these learning games. In addition, cell phones will make classrooms noisier. If everyone gets messages, plays games, or receives phone calls, think about how noisy classrooms will be.

We really do not need cell phones in our classrooms. It seems to me that the way our classrooms are right now is great. They are helping prepare me and other students for the future.

4. What is a key point difference in the two passages?

Ⓐ   Both passages think that cell phones are very bad to have at school.

Ⓑ   "Cell Phones in the Classroom" gives the positives and negatives of having cell phones at school. "Always Worked Fine Before" only tells the negatives of having cell phones at school.

Ⓒ   Both authors support the use of cell phones in the classroom.

Ⓓ   Both passages have a negative opinion of principals having the say-so of who gets to have cell phones at school.

5. What is a key similarity in the two passages?

Ⓐ   Both authors want cell phones used in the classroom as learning tools.

Ⓑ   Both passages are written by a student.

Ⓒ   Both authors dislike school and think that cell phones will make the learning experience more positive.

Ⓓ   Both authors are concerned that the use of cell phones could lead to students getting off task.

Question 6 and 7 are based on the passage below.

Madison Elementary
Madison Elementary has adopted a new uniform policy for students. The students are not happy about the policy. They decided to get together to write a letter to the school board to explain their feelings about uniforms. Each grade appointed one student to present the letter as a group to the school board at their next meeting. The school board listened to the group of students and told them that they would discuss it. The board members talked over the student's concerns and decided to get rid of the new policy. The students would not have to wear uniforms after all.

Jefferson Elementary
The Jefferson Elementary school board has written a new policy about school snacks. The board decided that students would no longer be able to bring snacks from home. The school would give the students healthy snacks such as fruits and vegetables instead. The students were not pleased with the new policy. They complained to their parents, their teachers, and the principal. Their parents, teachers, and principal all were in favor of the healthy snacks. So the students at Jefferson Elementary were stuck with the healthy snacks.

6. What is a similarity between the two passages?

Ⓐ Both passages are about a new policy on healthy snacks.
Ⓑ Both passages are about new policies that the schools have adopted.
Ⓒ Both policies were changed by the school board once the students expressed their dislike of the policies.
Ⓓ There were no similarities in the two passages.

7. What is the difference between the two passages?

Ⓐ The Madison Elementary school board changed the policy once the students talked to them about their concerns. Jefferson Elementary did not change their policy about healthy snacks after the students stated their concerns.
Ⓑ The Madison Elementary students did not go in front of the school to state their concerns. The Jefferson Elementary students went in front of the school board.
Ⓒ Madison Elementary policy on school uniforms was not changed but the Jefferson Elementary school policy on uniforms was changed.
Ⓓ There were no differences noted in these passages.

Question 8 is based on the passage below.

Fable A.

Once a gazelle was running as fast as she could possibly go to outrun the lion who was pursuing her. She had a good lead, and was probably going to outrun the lion, when she came to a river. Although she could swim, the water looked cold and uninviting. She hesitated on the bank of the river, not wanting to jump in. While she debated, the lion overtook her and she became his dinner.

Fable B.

Once a gazelle was running as fast as she could possibly go to outrun the lion who was pursuing her. She had a good lead, and was probably going to outrun the lion, when she came to a river. Without looking, she jumped into the water where a crocodile was waiting and she became his dinner.

8. Part A

What is a major difference in these two fables?

Ⓐ There are no differences in these fables the gazelle gets eaten in both fables.
Ⓑ The gazelle in fable A did not jump into the river and the gazelle in fable B did jumped right into the river.
Ⓒ The gazelle in fable A could not swim and the gazelle in fable B could swim.
Ⓓ The gazelle in fable A was eaten by a crocodile and the gazelle in fable B was eaten by a lion.

8. Part B

What is a major similarity in the two fables?

Ⓐ These two fables are not similar.
Ⓑ The gazelle in fable A and the gazelle in fable B both jumped into the river.
Ⓒ The gazelles in both fables were eaten in the end.
Ⓓ The gazelle in fable A and the gazelle in fable B were running away from a crocodile.

Question 9 and 10 are based on the passage below.

Picture Day

It is picture day at school and Sara is so excited. She is going to wear her new pink lace dress and shiny new black Mary Jane shoes. Sara's mom took extra time curling her hair this morning and even tied in a beautiful satin ribbon. Sara bound into the school feeling so pretty. She could hardly wait for her turn to get her picture taken.

Picture Day

Oh no! It's picture day at school. Melissa hates picture day, especially since her father lost his job. There is no money to buy a new dress, so she has to wear her sister's hand-me-downs. Melissa's mother tries to make her feel better by fixing her hair but nothing helps to change Melissa's mood. Melissa stomped into the school feeling ugly. Melissa was ready for this day to be over.

9. Which of the following answer choices describes a difference in the two passages?

Ⓐ Both girls are excited about picture day at school.
Ⓑ Sara is excited about picture day but Melissa is not excited about picture day.
Ⓒ Both girls wore new dresses for picture day.
Ⓓ The girls went to different schools.

10. What was one similarity in the two passages?

Ⓐ Both girls had shiny new black Mary Jane shoes.
Ⓑ Both girls were in bad moods when they entered school.
Ⓒ Both girls were going to have their pictures taken at school.
Ⓓ Both girls were in really good moods when they entered school.

Question 11 is based on the passage below.

Tess

Eight-year-old Tess heard her parents talking about her little brother Andrew. She realized something was wrong. Andrew was very sick, and they did not have enough money for his treatment. Tess heard her daddy say, "Only a miracle can save him now."

Tess went to her bedroom and retrieved a jar from its hiding place. There were a few coins in it. She counted them carefully. She then made her way to the drug store. The pharmacist there was too busy to pay her any attention. "And what do you want?" he asked, annoyed at her persistence. "Can't you see that I am talking to my brother? He is here from Chicago."

Tess persisted, "My brother's really sick …….. and I want to buy a miracle. His name is Andrew. He has something bad growing inside his head and my daddy says only a miracle can save him now. So, how much does a miracle cost?" rambled Tess.

The pharmacist's brother, a well-dressed man, stooped down and asked the girl. "What kind of miracle does your brother need?" "Don't know," replied Tess, eyes welling up with tears. "I just know Mommy says he needs an operation. But my daddy can't pay for it. So, I want to use my money."

The man from Chicago asked, "How much money do you have?" "One dollar and 11 cents," said Tess. "Well, what a coincidence," smiled the man. "A dollar and 11 cents is the exact price of a miracle for your little brother." He took her money in one hand and grasped Tess's hand in the other. "Take me to where you live. "I want to see your brother and meet your parents. Let's see if I have the kind of miracle you need."

That well-dressed man was Carlton Armstrong, a neurosurgeon. He operated upon Andrew without charging any money. It wasn't long until Andrew was home and well again. "I wonder how much the surgery cost?" said Mother.

Tess smiled to herself. She knew exactly how much the miracle cost- one dollar and 11 cents….plus the immense faith of a little child.

Devon

Devon was a 3rd grader at Lincoln Elementary School. Devon had a younger sister, Heather. One day when Devon came home from school he overheard his parents talking. Devon's mother was crying. She said, "I don't know what we are going to do. We don't have that kind of money," she continued. Devon's father had his head in his hands and said nothing.

Devon spoke up and asked what was wrong. Devon's mother said, "Your sister is very ill and we don't have the money for her medication."

"How much does the medicine cost?" asked Devon.

Devon's father muttered, "It cost one hundred fifty dollars for one month supply."

Devon went to his room to think about the situation. He decided that he was going to try and raise the money for the medication. Devon got up the next morning and went door to door in his neighborhood. He asked the neighbors for a donation for his sister's medication. Devon stayed out all day trying to get enough money to help his sister. Just before dark he returned home and went straight to his room. He laid the money out on his bed and began counting. As he counted he began to cry, there was not only enough money for a month supply of medication but there was enough money for three months. Devon ran to his parents' room with the good news. Both his parents threw their arms around him to thank him for his good deed. His sister would get the help she needed.

11. What is a key difference between the two passages? Circle the correct answer choice

Ⓐ Devon went out and asked for donations for his sister's medication. Tess found a doctor that would perform the surgery on her brother.

Ⓑ Devon did nothing to try and help his sick sister and Tess did everything to try and help her brother.

Ⓒ There were no differences in these passages.

Ⓓ Tess raised the money through donations to help her brother and Devon found a doctor that gave him free medication for his sister.

End of Reading: Informational Text

Answer Key and
Detailed Explanations

Chapter 3: Reading: Informational Text

Lesson 1: Explicitly Comprehension

Question No.	Answer	Detailed Explanations
1	C	The passage explicitly states that Robert Johnson was a Blues Musician from the Mississippi Delta. The passage does not mention Chicago or that Robert Johnson was from Africa. The 2nd paragraph is all about Robert Johnson.
2	B	The passage tells the reader that the Blues began in the Deep South. It mentions an African influence. It does not state that the origin of the Blues was Africa. The passage does not mention Europe or the Northern states of the U.S.
3	B	The passage explicitly describes that the Blues have influenced many types of music, especially Rock and Roll, Rap, and Country.
4	B	The passage states, "evaporation (liquid changes to a gas)"
5	A	Good Virtues is the best title given because it summarizes what the passage is talking about. The other choices, examination, stealing, and late coming are examples that support the main idea of how good virtues are rewarded and bad things cause negative reactions.
6	C	According to the first paragraph of the text, everyone likes a well mannered person because he is polite and gentle.
7	A	Doing what is right is what pleases others according to this selection. "All that is right pleases everyone. Therefore, we should do what is right always."
8	C	Late coming is a bad habit because people who are late can not be depended on. The text uses this example in the paragraph about "late coming."
9	A	According to this selection we do not like to be punished for our mistakes. Instead we like to be forgiven. This is found in paragraph 7 of the selection.
10	D	Pearl is a teenager. Since she is carrying the makeup, bus pass, and student ID card, she is neither a very young child nor an adult.
11		In the Pacific Ocean, This fact is found in the first paragraph.
12		In the Pacific Ocean, This fact is found in the first paragraph.
13	2	Answer is 2, Detail noted in list of states in ABC order. Tennessee and Texas are the two states.
14	B, E, J, Q, X, Y, Z	B, E, J, Q, X, Y, Z. These letters are not used as the first letters of states' names.
15	D	He should share with parents, counselor and friend since they were all concerned and wanted him to do better.

Lesson 2: The Main Idea Arena

Question No.	Answer	Detailed Explanations
1	D	Answer choice D "Every thing in nature follows a pattern" is the only answer choice that is a true fact according to the text.
2	B	The answer to this question is B, referencing how bees make patterns. The other choices are not possible according to this text.
3	B	If you selected B, you picked the right answer. Each detail in the passage tells of an area where robots can do something that a person could not do.
4	A	If you selected A you made the right choice. The responses B, C, and D tell of jobs that robots can do that would be dangerous or impossible for human beings. Each response gives details that support the main idea.
5	C	If you chose C, Sentence 6, you made the right choice. All the details support the main idea that Jeremy is colder than he has ever been.
6	A	If you chose A, Sentence 1, you made the best choice. The rest of the sentences are details telling what Jennifer likes.
7	D	If you chose D, Sentence 6, you found the main idea. Sentence 1 could be argued, because it makes the same point, but it is not one of your choices, so Sentence 6 is the best choice.
8	D	If you chose option D, Sentence 5, you made the best selection. All the other sentences are details leading up to that idea.
9	A	If you selected choice A, Sentence 1, you made the right choice. The other sentences are details that support the main idea.
10	D	If you selected D, Sentence 4, you picked the right answer. The other sentences are details leading up to that conclusion.
11	C	Although all of the answers show details in the passage, only C puts details together for a short summary that tells the most.
12		Using the recipe, you can write the steps in the correct order they appear. The correct order is, B, E, A, F, D, C.
13	B	B is the correct answer choice. The passage states that the monarch butterfly lives about 8-9 months after becoming an adult.
14		The sentence needs to include something to the effect that the refrigerated boats allow the captain to keep the boat out longer, and allows for a larger catch to be brought in. Saves time and money.
15	D	Answers A,B,C can all be summarizations of the passage, but D is not part of the passage nor a summary. D is the best answer to which is Not a summary.

Lesson 3: Cause and Effect

Question No.	Answer	Detailed Explanations
1	A	Before tourists could visit Kentucky for horse racing, there had to be horse racing facilities for tourists. Kentucky is known for the Kentucky Derby which takes place at Churchill Downs. Therefore, "Churchill Downs was built" is the correct answer.
2	B	Answer choice B is correct. Line number 2 of the first paragraph provides this answer. The word "but" signals she did not do as planned, go to college. The reason is included in this paragraph.
3	A	Answer choice A is correct. The other three were mentioned in the passage but they were NOT highlighted as being a positive effect.
4	A	Water falling back to the ground is rain. Rain is a type of precipitation. Answer choice A is correct.
5	A	Answer choice A describes evaporation. The sun changes water to a vapor. The other three choices are related to precipitation.
6	A	Condensation forms into clouds that later becomes too heavy for the clouds to hold.
7	A	Answer choice A is the most LIKELY reason why the Olympics are successful today. Paragraph 2 explains about the first Olympics and its success. The other answer choices happened afterwards, without the original Olympics none of the future games would be significant.
8	C	The asteroid belt was formed from the lumps of rocks that the planets left behind. Therefore, answer choice C "Ceres was identified and named" is correct.
9	D	The asteroid belt was formed from the lumps of rocks that the planets left behind. Therefore, the only answer choice possible is option A "The Earth was made".
10	D	If you picked D, you picked the best response. The two statements are not correct, and they are not different, so b and c are not good answers. It is true that the statements are similar, but they did not become famous because they are similar. They are famous for being wrong.
11		In the context of the passage, the students can imagine and give their response. The passage says that the Romans felt protected by the Alps, so they were not prepared for an attack. The passage also says that the Romans panicked because they had never seen animals like the elephants. If they were unprepared and panicky, it is more likely that Hannibal defeated the Romans than that the Romans defeated.

Lesson 4: Educational Expressions

Question No.	Answer	Detailed Explanations
1	C	Carnivore means meat eating animal, choice C. The reader can determine this by reading the first sentence, animals eat other animals. The next sentence states these animals are carnivores. Therefore, animals eating other animals would be carnivores.
2	C	Answer choice C, water heating up and turning into vapor, is the meaning of evaporation. "They" in the text refers to clouds. Clouds form when lots of vapors get together. Vapor is formed when the sun heats up water sources such as lakes, rivers, and puddles.
3	D	Population refers to the number of people, which is answer choice D. The reader can determine this by reading, "thousands of babies are being born adding to the population." Babies are human and considered part of a group or society of people. This is how an area's population is determined.
4	C	The word citizen is a noun used after the adjective German. The first sentence tells the reader that Hans lives in Germany. The conclusion for the meaning of citizen is, therefore, a person living in a particular country.
5	B	While A and D appear logical, the key words are "move to another country", so Answer B is the best answer. Answer C may or may not be correct because people who are at war may or may not leave a country.
6	C	The setting of a story means time and place that a story occurred, which is answer choice C. The context clues "in Mexico in 1870," help the reader determine the meaning of setting.
7	B	The word "sum" refers to the total of something. So if a teacher gives you numbers and wants their sum, he/she wants the numbers added together for a total. Answer choice B is correct.
8	C	Answer choice C is the best definition for summary. If a teacher reads a picture book and asks for a summary then he/she is asking for a few sentences describing what the story is about.
9	B	The use of the word "while" signals two things occurring. The prefix on "re" on main also means again or over and over. Therefore, the best answer choice for the meaning of remain is stay the same.
10	D	The opening sentence states, "over the past 100 years." This a clue for the meaning of century used in the next paragraph with the date 2008. Answer choice D is correct.

Question No.	Answer	Detailed Explanations
11	B	Basic in this sentence is used as an adjective describing tasks. Inside this paragraph with this sentence, the author describes things that people do to complete their jobs easier. Nothing extra or really hard is described with this sentence or paragraph. Boring is not relevant with the tasks used. The conclusion can then be drawn that basic means about the same as main, answer choice B.
12	C	In this context, legacy is like a gift. The paragraph that includes this word describes Earhart's contributions to history. These contributions were positive not negative. Contributions usually refer to one's actions or donations.
13	D	The phrase, "give students access to many resources," helps the reader determine that the meaning of access is connection, answer choice D. Schools often spend money on extra classroom resources, like dictionaries and calculators, to help students learn. If students have the ability to use the resources on a phone instead, they have an additional connection to the resources other than having to use the ones school's buy.

Lesson 5: Special Text parts

Question No.	Answer	Detailed Explanations
1	C	This author helps the reader locate information inside the text by numbering the sentences sequentially. Answer choice C is correct.
2	B	The first sentence of number 4 is about the jobs of bees. Answer B is correct.
3	B	This selection is about multiple ways to stay healthy, and answer choice B is correct. The other choices are examples of specific ways to stay healthy.
4	D	Answer choice D would not be helpful in teaching kids ways to be healthy. Most kids know all about junk foods and do not need additional ideas for foods or drinks to consume that are unhealthy.
5	C	The title tells the reader what this selection is going to be about, good manners. This title is at the beginning and is bold to catch the reader's attention. Italics or a header are not used. The second sentence just gives a reason why people like mannerly people. Answer choice C is correct.
6	A	Answer choice A would be a better title because the selection isn't really about the Amazon Rainforest, it's more about the red-eyed frog.
7	C	Answer choice C is correct. Since the paragraph is giving a description of the frog, an illustration would assist the reader in understanding this paragraph.
8	A	Answer choice A is correct since the text is all about matter.
9	B	Answer choice B is correct. Since matter can be found in all three examples listed in this choice, a picture would help the reader understand the different forms.
10	B	In this poem, the author uses apostrophes to break the words into syllables. For example, "yel'low" has the apostrophe between the double consonants which is a rule when dividing syllables of words with double consonants.

Lesson 6: What Did You Already Know?

Question No.	Answer	Detailed Explanations
1	B	The paragraph explains that hexagons are six sided figures. This math information is useful when writing about properties of a hexagon, answer choice B.
2	do not pick it up	The text explains that this frog is dangerous even if it is touched.
3	C	Based on the text, a person who enjoys shopping, might not enjoy a trip to Kentucky. Nowhere in the text can the reader find information about shopping. The other three answer choices provided in the text are enjoyable things to do in Kentucky.
4	C	The last few sentences of this text compare ostrich eggs to two dozen chicken eggs, but the author does not give the weight of chicken eggs. Therefore, answer choice C is correct.
5	C	Answer choice C is correct because it is the only opinion that is given in the answer choices. The word opinion means what is thought or felt but cannot be proven. The other answer choices are merely stating a fact that happened and can be proven.
6	C	Answer choice C is correct. The third paragraph of the text mentions texting, but this author is trying to give both pros and cons of using cell phones in classrooms. The parent who is worried about texting and wasting class time would most likely want cell phones banned.
7	A	Answer choice A is correct. The actual date that the world dates back to is often debated. The actual date is unknown. The other three choices, if disagreed with, the author could prove with pictures, historical and scientific research findings.
8	C	"We are bearers of the rain," is a line from the text with "we" in it. The bearers of the rain would be clouds because when moisture gathers in the air it forms clouds. When clouds become heavy with the moisture, it falls to Earth as rain. Answer choice C is correct.
9	C	Answer choice C is correct. If a person hates traveling then they are not going to agree with, "There is nothing better than hopping in a car or on a plane and setting off for an adventure." This is the author's opinion and if a person hates traveling they will not agree.
10	A	Answer choice A is correct because it is the ONLY fact that could be proven. The other choices use opinion words such as beautiful, will love, and most beautiful.
11		In lines 1 and 2 of the text, the reader is informed that Patty stays all day without her family and that the nearest house is miles away.

Lesson 7: Informational Instructions

Question No.	Answer	Detailed Explanations
1	A	"A" is the correct answer choice because Elizabeth would have to travel south on Vernon in order to reach Mill Street.
2	B	"B" is the correct answer choice because if Elizabeth was walking west on River Street she would travel on River, Hill, Grove, and School Streets in order to reach the school.
3	C	"C" is the correct answer choice because Venus and Mercury take fewer days than Earth to orbit the sun. You can find this information from the passage and the illustration.
4	D	"D" is the correct answer choice because it accurately describes that Mars climate is warmer than Uranus because Mars is closer to the sun. You can find this information in both the passage and the illustration.
5		Jupiter receives more sunlight than Neptune because Jupiter is closer to the sun. The correct answer can be found in the passage and illustration.
6	D	"D" is the correct answer choice because both the passage and the map tell you that primates are found in the wild in Central America, South America, Africa, and Asia.
7 Part A	A	"A" is the correct answer choice because both the passage and the chart tell you that monkeys and apes have dry noses and are active during the day. The other answer choices do not accurately describe similarities in apes and monkeys.
7 Part B	D	"D" is the correct answer choice because both the passage and the chart tell you that a difference is that prosimians have a lifespan of nineteen years and monkeys' lifespan is up to thirty. The other answer choices are not accurate differences between prosimians and monkeys.
8	D	"D" is the correct answer choice because both the passage and the timeline tell you that ice cream was first advertised in the U.S. in 1777.
9	C	"C" is the correct answer choice. It lists the two inventions that occurred with ice cream in the U.S. in the 1800s. Both can be identified from the passage and the time line. The other answer choices occurred before and after the 1800s.

Lesson 8: Connect the Dots

Question No.	Answer	Detailed Explanations
1	B	The author finds the ostrich extraordinary because he chose to write about it. Answer choice B is correct. Answer choices C and D cannot be correct based on the text.
2	A	Answer choice A is correct. The fourth sentence supplies the reader with this answer.
3	B	According to this text, answer choice B is correct. The other choices are NOT true based on the paragraph.
4	A	Answer choice A is correct. The paragraphs above are about nature's patterns and bees. Therefore, it could be included in a research paper about nature and bees.
5	B	Answer choice B is correct. The paragraph about hexagons tells about its properties. This text would not help to build a home or necessarily solve a math problem.
6	C	The author wants the reader to think about what a beehive looks like to help with the understanding of the text. Answer choice C is correct.
7	C	According to the text, answer choice C is correct. The bees all have jobs so they do not sit still. Numbers 3 and 4 from the text support this answer.
8	A	A speech usually includes information but is based on one's opinion. The other three choices are not speeches.
9	B	Answer choice B is correct. Jose wrote about similarities and differences of mosquitos and flies indicating that the piece is based on facts. Facts are used in informational pieces of writing.
10	C	A narrative piece can be based on one's own experiences. This would be true when Michael presents a PowerPoint about a trip he experienced. A fictional story is make-believe so that would not be correct. An information piece would be all facts and could be true but not likely when explained through observation. This PowerPoint will more than likely NOT be about Michael's opinion only. Therefore, answer choice C is the BEST.

Question No.	Answer	Detailed Explanations
11		When writing opinion pieces, including facts helps the author seem more knowledgeable about the subject. Facts just make opinions more convincing and help the reader make connections between the opinions being used.
12	B	This text is organized by cause and effect relationships. Each paragraph begins with the author's opinion and then facts that support the opinion. "Staying fit doesn't have to be hard," is the first sentence of the last paragraph. This is an opinion. Then the author follows it with examples of how to do this.
13	A	The author more than likely wrote this piece to express his/her opinion about cell phones in classrooms. It is NOT entertaining the reader with a fictional story and does NOT provide the history of cell phones. The author is also NOT telling about a past memory. Answer choice A is correct.
14	B	By ending the text with a question, the author wants the reader to answer the question for themselves. In order to do that, the reader must think about the information provided first.

Lesson 9: Compare & Contrast Important Details and Key Points

Question No.	Answer	Detailed Explanations
1	D	"D" is the correct answer choice because it is the only one that accurately describes a similarity in the two passages. "Both Cajuns and Creoles have impacted the Louisiana lifestyle." The other three answer choices are not accurate descriptions of a similarity.
2	A	"A" is the correct answer choice because it is the only one that accurately describes a difference in the two passages. "Cajuns fled Canada because they were not allowed to practice the Catholic religion. Creoles are people who live in New Orleans and are from French or Spanish family roots." The other three answer choices are not accurate descriptions of a difference.
3	C	"C" is the correct answer choice because it is the only one that accurately highlights a key detail from the passages. The others are not key points that are highlighted in both passages.
4	B	"B" is the correct answer choice because it is the only one that accurately highlights a key detail from the passages. The others are not key points that are highlighted in both passages.
5	D	"D" is the correct answer choice because it is the only one that accurately describes a similarity in the two passages. "Both authors are concerned that the use of cell phones could lead to students getting off task". The other three answer choices are not accurate descriptions of a similarity.
6	B	"B" is the correct answer choice because it is the only one that accurately describes a similarity in the two passages. "Both passages are about new policies that the schools have adopted." The other three answer choices are not accurate descriptions of a similarity.
7	A	"A" is the correct answer choice because it is the only one that accurately describes a difference in the two passages. The Madison Elementary school board changed the policy once the students talked to them about their concerns. Jefferson Elementary did not change their policy about healthy snacks after the students stated their concerns. The other three answer choices are not accurate descriptions of a difference.

Question No.	Answer	Detailed Explanations
8 Part A	B	This is the correct answer because the gazelle in fable A did not jump into the river and the gazelle in fable B did jump into the river. Answer choice A is incorrect because there are differences in the two fables. Answer choice C is incorrect because it states in fable A that the gazelle could swim she just didn't like how the water looked. Answer choice D is incorrect because the gazelle in fable A was eaten by a lion and the gazelle in fable B was eaten by a crocodile.
8 Part B	C	This is the correct answer choice because the gazelle in fable A was eaten by the lion and the gazelle in fable B was eaten by the crocodile. Answer choice A is incorrect because there were many similarities in the two fables. Answer choice B is incorrect because in fable A the gazelle did not jump into the river but the one in fable B did. Answer choice D is incorrect because in both fables the gazelle was running from the lion.
9	B	This answer choice is correct because in passage 1 Sara is very excited about picture day and in passage 2 Melissa is not excited about picture day. Answer choice A is incorrect because both girls are not excited about picture day at school. Answer choice C is incorrect because both girls did not wear new dresses for picture day. Melissa wore her sister's hand-me-down. Answer choice D is incorrect because neither passage said if the girls went to different schools or the same school, so this information was not provided.
10	C	This answer choice is correct because the main idea of both passages was that it was picture day at school and the girls were going to have their pictures taken. Answer choice A is incorrect because only Sara had new shiny black Mary Jane shoes to wear to school on picture day. Answer choice B is incorrect because only Melissa was in a bad mood on picture day. Answer choice D is incorrect because only Sara was in a good mood on picture day.
11	A	Answer choice A is the correct answer because Devon took up donations for his sister's medication and Tess found a doctor for her brother. Answer choice B is incorrect because Devon did something to help his sister. Answer choice C is incorrect because there are differences in the two passages. Answer D is incorrect because Tess found the doctor to help her brother and Devon raised money to help his sister.

LumosLearning.com

Chapter 4 - Language

The objective of the Language standards is to ensure that the student is able to accurately use grade appropriate general academic and domain specific words and phrases related to Grade 3.

To help students to master the necessary skills, we encourage the student to go through the resources available online on EdSearch to gain an in depth understanding of these concepts. The EdSearch page for each lesson can be accessed with the help of the URL or the QR code provided.

Chapter 4

Lesson 1: People, Places and Things

You can scan the QR code given below or use the URL to access additional EdSearch resources including videos and mobile apps related to *People, Places and Things.*

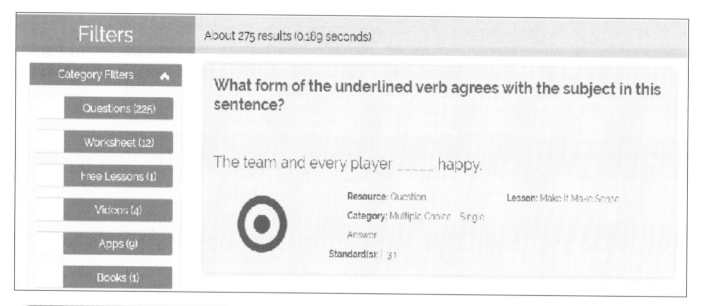

Filters	About 275 results (0.189 seconds)
Category Filters ▲	What form of the underlined verb agrees with the subject in this sentence?
Questions (225)	
Worksheet (12)	The team and every player _____ happy.
Free Lessons (1)	
Videos (4)	Resource: Question Lesson: Make It Make Sense
Apps (9)	Category: Multiple Choice Single Answer
Books (1)	Standard(s): L.3.1

ed Search   *People, Places and Things*

URL	QR Code
http://www.lumoslearning.com/a/l31	

1. What is the plural form of the word baby?

Ⓐ babys
Ⓑ babies
Ⓒ babes
Ⓓ babeys

2. What is the plural of day?

Ⓐ days
Ⓑ daies
Ⓒ daes
Ⓓ day

3. What is the plural form of butterfly?

4. How do you make tomato plural?

Ⓐ tomato
Ⓑ tomatoes
Ⓒ tomatos
Ⓓ tomati

5. Which word in this sentence is NOT a noun? Circle the correct answer choice.

Jose played soccer all day.

Ⓐ Jose
Ⓑ played
Ⓒ soccer
Ⓓ day

6. Which word from the sentence is NOT a noun?

Most of the time older dogs are the best pets for families with children to have.

Ⓐ older
Ⓑ dogs
Ⓒ families
Ⓓ children

7. Choose the possessive noun that BEST completes the following sentence.

Taking _____ pencil was not a nice thing to do.

- Ⓐ boy's
- Ⓑ boys
- Ⓒ Saads
- Ⓓ Saad's

8. Choose the noun that best completes the following sentence.

Her baby _____ are starting to fall out.

- Ⓐ teeth
- Ⓑ tooth
- Ⓒ teeths
- Ⓓ toothes

9. Choose the <u>proper noun</u> in the following sentence.

Dr. Martinez said that she would help me get an appointment for later next week.

- Ⓐ week
- Ⓑ Dr. Martinez
- Ⓒ said
- Ⓓ appointment

10. Choose the noun that BEST completes the following sentence.

The _____ are going to be late for practice again.

- Ⓐ girl
- Ⓑ girls
- Ⓒ female
- Ⓓ Yanire

11. Which of the words from this sentence is NOT a noun? Circle the correct answer choice.

All of the children were happy when their grandmother and aunt came to visit last Sunday.

- Ⓐ children
- Ⓑ happy
- Ⓒ aunt
- Ⓓ Sunday

Chapter 4

Lesson 2: Replace Those Nouns

You can scan the QR code given below or use the URL to access additional EdSearch resources including videos and mobile apps related to *Replace Those Nouns*.

ed Search	**Replace Those Nouns**
URL	**QR Code**
http://www.lumoslearning.com/a/l31	

1. A noun is a word that is the name of a person, place, animal or thing. Which word is a noun in the sentence below?

Charlene is the best forward on the team this season.

    Ⓐ   is
    Ⓑ   team
    Ⓒ   this
    Ⓓ   on

2. A pronoun is a word that takes the place of a noun. What are the pronouns in the sentence below?

Alice helped Jim with homework, and when he gave her a gift, she loved it.

3. When will Monica find out where _____ new school will be?

What pronoun best fits in the blank?

    Ⓐ   Jamie's
    Ⓑ   her
    Ⓒ   she
    Ⓓ   his

4. Charles lost _____ puppy in the park!

What pronoun best fits in the blank?

    Ⓐ   her
    Ⓑ   his
    Ⓒ   himself
    Ⓓ   herself

5. My pencil fell off of my desk and _____ broke in half.

What pronoun best completes this sentence?

    Ⓐ   it
    Ⓑ   he
    Ⓒ   she
    Ⓓ   its

6. Babies feel safest when _____ are close to _____ mothers.

What pair of pronouns fit best in this sentence?

- Ⓐ she, her
- Ⓑ he, his
- Ⓒ they, their
- Ⓓ we, our

7. Which of the following is a pronoun found in the sentence below?

I think they are going to drive over to the campsite tomorrow.

- Ⓐ think
- Ⓑ they
- Ⓒ drive
- Ⓓ tomorrow

8. Choose the pronoun that BEST completes the following sentence.

I want _____ to come over to my house too.

- Ⓐ him
- Ⓑ he
- Ⓒ me
- Ⓓ we

9. Choose the subject that could replace the underlined pronoun in the following sentence.

I saw them at the store about an hour ago.

- Ⓐ Ted
- Ⓑ Ted and Terry
- Ⓒ the boy
- Ⓓ we

10. Choose the pronoun that BEST completes the following sentence.

Crying isn't going to solve _____ problem.

- Ⓐ the
- Ⓑ her
- Ⓒ she
- Ⓓ they

11. Choose the pronoun that BEST replaces the underlined phrase in the following sentence.

<u>This math test</u> is going to be hard!

    Ⓐ They
    Ⓑ It
    Ⓒ Its
    Ⓓ Them

12. Choose the pronoun that BEST replaces the underlined phrase in the following sentence.

Please take <u>Amber, Billy, and Crystal</u> with you.

    Ⓐ they
    Ⓑ we
    Ⓒ them
    Ⓓ us

13. Choose the pronoun that best completes the following sentence.

_____ brought me a bouquet of flowers last week.

    Ⓐ They
    Ⓑ We
    Ⓒ Us
    Ⓓ She and I

Chapter 4

Lesson 3: Regular and Irregular Plural Nouns

You can scan the QR code given below or use the URL to access additional EdSearch resources including videos and mobile apps related to *Regular and Irregular Plural Nouns*.

URL	QR Code
http://www.lumoslearning.com/a/l31	

Regular and Irregular Plural Nouns

1. Which of the following is a plural noun written correctly?

Ⓐ childrens
Ⓑ mice
Ⓒ doctores
Ⓓ womans

2. Which of the words in the sentence below is a plural noun?

We saw four deer in the field on our hiking trip.

Ⓐ we
Ⓑ four
Ⓒ our
Ⓓ deer

3. Which answer choice demonstrates the correct plural spelling for the word "berry"?

Ⓐ berry
Ⓑ berries
Ⓒ berrys
Ⓓ berryes

4. Which of the words in the sentence below is a plural noun?

My mom baked a dozen loaves of bread yesterday.

Ⓐ loaves
Ⓑ baked
Ⓒ mom
Ⓓ bread

5. What is the correct way to make the word "cactus" plural?

Ⓐ cactus
Ⓑ cactues
Ⓒ cacti
Ⓓ cactuss

6. Which of the following demonstrate a noun correctly written in plural form?

 Ⓐ bookes
 Ⓑ boats
 Ⓒ birdes
 Ⓓ brickes

7. Which of the following demonstrate a plural noun written <u>incorrectly</u>?

 Ⓐ jellies
 Ⓑ schools
 Ⓒ mooses
 Ⓓ apples

8. Which of the following nouns in the sentence below is written <u>incorrectly</u> as a plural noun?

They were sitting on the park bench when a bunch of acornes began to fall from the oak trees.

 Ⓐ acornes
 Ⓑ trees
 Ⓒ they
 Ⓓ bunch

9. What is the correct way to write the word "goose" as a plural?

10. Which of the following plural nouns is written <u>incorrectly</u>? Circle the correct answer choice from the options given below

 Ⓐ women
 Ⓑ bushs
 Ⓒ teeth
 Ⓓ grapes

11. Which of the following words is incorrectly transformed from the plural form to its singular form?

 Ⓐ Countries = Country
 Ⓑ Dwarfs = Dwarf
 Ⓒ Wifes = Wife
 Ⓓ Moose = Moose

Chapter 4

Lesson 4: Awesome Abstract Nouns

You can scan the QR code given below or use the URL to access additional EdSearch resources including videos and mobile apps related to *Awesome Abstract Nouns*.

 **Awesome Abstract Nouns**

URL	QR Code
http://www.lumoslearning.com/a/l31	

1. Which word in the following sentence is an abstract noun?

The crime was committed on the corner of Jackson Avenue and Main Street.

- (A) committed
- (B) Avenue
- (C) crime
- (D) corner

2. Which word in the following quotation is an abstract noun?

"Beauty is in the eye of the beholder."

- (A) beauty
- (B) eye
- (C) in
- (D) the

3. Which of the following is an example of an abstract noun?

- (A) dog
- (B) wisdom
- (C) apartment
- (D) teacher

4. Which of the following is an example of an abstract noun?

- (A) grandmother
- (B) humor
- (C) television
- (D) telephone

5. What is the abstract noun found in the sentence below?

What time are you going to Jeremy's house tomorrow?

- (A) going
- (B) Jeremy's
- (C) time
- (D) house

6. Which of the following is an example of an abstract noun?

Ⓐ girl
Ⓑ tractor
Ⓒ daisy
Ⓓ freedom

7. Which of the following is an example of an abstract noun?

Ⓐ bravery
Ⓑ camera
Ⓒ New York
Ⓓ Christy

8. Which of the following is <u>not</u> an abstract noun?

Ⓐ evil
Ⓑ despair
Ⓒ happiness
Ⓓ dress

9. Which of the following is <u>not</u> an abstract noun?

Ⓐ idea
Ⓑ coffee
Ⓒ dream
Ⓓ hope

10. Which of the following is an accurate definition of an abstract noun?

Ⓐ An abstract noun is a noun that names something that you cannot see, touch, taste, smell, or hear, and it usually names some idea or concept.
Ⓑ An abstract noun names a specific person, place, thing, or idea.
Ⓒ An abstract noun is a noun that you can touch, see, taste, smell, or hear.
Ⓓ An abstract noun names a person, place, or thing but does not name an idea because it engages one of the five senses.

11. Which of the following is an example of an abstract noun in the sentence below?

The relief that I felt when I found my puppy, Bruno, was safe is unexplainable.

- (A) Found
- (B) Puppy
- (C) Relief
- (D) Bruno

12. Which of the following words is an example of an abstract noun in the sentence below?

The memories that were made on our camping trip will last a lifetime.

13. Which of the following words in the sentence below is an example of an abstract noun?

The teacher used treats as motivation to encourage her students to increase their reading levels.

Chapter 4

Lesson 5: Show Me the Action

You can scan the QR code given below or use the URL to access additional EdSearch resources including videos and mobile apps related to *Show Me the Action*.

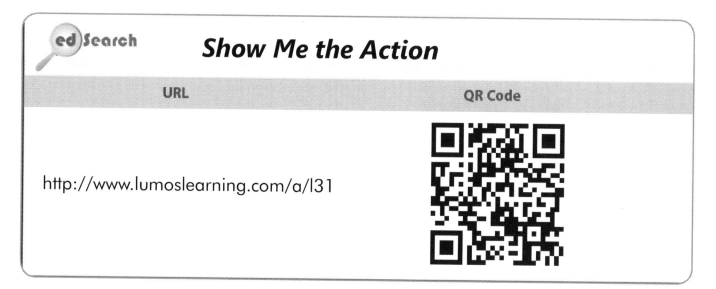

ed)Search

Show Me the Action

URL	QR Code
http://www.lumoslearning.com/a/l31	

1. Choose the correct form of the action word given below to fill in the blank.

The bear was _____ angrily.

- Ⓐ growl
- Ⓑ growled
- Ⓒ growling
- Ⓓ growls

2. Choose the correct form of the action word given below to fill in the blank.

The monkey was _____ on the branch of the tree.

- Ⓐ sleep
- Ⓑ slept
- Ⓒ sleeps
- Ⓓ sleeping

3. Choose the following word that correctly completes the sentence.

I often _____ into the woods to be with nature.

- Ⓐ wonder
- Ⓑ wander
- Ⓒ yonder
- Ⓓ ponder

4. What is the verb in this sentence?

Isabelle really hates spinach!

- Ⓐ Isabelle
- Ⓑ really
- Ⓒ hates
- Ⓓ spinach

5. What is the past tense form of the underlined verb?

I <u>think</u> about you often.

- Ⓐ think
- Ⓑ thinked
- Ⓒ thought
- Ⓓ am thinking

6. What is the past tense form of the underlined verb?

I <u>buy</u> lunch every day.

- Ⓐ buy
- Ⓑ will buy
- Ⓒ bought
- Ⓓ buyed

7. Which answer choice correctly changes this sentence to past tense?

I catch the ball every time.

- Ⓐ I catch the ball every time.
- Ⓑ I catched the ball every time.
- Ⓒ I will catch the ball every time.
- Ⓓ I caught the ball every time.

8. Which answer choice correctly changes this sentence to past tense?

I bring my lunch to school.

- Ⓐ I bringing my lunch to school.
- Ⓑ I bringed my lunch to school.
- Ⓒ I can bring my lunch to school.
- Ⓓ I brought my lunch to school.

9. Which answer choice correctly changes this sentence to past tense?

I break my pencil when I write too hard.

- Ⓐ I break my pencil when I write too hard.
- Ⓑ I breaked my pencil when I writed too hard.
- Ⓒ I broke my pencil when I wrote too hard.
- Ⓓ I breaked my pencil when I wrote too hard.

10. Which answer choice correctly changes this sentence to past tense?

I will drink all of the milk that I find in the refrigerator.

- Ⓐ I drinked all of the milk that I finded in the refrigerator.
- Ⓑ I will drank all of the milk that I find in the refrigerator.
- Ⓒ I drink all of the milk that I found in the refrigerator.
- Ⓓ I drank all of the milk that I found in the refrigerator.

11. How would this sentence be written if it happened yesterday?

I go to the store every day after school.

   Write your answer in the box below.

   ┌───┐
   │   │
   │   │
   └───┘

12. How would this sentence be written if it was to happen tomorrow?

I do all my homework every afternoon.

   Write your answer in the box below.

   ┌───┐
   │   │
   │   │
   └───┘

13. How would this sentence be written if it was to happen tomorrow?

I eat breakfast before school.

   Write your answer in the box below.

   ┌───┐
   │   │
   │   │
   └───┘

14. How would this sentence be written if it happened yesterday?

I drink three glasses of milk every day.

   Circle the correct answer choice

   Ⓐ   I drinked three glasses of milk yesterday.
   Ⓑ   I drank three glasses of milk yesterday.
   Ⓒ   I will drink three glasses of milk yesterday.
   Ⓓ   I drink three glasses of milk yesterday.

Chapter 4

Lesson 6: Simply Simple Verb Tenses

You can scan the QR code given below or use the URL to access additional EdSearch resources including videos and mobile apps related to *Simply Simple Verb Tenses*.

 **Simply Simple Verb Tenses**

URL	QR Code
http://www.lumoslearning.com/a/l31	

1. What is the past tense form of the verb "play"?

Ⓐ plays
Ⓑ played
Ⓒ will play
Ⓓ playing

2. Which verb tense is the underlined word written in the sentence below?

Jason <u>will try</u> to come to the party tomorrow.

Ⓐ present
Ⓑ past
Ⓒ future

3. Which of the following verbs is an example of a <u>present tense</u> verb?

Ⓐ speaks
Ⓑ jumped
Ⓒ will sing
Ⓓ driven

4. Which of the following verbs is an example of a <u>future tense</u> verb?

Ⓐ crying
Ⓑ cried
Ⓒ cries
Ⓓ will cry

5. What verb tense is the underlined word written in the sentence below?

My mom <u>threw</u> my favorite pair of jeans away because they had holes in the knees.

Ⓐ present
Ⓑ past
Ⓒ future

6. What is the <u>future tense</u> of the verb "chop"?

Ⓐ will chop
Ⓑ chopped
Ⓒ chop
Ⓓ chops

7. What is the present tense of the verb "sneeze"?

Ⓐ sneezed
Ⓑ will sneeze
Ⓒ sneeze
Ⓓ had sneezed

8. What is the verb tense of the underlined word written in the following sentence?

Daniel <u>shouted</u> for help because his foot was caught in a tree branch and he could not get down.

Ⓐ present
Ⓑ past
Ⓒ future

9. Which of the following verbs is an example of a past tense verb?

Ⓐ carry
Ⓑ sleeping
Ⓒ laughed
Ⓓ will shop

10. What is the present tense of the verb "write"?

Ⓐ write
Ⓑ written
Ⓒ wrote
Ⓓ will write

11. What is the future tense of the underlined verb in the following sentence?

Kale has <u>gone</u> to the doctor because the school nurse thinks she may have broken her arm.

Ⓐ Going
Ⓑ Will go
Ⓒ Goes
Ⓓ Gone

12. What is the past tense of the underlined verb in the following sentence?

Mrs. James said that she <u>will bake</u> cookies for the class party on Friday.

13. What is the present tense of the underlined verb in the following sentence?

We <u>rode</u> the merry-go-round at the mall five times.

Chapter 4

Lesson 7: Make It Make Sense

You can scan the QR code given below or use the URL to access additional EdSearch resources including videos and mobile apps related to *Make It Make Sense*.

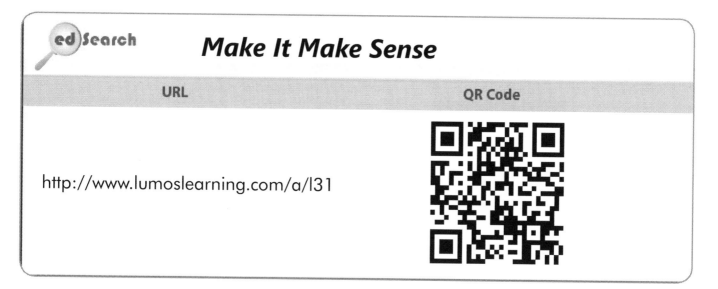

URL	QR Code
http://www.lumoslearning.com/a/l31	

1. Which sentence uses a subject and verb that agree?

Ⓐ My sister always help my mother.
Ⓑ My sister always helping my mother.
Ⓒ My sister always helps my mother.
Ⓓ My sister always am helping my mother.

2. Which sentence uses a subject and verb that agree?

Ⓐ My neighbor and his dogs walks every day.
Ⓑ My neighbor and his dog walk every day.
Ⓒ My neighbor and his dog walking every day.
Ⓓ My neighbor and his dog do walks every day.

3. What form of the underlined verb agrees with the subject in this sentence?

My sister and her friend <u>goes</u> to the park.
Ⓐ goes
Ⓑ going
Ⓒ go
Ⓓ goed

4. What form of the underlined verb agrees with the subject in this sentence?

My brother and I <u>does</u> all the work at my house.

Ⓐ does
Ⓑ do
Ⓒ doing
Ⓓ done

5. Which sentence uses a subject and verb that agree? Circle the correct answer choice.

Ⓐ Steven and Mario walk to school together.
Ⓑ Steven and Mario walks to school together.
Ⓒ Steven and Mario walking to school together.
Ⓓ Steven and Mario do walk to school together.

6. Which sentence uses a subject and verb that agree? Circle the correct answer choice.

Ⓐ The bag of cookies are on the counter.
Ⓑ The bag of cookies is on the counter.
Ⓒ The bag of cookies am on the counter.
Ⓓ The bag of cookies be on the counter.

7. What form of the underlined verb agrees with the subject in this sentence?

Lexi <u>plant</u> flowers in the garden.

- Ⓐ plant
- Ⓑ plants
- Ⓒ planting
- Ⓓ am planting

8. What form of the underlined verb agrees with the subject in this sentence?

Brian <u>cries</u> when he fell off of the slide last Tuesday.

- Ⓐ cries
- Ⓑ crying
- Ⓒ cried
- Ⓓ cry

9. What form of the underlined verb agrees with the subject in this sentence?

My day <u>beginned</u> badly when I missed the school bus.

- Ⓐ beginned
- Ⓑ begins
- Ⓒ began
- Ⓓ beginning

10. Choose the word that BEST completes the following sentence.

Your essay _____ very well written.

- Ⓐ was
- Ⓑ will
- Ⓒ are
- Ⓓ ain't

11. What form of the underlined verb agrees with the subject in this sentence?

The team and every player _____ happy.

12. Fill in the blank with the correct verb form

Eating these foods _____ her more energy for the race.

Chapter 4

Lesson 8: Tell Me More

You can scan the QR code given below or use the URL to access additional EdSearch resources including videos and mobile apps related to *Tell Me More*.

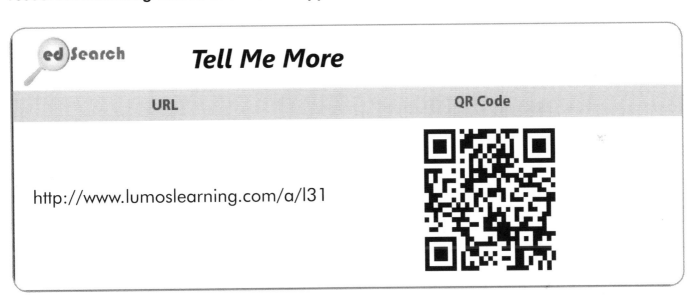

ed Search

Tell Me More

URL	QR Code
http://www.lumoslearning.com/a/l31	

1. Bears are so 'growly' means that _____.

- (A) bears roar
- (B) bears shout
- (C) bears growl
- (D) bears howl

2. Fill in the blanks with the correct descriptive word.

Giraffes have _____ necks.

- (A) longer
- (B) long
- (C) elongate
- (D) short

3. An adjective is a word that describes a noun or pronoun. What is the adjective in the sentence below?

The assignment was confusing, so I didn't do it.

- (A) assignment
- (B) confusing
- (C) I
- (D) do

4. An adverb is a word that describes a verb, an adjective, or another adverb. What is the adverb in the sentence below?

Joe was whistling merrily all morning.

- (A) Joe
- (B) whistling
- (C) merrily
- (D) morning

5. What are the two adverbs in this sentence?

I am really too busy to go to the party.

- (A) too, busy
- (B) really, too
- (C) really, busy
- (D) busy, party

6. Fill in the blanks with the correct descriptive word.

Ashley had to sharpen her pencil because it was _____.

   Ⓐ sharpened
   Ⓑ broken
   Ⓒ yellow
   Ⓓ old

7. Fill in the blanks with the correct descriptive word.

Strawberries are my favorite fruit. They are very _____.

   Ⓐ sour
   Ⓑ rotten
   Ⓒ bitter
   Ⓓ tasty

8. Fill in the blanks with the correct descriptive word.

Aaron knew he was in trouble when he saw the _____ look on his mother's face.

   Ⓐ confused
   Ⓑ happy
   Ⓒ smiling
   Ⓓ angry

9. Choose the adverb from the following sentence. Circle the correct answer choice.

The boys entered the room very slowly. I think they knew that they were in big trouble.

   Ⓐ entered
   Ⓑ slowly
   Ⓒ boys
   Ⓓ The

10. Choose the adjective from the following sentence.

Andy made a delicious apple pie for us last night.

   Ⓐ Andy
   Ⓑ made
   Ⓒ a
   Ⓓ delicious

11. Choose the word that is acting as an adjective in the following sentence.

My dear friends, I want to see you again soon.

☐

12. Choose the word that is acting as an adverb in the following sentence.

Her behavior only mildly disrupted the actors.

☐

Chapter 4

Lesson 9: Subordinating and Coordinating Conjunctions

You can scan the QR code given below or use the URL to access additional EdSearch resources including videos and mobile apps related to *Subordinating and Coordinating Conjunctions.*

Subordinating and Coordinating Conjunctions

URL	QR Code
http://www.lumoslearning.com/a/l31	

1. Is the underlined conjunction in the sentence below an example of a coordinating or subordinating conjunction?

We will be going shopping today <u>rather than</u> going shopping on Saturday.

- Ⓐ coordinating
- Ⓑ subordinating

2. What word in the following sentence is an example of a subordinating conjunction?

Francis was watching television until her friend Maris came over.

- Ⓐ watching
- Ⓑ was
- Ⓒ came
- Ⓓ until

3. What is the correct definition of a coordinating conjunction?

- Ⓐ A conjunction that links words, phrases, and clauses that have equal importance.
- Ⓑ A conjunction that introduces a coordinating clause.
- Ⓒ A conjunction that introduces a subordinating clause.
- Ⓓ A conjunction that shows the action that the subject is doing in a sentence.

4. Which of the following words is an example of a coordinating conjunction?

- Ⓐ whereas
- Ⓑ but
- Ⓒ since
- Ⓓ as soon as

5. What is the coordinating conjunction in the sentence below?

You left your backpack in Ms. Thomas' class and you left your jacket in Mr. Carson's class.

- Ⓐ in
- Ⓑ left
- Ⓒ your
- Ⓓ and

6. **Which of the following answer choices is an example of a subordinating conjunction?**

Ⓐ nor
Ⓑ or
Ⓒ even if
Ⓓ yet

7. **What is the correct definition of a subordinating conjunction?**

Ⓐ A conjunction that introduces a coordinating clause.
Ⓑ A conjunction that introduces a subordinating clause.
Ⓒ A conjunction that links a word, phrase, or clause that have equal importance.
Ⓓ A conjunction is a word that refers back to the subject of a sentence.

8. **What is the subordinating conjunction in the following sentence?**

Travis will be going to Denver since his flight to Tampa was canceled.

Ⓐ going
Ⓑ was
Ⓒ will be
Ⓓ since

9. **What is the coordinating conjunction in the following sentence?**

I thought I was prepared for my math test yet when I got the test I didn't remember how to set the problems up correctly.

Ⓐ got
Ⓑ how
Ⓒ yet
Ⓓ when

10. **What is the subordinating conjunction in the following sentence?**

The children anxiously waited for the bell to ring; as soon as it rang they darted out the door.

Ⓐ as soon as
Ⓑ waited for
Ⓒ for
Ⓓ as it

11. Is the underlined conjunction in the sentence below an example of a coordinating or subordinating conjunction?

LaTonya said that she was getting a new bike <u>and</u> a new purse for her birthday.

12. What is the coordinating conjunction in the following sentence?

My mom cooked spaghetti for dinner but I really wanted lasagna.

Chapter 4

Lesson 10: Mix Up Those Sentences

You can scan the QR code given below or use the URL to access additional EdSearch resources including videos and mobile apps related to *Mix Up Those Sentences*.

Search

Mix Up Those Sentences

URL	QR Code
http://www.lumoslearning.com/a/l31	

1. Giraffes are long-legged and meek.

What type of sentence is this?

- Ⓐ Descriptive (paints a picture in the reader's mind)
- Ⓑ Informative
- Ⓒ Interrogative (asks a question)
- Ⓓ Imperative (states a command or makes a request)

2. Sammy likes to play soccer, and he also likes to play basketball.

What type of sentence is this?

- Ⓐ simple
- Ⓑ compound
- Ⓒ complex

3. When I eat too much candy, I get a stomach ache.

What type of sentence is this?

- Ⓐ simple
- Ⓑ compound
- Ⓒ complex

4. Some children don't like to eat fruits and vegetables.

What type of sentence is this?

- Ⓐ simple
- Ⓑ compound
- Ⓒ complex

5. Laura and Beth were allowed to go outside and play after they finished their homework.

What type of sentence is this?

- Ⓐ simple
- Ⓑ compound
- Ⓒ complex

6. Jasmine and Donald are cousins.

What type of sentence is this?

Ⓐ simple
Ⓑ compound
Ⓒ complex

7. Our dogs can do many tricks when they want to.

What type of sentence is this?

Ⓐ simple
Ⓑ compound
Ⓒ complex

8. Choose the answer choice that is an example of a SIMPLE sentence.

Ⓐ The little bear likes berries.
Ⓑ Today is hot, but tomorrow will be even hotter.
Ⓒ Giraffes are herbivores; a carnivorous animal is a lion.
Ⓓ I think they are coming over, but you might want to call them just to be sure.

9. Choose the answer choice that is an example of a COMPOUND sentence.

Ⓐ Jeremiah likes fruits, but Jasmine prefers vegetables.
Ⓑ Please buy some toothpaste and shampoo.
Ⓒ I missed school last Monday, Tuesday, and Wednesday.
Ⓓ She forgot to study for the math test again; her grade is not going to be good, I am afraid.

10. Choose the answer choice that BEST combines the following simple sentences into one sentence.

I had math homework on Monday. I had a math project due on Tuesday. I had a math quiz on Wednesday.

Ⓐ I had math homework on Monday. I had a math project and quiz on Tuesday and Wednesday.
Ⓑ I had math homework on Monday, a math project due on Tuesday, and a math quiz on Wednesday.
Ⓒ I had math homework on Monday, a math project due on Tuesday a math quiz on Wednesday.
Ⓓ I had math homework, a project, and a quiz on Monday, Tuesday, and Wednesday.

11. Choose the word that BEST completes the following sentence.

The baby's bottle was missing _____ we looked through the entire car.

 Ⓐ ,but
 Ⓑ ,so
 Ⓒ ,and
 Ⓓ ,or

12. Choose the word that BEST completes the following sentence.

Alexander forgot his glasses on the counter _____ his mom was able to bring them to school for him.

 Ⓐ ,and
 Ⓑ ,but
 Ⓒ ,so
 Ⓓ ,like

Chapter 4

Lesson 11: Capitalization Dedication

You can scan the QR code given below or use the URL to access additional EdSearch resources including videos and mobile apps related to *Capitalization Dedication.*

ed Search

Capitalization Dedication

URL	QR Code
http://www.lumoslearning.com/a/l32	

1. Which word needs to be capitalized in this sentence?

i called my mom to come and pick me up when i got sick at school.

_____

2. Which sentence has correct capitalization?

Ⓐ i said, "i don't feel well, mom."
Ⓑ I said, "i don't feel well, mom."
Ⓒ I said, "I don't feel well, mom."
Ⓓ I said, "I don't feel well, Mom."

3. Which sentence has correct capitalization?

Ⓐ She said, "doctor, my child doesn't feel well."
Ⓑ She said, "Doctor, my child doesn't feel well."
Ⓒ She said, "Doctor, my Child doesn't feel well."
Ⓓ She said, "Doctor, My Child doesn't feel well."

4. Which word(s) need to be capitalized in this sentence?

i told grandma i was sorry.

Ⓐ i
Ⓑ i, grandma
Ⓒ grandma
Ⓓ i, grandma, sorry

5. Which word(s) need to be capitalized in this sentence?

dr. crane said it was just the flu.

Ⓐ dr.
Ⓑ dr., crane
Ⓒ dr., crane, flu
Ⓓ flu

6. How should this book title be written?

Ⓐ the lord of the rings
Ⓑ the Lord of the rings
Ⓒ The Lord of the Rings
Ⓓ The Lord Of The Rings

7. How should this book title be written?

- Ⓐ the chronicles of narnia
- Ⓑ The chronicles of narnia
- Ⓒ The Chronicles of narnia
- Ⓓ The Chronicles of Narnia

8. How should this book title be written?

- Ⓐ From the mixed-up files of mrs.basil e.frankweiler
- Ⓑ From the mixed-up files of Mrs. Basil E. Frankweiler
- Ⓒ From the Mixed-up Files of Mrs.Basil E. Frankweiler
- Ⓓ From The Mixed-up Files Of Mrs. Basil E. Frankweiler

9. Which word(s) need to be capitalized in this sentence?

grandma said she would call my dad.

- Ⓐ grandma
- Ⓑ she
- Ⓒ dad
- Ⓓ said

10. Read the book titles and make a tick mark in the column "Correct" or "Not Correct" as applicable.

	Correct	Not Correct
Little House on the Prairie		
A Wrinkle in Time		
The Lion King		
The Call of the Wild		

Chapter 4

Lesson 12: Punctuation Education

You can scan the QR code given below or use the URL to access additional EdSearch resources including videos and mobile apps related to *Punctuation Education.*

URL	QR Code
http://www.lumoslearning.com/a/l32	

Punctuation Education

1. Which address has correct punctuation?

Ⓐ   1345 Sycamore, Street Chicago IL 123452
Ⓑ   1345 Sycamore Street Chicago, IL 123452
Ⓒ   1345 Sycamore Street Chicago, IL, 123452
Ⓓ   1345 Sycamore, Street Chicago, IL, 123452

2. Which address has correct punctuation?

Ⓐ   8142 Brown, Avenue New York NY 14353
Ⓑ   8142 Brown, Avenue New York, NY 14353
Ⓒ   8142 Brown Avenue New York, NY 14353
Ⓓ   8142 Brown Avenue New York, NY, 14353

3. Which address has correct punctuation?

Ⓐ   800 Heartbreak Lane Las Vegas, NV 83902
Ⓑ   800 Heartbreak Lane Las Vegas, NV, 83902
Ⓒ   800 Heartbreak, Lane Las Vegas, NV 83902
Ⓓ   800 Heartbreak, Lane Las Vegas, NV, 83902

4. Which quotation is written correctly?

Ⓐ   "Where, is my cookie?" asked the little girl.
Ⓑ   "Where, is my cookie?," asked the little girl.
Ⓒ   "Where is my cookie?" asked the little girl.
Ⓓ   "Where is my cookie?" ,asked the little girl.

5. Which quotation uses commas correctly?

Ⓐ   "Bring me a snack," said the bratty little boy, "or I'll bite you."
Ⓑ   "Bring me a snack" said the bratty little boy, "or I'll bite you."
Ⓒ   "Bring me a snack," said the bratty little boy "or I'll bite you."
Ⓓ   "Bring me a snack" said the bratty little boy "or I'll bite you."

6. Which quotation uses commas correctly?

Ⓐ   "Please hand me that plate", said the waitress.
Ⓑ   "Please hand me that plate" said, the waitress.
Ⓒ   "Please hand me that plate," said the waitress.
Ⓓ   "Please hand me that plate", said, the waitress.

7. Choose the sentence that shows the dialogue punctuated CORRECTLY.

- Ⓐ What was that noise asked Jason
- Ⓑ "I think it was thunder" replied Junior
- Ⓒ "There it goes again," exclaimed Jason.
- Ⓓ "are you scared" asked Junior?

8. Choose the word that Best completes the following sentence.

The _____ report showed that her teeth were very clean.

- Ⓐ dentists
- Ⓑ dentists'
- Ⓒ dentist's
- Ⓓ dentists's

9. Choose the word that BEST completes the following sentence.

A _____ way of protecting itself is its awful smell.

- Ⓐ skunks
- Ⓑ skunks'
- Ⓒ skunk's
- Ⓓ skunk

10. Choose the word that BEST completes the following sentence.

My _____ car is going to be ready to pick up sometime tomorrow.

- Ⓐ parents'
- Ⓑ parents
- Ⓒ parent's
- Ⓓ parent

11. Choose the punctuation mark that should be added in the space shown in the following sentence.

"It is only 3:00_____" replied Leon.

- Ⓐ a period (3:00.")'
- Ⓑ a quotation mark (3:00"")
- Ⓒ a comma (3:00,")
- Ⓓ a question mark (3:00?")

12. Jamie screamed, There is a spider.

Punctuate the sentence correctly and write it in the box below.

Chapter 4

Lesson 13: The Comma and Quotation Dilemma

You can scan the QR code given below or use the URL to access additional EdSearch resources including videos and mobile apps related to *The Comma and Quotation Dilemma*.

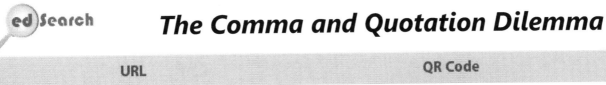

ed)Search   *The Comma and Quotation Dilemma*

URL	QR Code
http://www.lumoslearning.com/a/l32	

1. Which of the following answers correctly uses a comma and quotation marks?

Ⓐ "Did you find the ball, asked Thomas "if not I will look for it too."
Ⓑ Elizabeth, shouted I hate my little brother"
Ⓒ Grant asked, "Can I have some more pizza?"
Ⓓ "She said I hope, it snows tomorrow."

2. Which of the following answers correctly uses a comma and quotation marks?

Ⓐ "Amber said," we need to go to the movies on Sunday.
Ⓑ Perry asked, "Are you going to be at the meeting tonight?"
Ⓒ "He replied," "I want a computer for my birthday."
Ⓓ "Let's visit the neighbors tomorrow instead of today suggested, Sammie."

3. Which of the following answers correctly uses a comma and quotation marks?

Ⓐ "There will be a math test tomorrow," stated Mr. Thompson.
Ⓑ "there will be a math test tomorrow stated Mr. Thompson."
Ⓒ "There will be a math test tomorrow. Stated Mr. Thompson."
Ⓓ "There will be a math test tomorrow. stated" Mr. Thompson.

4. Which of the following answers correctly uses commas and quotation marks? Choose the correct answer from the options given below by circling it.

Ⓐ Grandmother said "we are going to the zoo next week."
Ⓑ "Did you see the meteor shower last night?, asked Randy."
Ⓒ Jill, said. "I don't like this chocolate cake.
Ⓓ "Hillary was not at school this week," stated Peter.

5. Which of the following answer choices accurately describes the correct placement of commas when used in dialogue?

Ⓐ Place a comma after the person has spoken if the quote follows.
   Ex. Mark asked, "Is it supposed to snow?"
Ⓑ Commas are not used in dialogue. Only quotation marks and ending punctuation should be used to set off quotations.
   Ex. Edward asked. "Do you have a pencil I can borrow?"
Ⓒ Place commas at the end of the quote and at the end of the sentence.
   Ex. "I am going to cook a pizza for lunch," said Terry,
Ⓓ Always place a comma after the person's name that is speaking.
   Ex. "My favorite toy truck broke." said Tony,
   Lawanda, said. "I got a bad grade on my science test."

6. Which of the following answer choices correctly punctuates the dialogue below?

Walker said it is going to be a long day

Ⓐ Walker said. "it is going to be a long day.
Ⓑ Walker said, "It is going to be a long day."
Ⓒ Walker, said. "It is going to be a long day?"
Ⓓ Walker "said, it is going to be a long day."

7. Which of the following answer choices correctly punctuates the dialogue below?

I hope that I get that new football video game for my birthday stated Perry

Ⓐ "I hope that I get that new football video game for my birthday stated Perry."
Ⓑ I hope that I get that new football video game for my birthday, "stated Perry."
Ⓒ "I hope that I get that new football video game for my birthday," stated Perry.
Ⓓ "I hope that I get that new football video game for my birthday" stated Perry.

8. Which of the following answer choices correctly punctuates the dialogue below?

May I have your attention said Mrs. Williams I would like to introduce a new student to our class

Ⓐ "May I have your attention," said Mrs. Williams, "I would like to introduce a new student to our class."
Ⓑ "May I have your attention said Mrs. Williams" I would like to introduce a new student to our class."
Ⓒ "May I have your attention, said Mrs. Williams, I would like to introduce a new student to our class."
Ⓓ May I have your attention, said Mrs. Williams. "I would like to introduce a new student to our class."

9. Which of the following answer choices correctly punctuates the dialogue below?

Come into the kitchen called my mom we need to make a list of ingredients to make cookies

Ⓐ "Come into the kitchen called my mom." We need to make a list of ingredients to make cookies.
Ⓑ "Come into the kitchen," called my mom. "we need to make a list of ingredients to make cookies."
Ⓒ "Come into the kitchen," called my mom, "we need to make a list of ingredients to make cookies."
Ⓓ "Come into the kitchen, called my mom, we need to make a list of ingredients to make cookies."

10. **Which of the following answer choices accurately describes why quotation marks are used in dialogue?**

   Ⓐ Quotation marks are not used in dialogue.
   Ⓑ Quotation marks are used to identify the exact words someone has spoken.
   Ⓒ Quotation marks are only used to identify what a person said if they are asking a question.
   Ⓓ Quotation marks are only used to identify what a person said if they are giving a command.

11. **Which of the following answers correctly uses commas and quotation marks? Choose the correct answer from the options given below by circling it.**

   Ⓐ "Bring me your papers said Mr. Golf, I need to grade them."
   Ⓑ "Bring me your papers, said Mr. Golf I need to grade them."
   Ⓒ "Bring me your papers said Mr. Golf I need to grade them."
   Ⓓ "Bring me your papers," said Mr. Golf, "I need to grade them."

Chapter 4

Lesson 14: Impressive Possessives

You can scan the QR code given below or use the URL to access additional EdSearch resources including videos and mobile apps related to *Impressive Possessives*.

URL	QR Code
http://www.lumoslearning.com/a/l32	

edSearch

Impressive Possessives

1. Which word best completes the following sentence?

My things are all _____.

- Ⓐ me's
- Ⓑ I's
- Ⓒ mine
- Ⓓ I

2. Which pronoun best completes the following sentence?

Lydia's things are _____.

- Ⓐ mine
- Ⓑ yours
- Ⓒ his
- Ⓓ hers

3. Which pronoun best completes the following sentence?

Billy and Tim's things are _____.

- Ⓐ mine
- Ⓑ his
- Ⓒ hers
- Ⓓ theirs

4. Which pronouns best complete the following sentence?

Bobby was doing _____ homework when I called, so he didn't take _____ call.

- Ⓐ his, his
- Ⓑ his, my
- Ⓒ my, his
- Ⓓ her, my

5. Which pronouns best complete the following sentence?

I was worried when _____ pencil broke during the test, but Ali loaned me one of _____.

- Ⓐ my, his
- Ⓑ my, her
- Ⓒ his, my
- Ⓓ my, mine

6. Which pronoun best completes the following sentence?

We were all excited when we moved into _____ new house.

- Ⓐ my
- Ⓑ our
- Ⓒ we
- Ⓓ their

7. Choose the word that BEST completes the following sentence.

My _____ dog ran away last night.

- Ⓐ friend's
- Ⓑ friends'
- Ⓒ friends
- Ⓓ friend

8. Choose the sentence that is NOT written correctly.

- Ⓐ Jim's grandparents are coming to visit next weekend.
- Ⓑ I cannot believe that she lost her's ring.
- Ⓒ Emily's backpack has my favorite colors.
- Ⓓ Please join me as I listen to the band's new song.

9. Choose the answer that BEST completes the following sentence.

They are going to bring over one of the _____ puppies for us later this evening.

- Ⓐ dog's
- Ⓑ dogs
- Ⓒ dogs'
- Ⓓ dog

10. Choose the word that BEST completes the following sentence.

The six _____ tires were all very similar in shape and size.

- Ⓐ bicycles
- Ⓑ bicycle's
- Ⓒ bicycle
- Ⓓ bicycles'

11. Choose the sentence that is written ENTIRELY correctly.

Ⓐ   We sent her a dozen roses to the hospital's.
Ⓑ   She is going to need a lot of medicine to get better was the doctors words.
Ⓒ   These paper's are getting wet in the rain.
Ⓓ   I forgot to invite Julian to my party.

12. Look at the answers given below. Choose the answer that BEST completes the following sentence and write it in the box given below.

They are going to bring over one of the _____ puppies for us later this evening.

Ⓐ   dog's
Ⓑ   dogs
Ⓒ   dogs'
Ⓓ   dog

Chapter 4

Lesson 15: Compelling Spellings

You can scan the QR code given below or use the URL to access additional EdSearch resources including videos and mobile apps related to *Compelling Spellings*.

ed Search

Compelling Spellings

URL	QR Code
http://www.lumoslearning.com/a/l32	

1. Which word is spelled correctly?

- Ⓐ hitchiker
- Ⓑ granddaughter
- Ⓒ naturaly
- Ⓓ mispelled

2. Which word is misspelled?

- Ⓐ hiker
- Ⓑ driver
- Ⓒ writer
- Ⓓ ridder

3. Which word is misspelled?

- Ⓐ field
- Ⓑ chief
- Ⓒ niece
- Ⓓ theif

4. Which of the following sentences describes a "homophone"?

- Ⓐ Words that have same spelling, same meaning, and same sound.
- Ⓑ Words that have same spelling but different meanings and different sounds.
- Ⓒ Words that have different spellings, different meanings and different sounds.
- Ⓓ Words that have different spellings, different meanings, but the same sounds.

5. Which of the following pairs of words are homophones?

- Ⓐ flower, plant
- Ⓑ plant, bush
- Ⓒ flower, flour
- Ⓓ flower, buds

6. Which of these words are spelled correctly? Circle the correct answer choice.

- Ⓐ dissappear
- Ⓑ dissapprove
- Ⓒ disappoint
- Ⓓ disscuss

7. **Which of the following sentences have all of the words spelled correctly? Circle the correct answer choice.**

(A) A night used to go riding every knight.
(B) A night used to go riding every morning.
(C) A knight used to go riding every night.
(D) A knight used to go riding every knight.

8. **Which of these words are misspelled?**

(A) mistake
(B) misunderstand
(C) misspell
(D) missbehave

9. **Which word in the following sentence is misspelled?**
   Write the word in the box given below

Tommorrow I will be a few minutes late for work because I have an appointment.

10. **Which word in the following sentence is misspelled?**
    Write the word in the box given below

Please write the date on the board: Febuary 8, 2012.

Chapter 4

Lesson 16: Syllable Patterns

You can scan the QR code given below or use the URL to access additional EdSearch resources including videos and mobile apps related to *Syllable Patterns*.

ed Search

Syllable Patterns

URL	QR Code
http://www.lumoslearning.com/a/l32	

1. How many syllables are in the word telescope?

An astronomer used to go out every night to observe stars. He would often be seen with a telescope in one hand and a notebook in the other.

Ⓐ one
Ⓑ two
Ⓒ three
Ⓓ four

2. How many syllables are in the word astronomer?

An astronomer used to go out every night to observe stars. He would often be seen with a telescope in one hand and a notebook in the other.

Ⓐ one
Ⓑ two
Ⓒ three
Ⓓ four

3. Which of the words in the following sentence has FOUR syllables?

I cannot attend your graduation party.

Ⓐ cannot
Ⓑ attend
Ⓒ graduation
Ⓓ party

4. Choose the word in the following sentence that have FIVE syllables.

Your helpful assistance during this trying time is very much appreciated.

Ⓐ helpful
Ⓑ assistance
Ⓒ trying
Ⓓ appreciated

5. Choose the word in the following sentence that has only ONE syllable.

Tuesday is going to be an eventful day for my family and me.

- Ⓐ going
- Ⓑ eventful
- Ⓒ day
- Ⓓ family

6. Choose the answer choice that shows the underlined word in the following sentence correctly divided into syllables.

Her <u>elbow</u> was not broken, only badly bruised.

- Ⓐ elbow
- Ⓑ el-bow
- Ⓒ e-l-bow
- Ⓓ e-lbow

7. Which word in the following sentence that has THREE syllables? Identify the word and write it in the box given below.

The boys went on an exciting journey last weekend.

8. Circle the answer choice that shows the underlined word in the following sentence correctly divided into syllables.

The <u>excursion</u> cost my family a lot of money, but it was so much fun.

- Ⓐ excur-sion
- Ⓑ ex-cursion
- Ⓒ excur-sion
- Ⓓ ex-cur-sion

9. Circle the word in the following sentence that has TWO syllables.

Tim and Trent were late for basketball practice this afternoon.

Ⓐ Tim
Ⓑ Trent
Ⓒ basketball
Ⓓ practice

10. Choose the word in the following sentence that has THREE syllables.

Yellow and orange are cheerful colors that are some of my family members' favorites.

Ⓐ yellow
Ⓑ cheerful
Ⓒ colors
Ⓓ favorites

11. How many syllables are in the word ostrich?

The ostrich is the largest bird in the world, but it cannot fly.

Chapter 4

Lesson 17: What's Your Reference Preference

You can scan the QR code given below or use the URL to access additional EdSearch resources including videos and mobile apps related to *What's Your Reference Preference.*

 **What's Your Reference Preference**

URL	QR Code
http://www.lumoslearning.com/a/l32	

The teacher asked students in her class to write a research paper on the American Civil War. She also asked the students to list all sources of information on their papers. Nia, a student, went to the library and read books on the history of the United States of America, and a book on the history of the American Civil War.

1. Where else can Nia get information for her paper?
   Circle the correct answer from among the options given below.

   Ⓐ A fashion magazine
   Ⓑ A program on Civil War aired on the History Channel
   Ⓒ A book on the history of Europe
   Ⓓ A book on the Constitution of United States of America

2. What other sources would be most helpful for Nia to use to help her write her research paper?

   Ⓐ An Internet search on facts about the Civil War in the United States.
   Ⓑ Read a fiction story about the Civil War.
   Ⓒ Get ideas by reading about the civil war of another country.
   Ⓓ Interview the school principal.

Beautiful seashells that are washed ashore on beaches by ocean waves have always fascinated human beings. Shells come in a wonderful array of shapes, sizes, and colors. Shells are actually made by marine creatures to serve as their homes.

3. If you were asked to do further research on seashells, where would you look for more information?

4. Where would you be able to find the meaning of the word "marine"?

Ⓐ Try to understand it from the passage.
Ⓑ Ask a friend in your class.
Ⓒ Look up the word in the dictionary.
Ⓓ Just make up your own meaning.

5. To look up the meaning of the word "marine" in the dictionary, which page would you turn to?

Ⓐ Page with the words beginning with s
Ⓑ Page with the words beginning with sea
Ⓒ Page with the words beginning with ma
Ⓓ None of the above.

6. What is the dictionary used for?

Ⓐ To look up the meaning of dictionary.
Ⓑ To look up the meaning and the sound of a word.
Ⓒ To locate factual information about topics.
Ⓓ None of the above.

7. Where would you be able to find more information about how to safely handle bees?

It is not quite safe for children to handle bees. They use their stingers as a defensive tool.

Ⓐ in a book about beekeeping
Ⓑ in an article about how to treat bee stings
Ⓒ in a fiction book about a hive of bees
Ⓓ in a story about a man who died from bee stings

8. Helen and her mother have to bake cookies for a school fundraiser. Which of the following reference materials would NOT be helpful to them?

Ⓐ a cookbook
Ⓑ an instructional manual on how to use a mixer
Ⓒ an article about fun crafts
Ⓓ a website of cookie recipes

The tiger is a giant cat. His body is nearly covered with black stripes. Unlike the lion, he runs so fast that the swiftest horse can not overtake him. He goes over the ground by making bounds or springs, one after another.

9. Where would you be able to find more information about lions?
Look at the options below, and write the correct answer in the box given below.

Ⓐ   in an encyclopedia article about tigers
Ⓑ   in a book about big cats
Ⓒ   in a fable about a lion and a tortoise
Ⓓ   in a website about pet cats

Look at the information provided in the three boxes below. Then, choose the answer choice that best answers each question.

#1	#2	#3
wander - to move around with no specific destination	wander - synonyms: leave, walk, onward	area: amount of space inside a shape
width - measurement from side to side.	width - synonyms: side, breadth	length: measurement from top to bottom
wrap - to hide.	wrap - synonyms: cover, conceal, hide	width: measurement from side to side
wrist - a body part located between one's hand and forearm.	wrist - synonyms: body part, arm	
yield - to pause.	yield - synonyms: pause, stop	

10. What type of resource does box #1 likely show?

Ⓐ   an index
Ⓑ   a dictionary
Ⓒ   a thesaurus
Ⓓ   a map

Look at the information provided in the three boxes below. Then, choose the answer choice that best answers each question.

#1	#2	#3
Wander - to move around with no specific destination width - measurement from side to side. wrist - a body part located between one's hand and forearm. yield - to pause.	wander - synonyms: leave, walk, onward width - synonyms: side, breadth wrap - synonyms - cover, conceal wrist - synonyms: body part, arm yield - synonyms: pause, stop	Area: amount of space inside a shape Length: measurement from top to bottom Width: measurement from side to side

11. Which box would contain a synonym for the word "Conceal"?

    Ⓐ   Box # 1

    Ⓑ   Box # 2

    Ⓒ   Box # 3

Chapter 4

Lesson 18: Connect the Word for Effect

You can scan the QR code given below or use the URL to access additional EdSearch resources including videos and mobile apps related to *Connect the Word for Effect*.

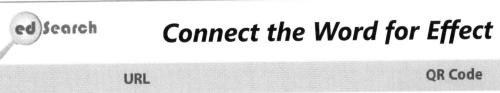

ed Search   *Connect the Word for Effect*

URL	QR Code
http://www.lumoslearning.com/a/l33	

Marina knew it would be a long time before she saw her mother's face again. When her grandmother asked her if she wanted to go on a two-week cruise to Alaska, Marina wasn't sure how to answer. Marina loved spending time with her grandma, but she had never been away from her mother and father for more than one night. Marina was sure that she would feel _____ because she couldn't see her parents for so long.

1. Which word best fills in the blank that will clearly show Marina's feelings at this point in the passage?

Ⓐ happy
Ⓑ concerned
Ⓒ sad
Ⓓ confused

I was ready for the competition this time. Last year during the kite flying competition, I was nervous and unprepared. I forgot my kite string and I had to borrow one from the judges. Once I got my kite into the air, I didn't do a very good job of controlling it, and it crashed into another kite. The two kites were tangled together, and the other flier and I were disqualified from the competition. This year was _____. I checked my kite for tears. It was perfect. I checked to make sure that the kite string was tied to the kite tightly, and that it was wound around the handle neatly.

2. Which word best fills in the blank that clearly completes the writer's thought?

Ⓐ different
Ⓑ the same
Ⓒ cloudy
Ⓓ nervous

Fauntleroy wanted to be as _____ a dragon, as his father. He had learned from an early age that dragons were meant to destroy things. His father was a fire-breather and had burned down many villages. Fauntleroy wanted to be just as dangerous and destructive as his father.

3. Which word best fills in the blank to tell what kind of dragon Fauntleroy dreams of becoming?

Ⓐ friendly
Ⓑ ferocious
Ⓒ large
Ⓓ fiery

When he saw the world, the duckling wanted to crawl back into his shell. There were bright lights shining in his face. There were noises like he'd never heard before. Plus, he was cold, so cold. The duckling started crying. "What's wrong, my little baby? " a voice asked.

The duckling wiped the tears from his eyes with his wing. He focused his new eyes and saw a big, beautiful duck smiling down at him. "I'm...I'm...sad and scared! It was dark, warm, and quiet in my shell. Now it's bright, cold, and _____ out here. I want to go back into my old home!" the duckling said, and he began to cry again.

4. Which word best fills in the blank to complete the duckling's thought?

Ⓐ quiet
Ⓑ noisy
Ⓒ bright
Ⓓ hot

The troll was not happy. He had been trying to build a fence around his home for days, but it kept falling over. You see, the troll didn't like anyone. He wanted to build a fence, so that his neighbors couldn't visit him. He cut down many trees and then cut them into posts for his fence. He dug holes in the ground and put the posts in them. Then he laid long logs on top of the posts, but the logs kept falling down.

5. As the troll was sitting on a log, feeling _____ about the unfinished fence, one of his neighbors walked by.

Ⓐ happy
Ⓑ joyous
Ⓒ glad
Ⓓ upset

The ostrich is the largest bird in the world, but it cannot fly. Its legs are so _____ and long that it can travel faster by running. Ostriches use their wings to help them to gather speed when they start to run. They also use them as brakes in turning and stopping.

6. Which word best fills in the blank and clearly completes the author's thought?

Ⓐ weak
Ⓑ lengthy
Ⓒ powerful
Ⓓ short

7. Choose the statement that best describes an angry child.

Ⓐ He was like an angry lion, roaring in the distance.
Ⓑ It was peaceful, like a slow falling rain.
Ⓒ I could hear him from a long way off.
Ⓓ He was like a fast-paced rabbit, here and then gone.

8. Choose the statement that best describes a sunrise.

Ⓐ It was like a beacon of light appearing in the east.
Ⓑ It spreads warmth all around us.
Ⓒ It was warm.
Ⓓ It was bright.

9. Choose the word that BEST explains the boy's feelings and completes the following sentence.

Jeremiah's balloon escaped. He felt _____ as he saw it float into the sky.

Ⓐ excited
Ⓑ sad
Ⓒ sick
Ⓓ hungry

10. Choose the statement that BEST describes a waterfall.

Ⓐ The clear liquid flowed from top to bottom, creating peaceful sounds.
Ⓑ The waterfall was pretty.
Ⓒ The noise was loud.
Ⓓ The water was foamy.

11. Choose the word that BEST completes the title of a speech that Andy is delivering to his friends about recess.

Recess Time is _____.

Circle the correct answer choice from the options given below.

Ⓐ Educationally Rewarding
Ⓑ Time for Fun
Ⓒ A Waste of Learning
Ⓓ Too Long

12. Choose the word(s) that BEST completes a title for a speech that Mrs. Smith is giving to her third-grade students.

Eating Healthy is _____

    Ⓐ Gross
    Ⓑ Rewarding
    Ⓒ Costly
    Ⓓ Not My Thing

Chapter 4

Lesson 19: Difference in Spoken and Written Language

You can scan the QR code given below or use the URL to access additional EdSearch resources including videos and mobile apps related to *Difference in Spoken and Written Language.*

 **Difference in Spoken and Written Language**

URL	QR Code
http://www.lumoslearning.com/a/l33	

1. **Which of the following answer choices would be the correct way to write a sentence that would clarify the dialogue below?**

That dessert was a killer.

- Ⓐ That dessert committed murder.
- Ⓑ That dessert was excellent.
- Ⓒ That dessert almost killed me.
- Ⓓ That dessert was awful.

2. **If you were asked to verbalize the sentence below, what might you say?**

Jameson was out of touch about the story of the airplane crash.

- Ⓐ Jameson was clueless.
- Ⓑ Jameson is stupid.
- Ⓒ Jameson knew some facts about the plane crash.
- Ⓓ Jameson knows everything.

3. **If someone says "it's in the bag", what are they saying?**

- Ⓐ You have something in a sack.
- Ⓑ You found the item in a bag.
- Ⓒ A situation has been solved or completed.
- Ⓓ You have lost something.

4. **Which of the following answers correctly uses a comma and quotation marks?**
   Circle the correct answer choice from the options given below.

Come on it's time to split.

- Ⓐ It is time to go.
- Ⓑ It is time to tear it in half.
- Ⓒ It is time to arrive.
- Ⓓ It is time for us to separate from one another.

5. **If someone says you are "flaky", what are they saying about you?**
   Circle the correct answer choice from the options given below.

- Ⓐ Your skin is peeling.
- Ⓑ You are cute.
- Ⓒ You are very smart.
- Ⓓ You are unreliable.

6. What does the following sentence mean?

Andre is an absolute riot.

    Ⓐ   Andre likes to fight.
    Ⓑ   Andre likes to damage things.
    Ⓒ   Andre is really funny.
    Ⓓ   Andre is nice.

7. What does the following sentence mean? Summarize the sentence as if you are telling someone the information found in the sentence without changing the meaning.

The gorgeous young woman captured the elite title of homecoming queen.

    Ⓐ   An ugly girl won the crown of homecoming queen.
    Ⓑ   A pretty girl won the title of homecoming queen.
    Ⓒ   This girl I know stole the title of homecoming queen.
    Ⓓ   A pretty girl stole my title of homecoming queen.

8. If someone says "no sweat", what are they saying?

    Ⓐ   They are not sweating.
    Ⓑ   They are cold.
    Ⓒ   No problem!
    Ⓓ   They are scared.

9. What sentence describes someone as a "chicken"?

    Ⓐ   My brother is too scared to go on an airplane.
    Ⓑ   My brother loves to eat fried chicken.
    Ⓒ   My brother loves to fly like a chicken.
    Ⓓ   My brother is very brave.

10. What sentence describes something as "grungy"?

    Ⓐ Kenny's clothes are always so clean.
    Ⓑ Sara's dog always smells so good.
    Ⓒ Peter and Pam have a nice new car.
    Ⓓ James had on a pair of really dirty pants at school.

Chapter 4

Lesson 20: Same Name, Different Game

You can scan the QR code given below or use the URL to access additional EdSearch resources including videos and mobile apps related to *Same Name, Different Game*

ed Search   **Same Name, Different Game**

URL	QR Code
http://www.lumoslearning.com/a/l34	

1. Read the poem and answer the question.

Camels are bumpy,
Their backs are all lumpy,
Giraffes are long- legged and meek:
Bears are so growly,
Hyenas are holy,
Dolphins are slippery and sleek.

Kangaroos have a pocket,
But no way to lock it,
Their babies can look out and peep,
But monkeys are funny
I wish I had money,
Enough to buy one and keep.

What's a kangaroo's pocket called in this poem?

Ⓐ a purse
Ⓑ a pouch
Ⓒ a packet
Ⓓ a parcel

2. Patterns in nature are not just pretty adornments. They do serve a purpose that has helped nature survive and flourish.

What does *survive* mean as it is used in this sentence?

Ⓐ Die
Ⓑ Go away
Ⓒ Stay alive
Ⓓ Perish

3. Read the passage and answer the question.

The ostrich is the largest bird in the world, but it cannot fly. Its legs are so strong and long that it can travel faster by running. Ostriches use their wings to help them gather speed when they start to run. They also use them as brakes in turning and stopping.

Ostriches have been known to run at speeds of 96 kms per hour. So, they can run faster than horses and match the average speed of car drivers on a highway.

These huge birds stand as tall as horses and sometimes weigh as much as 135 pounds. In North Africa, they are often seen with other larger animals. The zebra, which is also a fast runner, seems to be one of their favorite companions.

Each ostrich egg weighs as much as two dozen chicken eggs, or one and a half kg. Ostrich eggs are delicious and are often used for food by people in Africa. The shells also are made into cups and <u>ornaments</u>.

What does ornaments mean as it is used in this paragraph?

Ⓐ Statues
Ⓑ Jewelry
Ⓒ Books
Ⓓ Caps

4. What does this sentence mean?
The Constitution says that a citizen has the right to bear arms.

Ⓐ A citizen has the right to wear sleeveless clothing.
Ⓑ A citizen has the right to carry weapons.
Ⓒ A citizen must have two arms.
Ⓓ A citizen has the right to ask questions about someone's arms.

5. What does this sentence mean?
Betty bought a new dress for the ball.

Ⓐ Betty bought a new dress for the formal dance.
Ⓑ Betty bought a new dress to play ball.
Ⓒ Betty bought a new dress to go shopping for a new ball.
Ⓓ Betty tore her dress playing ball, so she had to buy a new one.

6. What is the meaning of this sentence?
The robber buried his money in the bank.

Ⓐ The robber buried his money in the financial office.
Ⓑ The robber buried his money beside the river.
Ⓒ The robber felt guilty, so he took his money back to the bank.
Ⓓ The robber dug a hole underneath the bank, where he placed his money.

7. What does *batter* mean as it is used in this sentence?
The batter was too thick.

Circle the correct answer choice from the list given below

Ⓐ mixture used for cakes
Ⓑ a baseball player who was up to bat
Ⓒ the baker that was trying to learn to play baseball
Ⓓ someone who bakes cakes

8. What does *bill* mean as it is used in this sentence?
   The bill was very expensive.

   Ⓐ a duck's beak
   Ⓑ money owed
   Ⓒ the man
   Ⓓ money

9. What does *die* mean as it is used in this sentence?
   We can't continue the game until we find the die.

   Ⓐ One of the dice
   Ⓑ No longer living
   Ⓒ A chemical used for changing the color of an item
   Ⓓ A player

10. What is the meaning of this sentence?
    We have to find a fair way to divide the cookies.

    Ⓐ We have to divide the cookies the way they do at the fair.
    Ⓑ We have to divide the cookies equally.
    Ⓒ These cookies must be created the same way they are at the fair.
    Ⓓ One person is going to receive more cookies than the others.

11. What prefix should be added to the word "game" to mean before the game?

12. What prefix should be added to the word "tell" to show that the student told the story again?

Chapter 4

Lesson 21: Context Clue Crew

You can scan the QR code given below or use the URL to access additional EdSearch resources including videos and mobile apps related to *Context Clue Crew.*

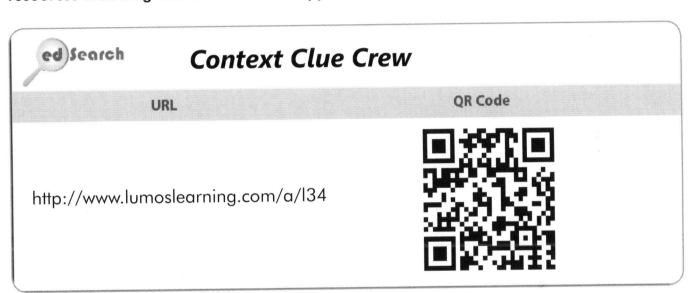

ed Search	**Context Clue Crew**
URL	**QR Code**
http://www.lumoslearning.com/a/l34	

1. Which word means "time of day after the morning, but before the night"?

Ⓐ afternoon
Ⓑ noonafter
Ⓒ aftermoon
Ⓓ dawn

Amy, Ingrid, and Rebecca were friends. They went to school together. They had to cross a river on the way to school. The only way that they could cross it was by walking on a narrow tree trunk.

2. In the above paragraph, what is the meaning of the word "narrow"?
   Circle the correct answer choice from among the options given below.

Ⓐ the size of a bus
Ⓑ very large
Ⓒ not so wide
Ⓓ the size of a car

Amy and her friends were off to school as usual. As they were crossing the narrow bridge, Rebecca, who was right in the back of the line, slipped on the narrow bridge. She gave a frightened scream, clutching hold of Ingrid who was in front of her. Both of them lost their balance and fell into the river. Amy clutched her mother in fright. For a moment, she hesitated and then threw herself into the river after her friends, determined to save them.

3. Which of the following words have the same meaning as "frightened"?

Ⓐ afraid
Ⓑ brave
Ⓒ strong
Ⓓ timid

The pharmacist's brother, a well-dressed man, stooped down and asked the girl about her brother.

4. What does "stooped" mean in this sentence?

Ⓐ flew
Ⓑ sat
Ⓒ bent
Ⓓ lay

5. When you "annoy" a person, that person _____ .

Ⓐ is thankful.
Ⓑ is irritated.
Ⓒ is happy.
Ⓓ is friendly.

When the judge asked the woman to explain why she didn't pay the doctor, the woman said, "Sir, before the operation, I was partially blind, but at least I could see the things in my room."

6. What is the meaning of the word "partially" according to the above sentence?

Ⓐ partly
Ⓑ completely
Ⓒ not so clear
Ⓓ clearly

Once upon a time there was a wealthy woman that could not see clearly. She called a doctor to treat her and restore her eyesight.

7. What does the phrase "restore her eyesight" mean?

Ⓐ Make her completely blind.
Ⓑ Make her able to see well again.
Ⓒ Make her able to see objects that are near.
Ⓓ Make her able to see objects that are far.

Kamil's mom told him that he had <u>bitten off more than he could chew</u>.

8. What does the underlined phrase in this sentence most likely mean?

Ⓐ He had taken too big of a bite.
Ⓑ He was wasting his time.
Ⓒ He had taken on too many new responsibilities.
Ⓓ He is not eaten enough.

(1) Andy wants to learn how to ride his bike. (2) His dad tried to teach him on Monday, but Andy was inattentive. (3) His dad tried to teach him on Tuesday, but he was inattentive. (4) His dad tried to teach him on Wednesday, but he was inattentive. (5) Andy's inattentiveness happened over and over again. (6)Now, when he tries to go down the hills, he <u>accelerates</u> too fast, which leaves him frightened. (7)When his dad returns from work, he is going to try to <u>persuade</u> him to show him the basics of riding a bike. (8) This time, he plans to follow his dad's instructions, instead of not listening carefully.

9. What does the underlined word in sentence 6 (accelerates) MOST LIKELY mean?

Ⓐ speeds up
Ⓑ slows down
Ⓒ stops
Ⓓ wrecks

10. What does the underlined word in sentence 7 (persuade) MOST LIKELY mean?

Ⓐ make him
Ⓑ convince
Ⓒ violently force
Ⓓ ignore

[1]Maria is a very intelligent third-grade student at Sunshine Elementary. [2]She is a <u>diligent</u> worker that wants to make straight A's. [3]Last night; she had a plethora of homework that took her several hours to finish. [4]She had two pages of math homework to complete. [5]She had a spelling worksheet. [6]She had a page of science homework. [7]She had one page of social studies homework to complete. [8]Her parents understand that she attends one of the top schools in the state and this requires a lot of hard work. [9]However, they feel that this amount of work is a bit absurd. [10]There is no time for their daughter's extracurricular activities. [11]They are going to call the school later today to discuss their concerns.

11. What does the underlined word in sentence 2 (diligent) MOST LIKELY mean?
Write your answer in the box given below.

Lesson 22: The Root and Affix Institute

You can scan the QR code given below or use the URL to access additional EdSearch resources including videos and mobile apps related to *The Root and Affix Institute*.

 **The Root and Affix Institute**

URL	QR Code
http://www.lumoslearning.com/a/l34	

1. What is the prefix in the word *bewailed*?

Ⓐ be-
Ⓑ bew-
Ⓒ -ed
Ⓓ wail

2. What is a *telescope*?

Ⓐ An instrument that helps us to see small objects by making them look bigger
Ⓑ An instrument that helps us to get a closer view of objects far away
Ⓒ An instrument that helps us to measure speed of a vehicle
Ⓓ An instrument that helps us to keep things cold and preserve them

3. Which part of the word *treatment* is a suffix?

Ⓐ -ment
Ⓑ treat-
Ⓒ trea-
Ⓓ -atment

4. In the word *coincidence*, 'co-' is the _____.

Ⓐ suffix
Ⓑ root word
Ⓒ prefix
Ⓓ helping word

5. How many legs does a tripod have?

Ⓐ one
Ⓑ two
Ⓒ three
Ⓓ four

6. Look at the following pairs of words.

    happy - unhappy
    cover - uncover
    lock - unlock
    When the prefix 'un' is added to the word, what happens to its meaning?

  Ⓐ The meaning remains the same.
  Ⓑ The meaning becomes opposite of the given word.
  Ⓒ The word becomes a synonym of the given word.
  Ⓓ The word becomes clear to understand.

7. Based on the following sentences, what does the prefix "anti-," mean?

    The abolitionists were <u>antislavery</u>.
    The peace marchers are <u>antiwar</u>.
    He doesn't like to go to parties; he is <u>antisocial</u>.

  Ⓐ in favor of
  Ⓑ against
  Ⓒ before
  Ⓓ after

8. Based on the following sentences, what does the prefix "micro," mean?

    A <u>microchip</u>, a tiny part of an electronic or computer device.
    A <u>microscope</u> looks at tiny creatures.
    A <u>microphone</u> makes a soft sound louder.

  Ⓐ creature
  Ⓑ larger
  Ⓒ loud
  Ⓓ small

9. Based on the following sentences, what does the prefix "tele-," mean?

    A <u>telescope</u> is used to look at distant things.
    A <u>telephone</u> is used to place long distance calls.
    A <u>television</u> receives a signal from far away.

  Ⓐ again
  Ⓑ distant
  Ⓒ nearby
  Ⓓ short

10. Based on the following sentences, what does the prefix "un-," mean?
    The heavy jacket is <u>uncomfortable</u> in hot weather.
    Karla was <u>unhappy</u> when her dog died.
    He couldn't tell which answer was right; he felt <u>uncertain</u>.

    Ⓐ comfortable
    Ⓑ very
    Ⓒ not
    Ⓓ sure

11. Match the word to its Prefix.

    Write the prefix to match the word in the blank boxes.

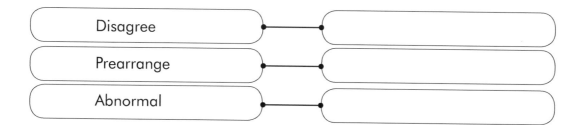

12. Write the Prefix, Root word and Suffix in the correct order for the word "Disagreeable" in the boxes given below.

    Prefix   **Root Word**   **Suffix**

Chapter 4

Lesson 23: Referring to References

You can scan the QR code given below or use the URL to access additional EdSearch resources including videos and mobile apps related to *Referring to References*

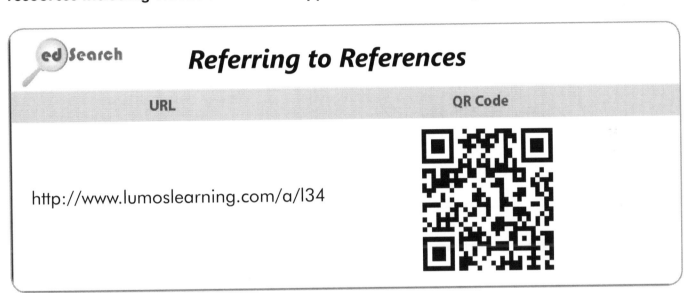

ed Search

Referring to References

URL	QR Code
http://www.lumoslearning.com/a/l34	

View the dictionary excerpt and answer the question.
Main Entry: wrap
Pronunciation: 'rap
Function: verb

1 (a): to cover especially by winding or folding (b): to and secure for transportation or storage : BUN-DLE (c) : ENFOLD, EMBRACE (d): to coil, fold, draw, or twine (as string or cloth) around something
2 a : to involve completely : ENGROSS
3 : to conceal or obscure as if by enveloping
4 : to finish filming or videotaping <wrap a movie>

1. Which definition of the word wrap is used in the sentence below?

Jenny was so wrapped up in the movie that she did not hear the phone ringing.

- Ⓐ   to envelop and secure for transportation or storage
- Ⓑ   to involve completely: ENGROSS
- Ⓒ   to conceal or obscure as if by enveloping
- Ⓓ   to finish filming or videotaping

2. Which of the following definitions best describes "strange".

The strange sound was coming from the basement door as we walked down the hall.

- Ⓐ   of, relating to, or characteristic of another country
- Ⓑ   not before known, heard, or seen
- Ⓒ   ill at ease
- Ⓓ   having the major characteristic of strangeness

Use the excerpt from a glossary found in a math book to answer the following question.

Addend: any number being added
A.M.: Times between 12:00 (midnight) and 12:00 (noon)
Area: A measurement of square units of the inside of a plane figure.
Array: The arrangement of objects that are in equal rows.
Bar graph: Is a graph that uses rectangles to compare the amounts of data.

3. Which of the words from the glossary is an example of a measurement of time?

- Ⓐ   bar graph
- Ⓑ   array
- Ⓒ   a.m.
- Ⓓ   Area

Use the excerpt from a glossary found in a math book to answer the following question.

Addend: any number being added
A.M.: Times between 12:00 (midnight) and 12:00 (noon)
Area: A measurement of square units of the inside of a plane figure.
Array: The arrangement of objects that are in equal rows.
Bar graph: Is a graph that uses rectangles to compare the amounts of data.

4. Which of the words from the glossary is a way to compare data?
- Ⓐ array
- Ⓑ addend
- Ⓒ area
- Ⓓ bar graph

View the glossary excerpt from a 3rd grade ELA text book and answer the questions.

diagram:
A drawing the shows a schematic representation of how something works or shows a relationship

dialogue:
1. A conversation between characters in literary work.
2. The exact words someone has spoken.

distinction:
A difference made between two or more individuals, ideas, or everts.

distinguish:
To mark off as different; to recognize the prominent features of

domain-specific vocabulary:
Vocabulary specific to a particular field of study (domain)

5. Which two words tells the difference in something?

6. Which of the words from the glossary describes words that are found in a particular area of study?

Ⓐ dialogue
Ⓑ diagram
Ⓒ domain-specific vocabulary
Ⓓ distinction

View the dictionary excerpt and answer the question.
Main Entry: **sev•er•al**
Pronunciation: **'sev-r&l, 'se-v&-**

Function: adjective
1 a : separate or distinct from one another <federal union of the several states> b (1) : individually owned or controlled (2) : of or relating separately to each individual involved <a several judgment> c : being separate and distinctive

2 a : more than one <several please> b : more than two but fewer than many <moved several inches> c chiefly dialect : being a great many

7. Which of the definitions of the word several tells you the amount?

Ⓐ 2a: more than one, 2b: more than two but fewer than many, 2c: being of great many
Ⓑ 1a: separate or distinct from one another, 1b(1): individually owned or controlled
Ⓒ 1c: being separate and distinctive
Ⓓ 1b (2): of or relating separately to each individual involved

View the dictionary excerpt and answer the question.
Main Entry: **fan•cy**
Pronunciation: 'fan(t)-sE
Function: transitive verb
Inflected Form(s): **fan•cied; fan•cy•ing**
1 : to have a fancy for : **LIKE**
2 : to form a conception of : **IMAGINE** <fancy our embarrassment>
3 a : to believe mistakenly or without evidence b : to believe without being certain <she fancied she had met him before>
4 : to visualize or interpret as <fancied myself a child again>
synonym see THINK

8. From the dictionary excerpt, which of the following would be a synonym for the word fancy?

- Ⓐ unpleasant
- Ⓑ elegant
- Ⓒ plain
- Ⓓ unwanted

View the dictionary excerpt and answer the question.
Main Entry: **fan•cy**
Pronunciation: 'fan(t)-sE
Function: transitive verb
Inflected Form(s): **fan•cied; fan•cy•ing**
1 : to have a fancy for : **LIKE**
2 : to form a conception of : **IMAGINE** <fancy our embarrassment>
3 a : to believe mistakenly or without evidence b : to believe without being certain <she fancied she had met him before>
4 : to visualize or interpret as <fancied myself a child again>
synonym see **THINK**

9. Which definition states that fancy can mean to interpret as?

- Ⓐ 2: to form a conception of
- Ⓑ 1: to have a fancy for: Like
- Ⓒ 4: to visualize or interpret as
- Ⓓ 3b: to believe without being certain

View the glossary excerpt from a 3rd grade science text book and answer the question

capacity: the volume of a container measured in liquid units.
chlorophyll: the green coloring of leaves and plants
classify: to place materials that share properties together in groups.
compost: A mix of decaying leaves, vegetables, and other living matter
constellation: a group of stars that is shaped somewhat like an animal, person, or object
crescent: the shape of the moon as it appears in its first or last quarter, with curved edges ending in points

10. Part A

Which of the words from the glossary would help you understand what the shape of a group of stars is called?

Ⓐ Crescent
Ⓑ Classify
Ⓒ Compost
Ⓓ Constellation

Part B

Which two words from the science glossary tells you the definition of words that are things found in the sky?

Ⓐ Crescent, Classify
Ⓑ Constellation, Crescent
Ⓒ Crescent, Capacity
Ⓓ Classify, Constellation

Chapter 4

Lesson 24: Making Words Work

You can scan the QR code given below or use the URL to access additional EdSearch resources including videos and mobile apps related to *Making Words Work*.

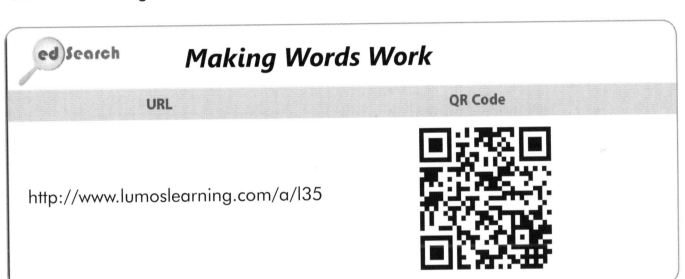

Making Words Work

URL	QR Code
http://www.lumoslearning.com/a/l35	

1. Which list of words rhyme?

Ⓐ toil, boil, soil
Ⓑ soil, bail, tail
Ⓒ twin, win, swing
Ⓓ song, hung, sung

2. What word is a synonym for anxiously? Choose the correct word and circle it.

Maria waited anxiously for the concert to begin.

Ⓐ unfriendly
Ⓑ uneasily
Ⓒ easily
Ⓓ happily

3. What word is an antonym for the bold word in the sentence?

He couldn't believe his luck. "Ha! Ha!" he **laughed**.

Ⓐ happy
Ⓑ unhappy
Ⓒ cried
Ⓓ giggled

4. Which set of words rhymes with "brought"?

Ⓐ bought, bring
Ⓑ thought, sought
Ⓒ bringing, buy, bring
Ⓓ None of the above

5. What is a homophone for "there"?

Ⓐ them
Ⓑ their
Ⓒ those
Ⓓ this

6. Which word is a synonym for "quarreled"?

Kelsey and Maya quarreled again. They both wanted to play with the soccer ball.

Ⓐ discussed
Ⓑ yelled
Ⓒ fought
Ⓓ fit

7. What is the antonym of "night"?

- Ⓐ dark
- Ⓑ light
- Ⓒ sleep
- Ⓓ morning

8. What list of words contains antonyms for the word "wrong"?

- Ⓐ right, correct
- Ⓑ wrong, strong
- Ⓒ amazed, right
- Ⓓ write, right

9. Which list of words contains rhyming words?

- Ⓐ brother, another, strong
- Ⓑ along, wrong, right
- Ⓒ black, brother, back
- Ⓓ slight, right, night

10. What is an antonym of the word "deep"?

- Ⓐ profound
- Ⓑ shallow
- Ⓒ meaningful
- Ⓓ secret

11. Which word means the opposite of *whisper*? Circle the correct answer choice.

- Ⓐ talk
- Ⓑ look
- Ⓒ quiet
- Ⓓ scream

12. What is the antonym of the word "Carefully"? Write your answer in the box below.

Chapter 4

Lesson 25: Shades of Words Meanings

You can scan the QR code given below or use the URL to access additional EdSearch resources including videos and mobile apps related to *Shades of Words Meanings*.

Shades of Words Meanings

URL	QR Code
http://www.lumoslearning.com/a/l35	

1. Completes the analogy?

Clear is to sunny
as gloomy is to _____

Write your answer in the box below.

[   ]

2. Which of the following answer choices could replace the underlined words without changing the meaning of the sentence? Circle the correct answer choice from the options given.

The spaghetti was <u>rich with flavor</u>.

Ⓐ   tasty
Ⓑ   bland
Ⓒ   vanilla
Ⓓ   nasty

3. Which of the following answer choices could replace the underlined words without changing the meaning of the sentence? Circle the correct answer choice from the options given.

Derrick is <u>very funny</u>.

Ⓐ   serious
Ⓑ   boring
Ⓒ   somber
Ⓓ   hilarious

4. Which of the following answer choices is being described in the sentence below?

Lily was <u>elegant</u> as she moved across the dance floor.

Ⓐ   awkward
Ⓑ   graceful
Ⓒ   rigid
Ⓓ   careless

5. Which of the following answer choices is being described in the sentence below?

The tightrope walker was very <u>bold</u> as he walked along the high wire a hundred feet up in the air.

- Ⓐ timid
- Ⓑ cautious
- Ⓒ daring
- Ⓓ cowardly

6. Which of the following answer choices complete the following sentence keeping with the context of the sentence?

Many Americans throw away a lot of uneaten food every year, some say they are _____.

- Ⓐ wasteful
- Ⓑ economical
- Ⓒ saving
- Ⓓ practical

7. Which of the following answer choices completes the following sentence keeping with the context of the sentence?

The wrestler had large muscles and _____ strength.

- Ⓐ normal
- Ⓑ tremendous
- Ⓒ ordinary
- Ⓓ powerless

8. Which of the following answer choices complete the following sentence keeping with the context of the sentence?

The sight of the ruby encrusted necklace was almost _____.

- Ⓐ shabby
- Ⓑ pitiful
- Ⓒ tacky
- Ⓓ majestic

9. **Which of the following answer choices means the opposite of the underlined word in the sentence below?**

Jessica's baby sister is just <u>precious</u>.

- (A) adorable
- (B) obnoxious
- (C) delightful
- (D) darling

10. **Which of the following answer choices means the opposite of the underlined word in the sentence below?**

The look on Ms. Morris' face after the test results were in was almost <u>a snarl</u>.

- (A) glare
- (B) scowl
- (C) smile
- (D) grimace

Chapter 4

Lesson 26: Connecting Related Words

You can scan the QR code given below or use the URL to access additional EdSearch resources including videos and mobile apps related to *Connecting Related Words*.

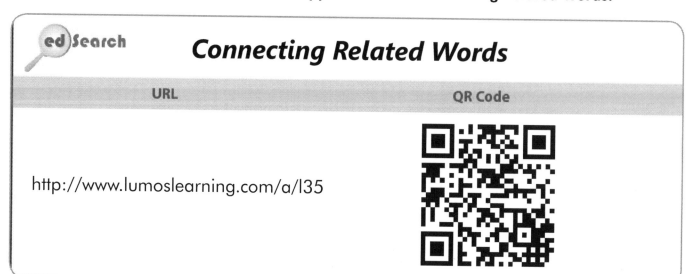

ed Search

Connecting Related Words

URL	QR Code
http://www.lumoslearning.com/a/l35	

1. Which of the following sentences has the same meaning as the sentence below?

The principal was infuriated that someone had pulled the fire alarm.

- Ⓐ The principal was calm when someone pulled the fire alarm.
- Ⓑ The principal was relaxed when someone pulled the fire alarm.
- Ⓒ The principal was enraged that someone had pulled the fire alarm.
- Ⓓ The principal was excited that someone had pulled the fire alarm.

2. Read the below list of words:
    A. Enormous
    B. Slight
    C. Minute
    D. Average

There were a <u>tremendous</u> number of people at the concert last night.

Which word is similar to the underlined word in the above sentence? Write the correct answer in the box given below.

```
┌─────────────────────────────────┐
│                                 │
└─────────────────────────────────┘
```

3. Which word is most extreme in its meaning?

- Ⓐ cheerful
- Ⓑ happy
- Ⓒ delighted
- Ⓓ overjoyed

4. Which answer choice is similar to "whisper"?

- Ⓐ screech
- Ⓑ chatter
- Ⓒ murmur
- Ⓓ scream

5. Which of the following sentences has the same meaning as the sentence below?

During the scavenger hunt our team had a hard time finding a sphere.

- Ⓐ During the scavenger hunt our team had a hard time finding a cone.
- Ⓑ During the scavenger hunt our team had a hard time finding an orb.
- Ⓒ During the scavenger hunt our team had a hard time finding a cylinder.
- Ⓓ During the scavenger hunt our team had a hard time finding a cube.

6. Which of the answer choices has a similar meaning as "slippery"?

Ⓐ dry
Ⓑ slick
Ⓒ tacky
Ⓓ rough

7. Which of the following words is the least extreme in its meaning? Circle the correct answer choice.

Ⓐ enemy
Ⓑ attacker
Ⓒ rival
Ⓓ competitor

8. Which of the following sentences does NOT have the same meaning as the sentence below?

Lily froze in her tracks when she saw the large scary dog approaching.

Ⓐ Lily halted in her tracks when she saw the large terrifying dog approaching.
Ⓑ Lily stopped in her tracks when she saw the large dangerous looking dog approaching.
Ⓒ Lily darted when she saw the large frightening dog approaching.
Ⓓ Lily stopped in her tracks when she saw the large horrifying dog approaching.

9. Which of the following answer choices has a similar meaning to the word "possible"?

Ⓐ potential
Ⓑ impossible
Ⓒ unlikely
Ⓓ unattainable

10. Which of the following answer choices is least like the word "naughty"?

Ⓐ rowdy
Ⓑ behaved
Ⓒ evil
Ⓓ unruly

Chapter 4

Lesson 27: Vocabulary Acquisition

You can scan the QR code given below or use the URL to access additional EdSearch resources including videos and mobile apps related to *Vocabulary Acquisition*.

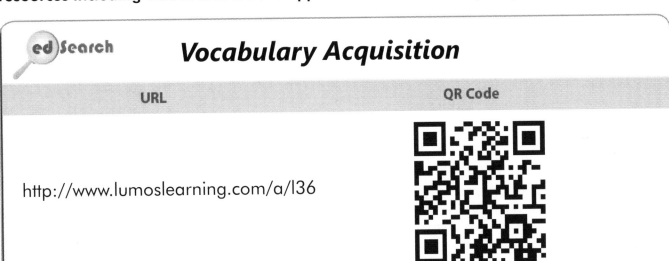

URL	QR Code
http://www.lumoslearning.com/a/l36	

1. **Which of the following domain specific words means "the number below the line in a fraction and tells how many equal parts there are in the whole"? Circle the correct answer choice**

   Ⓐ fragment
   Ⓑ denominator
   Ⓒ reproduction
   Ⓓ difference

2. **In which class would you most likely talk about "mammals"?**

   Ⓐ Math
   Ⓑ Social Studies
   Ⓒ English Language Arts
   Ⓓ Science

3. **If your teacher asked you to list a "sequence of events" from a story that you just read, what is she asking you to do?**

   Ⓐ The teacher wants you to put the events in order as they occurred in the story.
   Ⓑ The teacher wants you to summarize the story in your own words.
   Ⓒ The teacher wants you to list the main idea and the supporting points from the story.
   Ⓓ The teacher wants you to write your own story that has a similar plot as the story you read.

4. **In which class would you most likely hear the domain-specific word "hyperbole"?**

   Ⓐ Math
   Ⓑ Science
   Ⓒ Social Studies
   Ⓓ English Language Arts

5. **If your teacher asked you to "estimate" the amount of time you spent studying for the spelling test, what is he asking you to do?**

   Ⓐ The teacher wants you to write a detailed report of your study habits.
   Ⓑ The teacher wants you to give an approximate amount of time that you have spent studying.
   Ⓒ The teacher wants an exact amount of time you spent studying.
   Ⓓ The teacher wants you to write your spelling words down and study them.

6. **If the directions of an assignment require you to provide "evidence" to support your short answer responses, what information are you being asked to provide?**

   Ⓐ The directions are asking you to write your opinion of what you think is the correct answer to the question.
   Ⓑ The directions want you to show the sources that support the answer responses.
   Ⓒ The directions want you to give the answer that you think is correct.
   Ⓓ The directions want you to find the key points of the chapter you are studying.

7. Mrs. Johnson's science class is studying "moon phases". Which of the following is an accurate definition of "moon phases"?

Ⓐ Moon phases- the path that the moon follows as it rotates around the planets.
Ⓑ Moon phases- a chart that tells you when the moon will rise every day.
Ⓒ Moon phases- the appearance of the lit portion of the moon as seen by an observer.
Ⓓ Moon phases- the type of weather the Earth will be experiencing with the moon.

8. What does the academic word "maximum" mean?

Ⓐ The smallest amount required
Ⓑ The average number that needs to be provided
Ⓒ The range of numbers that is required
Ⓓ The largest number of items that can be provided

9. In which class would you most likely learn about "subordinating conjunctions"?

Ⓐ Social Studies
Ⓑ English Language Arts
Ⓒ Math
Ⓓ Science

Mr. Nelson separated his class into groups. There were four in each group. Each member of the group was assigned to write a "verse" of a poem about the seasons.

10. What will each student have to write?

Ⓐ Each student will to write one line for the group's poem.
Ⓑ Each student will write four lines for the group's poem.
Ⓒ Each student will write a separate poem and edit each other's work.
Ⓓ Each student will to write a single word for the group's poem.

11. If your teacher wants you to "justify" your answer, what is your teacher asking you to do?

End of Language

Answer Key and Detailed Explanations

Chapter 4: Language

Lesson 1: People, Places and Things

Question No.	Answer	Detailed Explanations
1	B	If you chose B, you picked the right answer. If a word ends in a consonant followed by a y, change the y to "i" and add "-es."
2	A	If you chose A, you picked the correct spelling. If the word ends in a vowel followed by a y, do not change the y to "i". Just add "-s."
3	Butterflies	Remember to change the y to "i," and add "-es," if the letter before the y is a consonant, not a vowel.
4	B	If you selected B, you got the answer. Like "heroes," "potatoes," and "zeroes," the plural of "tomatoes" is formed by adding "-es."
5	B	Since "played" shows action, it is not a noun. A noun names a person, place, thing, or idea. It DOES NOT show action.
6	A	"Older" is not a person, place, thing, or idea. In this sentence, it is describing a noun. This makes it an adjective.
7	D	There is only one pencil, so it can only belong to one person. "Boy's" is a singular possessive noun, but it does not fit the sentence without using "the" in front of it. "Saads" does not contain an apostrophe to show ownership or possessiveness. "Boys" is plural, but there are not multiple pencils. "Saad's" is the correct answer.
8	A	Given the verb "are", it is not going to be "tooth". "Toothes" and "teeths" are not real words. The correct plural noun for this sentence is teeth.
9	B	A proper noun name a specific person place, thing, or idea. It also requires capitalization, even if it is NOT at the beginning of the sentence. Dr. Martinez is the proper noun.
10	B	Given the use of the word "are" as a verb in the sentence, the noun needs to be plural. The other choices are singular. Girls is the correct plural noun to complete this sentence.
11	B	Happy is not a person, place, thing, or idea. It is describing a noun. This makes it an adjective.

Lesson 2: Replace Those Nouns

Question No.	Answer	Detailed Explanations
1	B	"Team" refers to the group of players. Charlene is also a proper noun, but is not one of the answer choices.
2	He, her, she, and it	He, her, she and it are the pronouns that replace the nouns Alice, Jim, and gift.
3	B	We need a pronoun to replace Monica. The correct choice is "her".
4	B	Charles is a boy. We need a possessive pronoun to take the place of Charles and show that the puppy belongs to him. "His" is the correct pronoun to complete the sentence.
5	A	Pencil is a thing. The word that takes its place is "it".
6	C	Since the word babies are plural, the pronoun for the first blank that takes the place of babies is "they." "Their" is the correct word for the second blank, as it is a possessive pronoun. Possessive pronouns show that something belongs to someone. In this case, the babies belong to their mothers.
7	B	"They" is a pronoun because it takes the place of some people that are driving to the camp site.
8	A	"Him" is the only pronoun that makes the sentence grammatically correct.
9	B	The pronoun "them" refers to two people. The proper nouns that could be placed in the sentence if the pronoun was removed would be "Ted and Terry".
10	B	While the word "the" does sound correct in the sentence, it is NOT a pronoun. The pronoun "her" is the correct word to complete this sentence.
11	B	If you read through the choices, them and they are too personal and lifelike to replace "the math test". Its is grammatically incorrect. "It" is the best pronoun to replace "the math test".
12	C	Since the three names are listed in third person, "them" is the correct pronoun.
13	A	"We", "us" and "She and I" are all second person pronouns. Since the flowers were brought to "me", the speaker would not use a second person pronoun. The best pronoun to complete this sentence is "they".

Lesson 3: Regular and Irregular Plural Nouns

Question No.	Answer	Detailed Explanations
1	B	This answer choice B is correct because the plural form of "mouse" is mice. Answer choice A is incorrect because children is the correct plural form not childrens. Answer C is incorrect because "doctors" is the correct plural form and doctores is not. Answer D is incorrect because "women" is the correct plural form and womans is not.
2	D	This answer choice is correct because "deer" is the only answer choice that is used as a plural noun in the sentence. "We" is a pronoun so it is not the correct answer.
3	B	This is the correct answer because "berries" is the correct plural form of the word "berry."
4	A	The word "loaves" is the only answer choice that is a plural noun found in the sentence.
5	C	This is the correct answer because the plural form of the irregular noun cactus is "cacti".
6	B	This is the correct answer because boats is the only answer choice that is in the correct plural form.
7	C	This answer demonstrates "mooses," as the only incorrect plural form. The rest of the answer choices are correctly spelled.
8	A	This answer choice acornes is the only plural noun written incorrectly.
9	geese	The correct plural form of "goose" as "geese".
10	B	This answer choice bushs is the answer choice that contains an incorrect plural noun. This is the correct way to spell "bushes".
11	C	This is the only answer choice that incorrectly changes a plural noun to its singular form. Wifes=Wife

Lesson 4: Awesome Abstract Nouns

Question No.	Answer	Detailed Explanations
1	C	This is the correct answer choice because the word crime is the only example of an abstract noun.
2	A	This answer choice listed as "beauty" is the only abstract noun.
3	B	The correct answer is "wisdom" because it is the answer choice that is an abstract noun. The other answer choices give examples of concrete nouns a noun that can be seen, touched, smelled, or heard.
4	B	This is the only answer choice that gives an abstract noun. The other three answer choices are examples of concrete nouns, a noun that can be seen, touched, smelled, or heard.
5	C	"Time" is an example of an abstract noun that is found in the given sentence.
6	D	"Freedom" is an example of an abstract noun. The other answer choices "girl, tractor, and daisy" are all concrete nouns that engage one of the 5 senses.
7	A	"Bravery" is the only answer choice that is an example of an abstract idea because it does not engage one of the 5 senses. The other answer choices "camera, New York, and Christy" all name concrete nouns.
8	D	The word "dress" an example of a concrete noun; the rest of the answer choices are abstract nouns.
9	B	This answer choice "coffee" is the only non-abstract noun. The rest of the answer choices are abstract.
10	A	This answer choice is the only choice given that accurately defines an abstract noun.
11	C	"Relief" is the only answer given that is found in the given sentence that is an example of an abstract noun.
12	Memories	"Memories" is the abstract noun found in the given sentence. .
13	Motivation	"Motivation" is the only abstract noun given that is found in the sentence.

Lesson 5: Show Me the Action

Question No.	Answer	Detailed Explanations
1	C	"Angrily" is an adverb to explain how the verb was acting. We need a verb to complete the sentence. Since the sentence is currently occurring, "growling" is correct.
2	D	If you read through the choices, only one is grammatically correct. "Sleeping" is the correct verb choice. "The monkey was sleeping on the branch of the tree" is the complete sentence.
3	B	"Wander" refers to just walking around without a real plan. "Wonder" refers to think about or ponder. "Yonder" refers to a distant location.
4	C	Clearly, hates is the action here.
5	C	The past tense of think is thought.
6	C	Lunch purchased previously was "bought".
7	D	The verb "caught" is the past tense form of catch.
8	D	The past tense of bring is "brought".
9	C	The past tense of break is broke and the past tense of write is wrote.
10	D	This sentence requires that "drink" and "find" must be changed to a past tense. The correct verbs are "drank" and "found".
11		If we are referring to the day before, the correct reference to that would be: "I went to the store yesterday after school."
12		"I will do all my homework tomorrow afternoon." The verb phrase "will do" refers to a future action.
13		"I will eat breakfast tomorrow before school." The verb phrase "will eat" refers to a future action.
14	B	"I drank three glasses of milk yesterday." "Drank" is the past tense form of the verb drink.

Lesson 6: Simply Simple Verb Tenses

Question No.	Answer	Detailed Explanations
1	B	This answer choice is correct because it is the past tense form of "play".
2	C	This answer choice correctly labels "will try" as future tense.
3	A	This answer choice is correct because "speaks" is the present tense of the verb.
4	D	"Will cry" is the answer choice that is written in future tense.
5	B	This answer choice is correct because "threw" is past tense.
6	A	"Will chop" is the future tense verb given as an answer choice.
7	C	This answer choice is correct because "sneeze" is in the present tense.
8	B	This choice is correct because "shouted" is a past tense verb.
9	C	This answer choice "laughed". It is the only past tense verb.
10	A	This is the correct answer because "write" is in the present tense.
11	B	This answer choice B is correct because the question asks you to change "gone" to future tense. This answer correctly changes "gone" to "will go".
12	Baked	The question asked you to change "will bake" to its past tense form. "Mrs. James said that she baked cookies for the class party on Friday." This answer correctly does that because it changes to "baked".
13	Ride	The question ask for you to change the word "rode" to its present tense. "We ride the merry-go-round at the mall five times." This answer correctly does that because it changes to "ride"

Lesson 7: Make It Make Sense

Question No.	Answer	Detailed Explanations
1	C	The subject of the sentence "my sister" is singular, and needs a plural verb. The sentence that is written correctly is "My sister always helps my mother."
2	B	Since "my neighbor and his dog" refers to two subjects, the verb needs to be singular. The sentence that has an agreeing subject and verb is "My neighbor and his dog walk every day."
3	C	The word that completes the sentence properly is "go".
4	B	"Does" should be replaced with "do". If you read through the other options, they do not create a sentence that makes sense.
5	A	"Steven and Mario" are referring to two people, and the verb needs to be singular. The sentence that is written correctly is: "Steven and Mario walk to school together."
6	B	The word "bag" is singular, and needs to be paired with the verb "is".
7	B	"Plants" is the word that makes sense. The other verbs do not match the action that is occurring in the sentence. This action is occurring now, so "plants" is the present tense verb that is needed to complete this sentence.
8	C	The action occurred last week, and the verb needs to be past tense. "Cried" is the correct verb to show that the action has already happened.
9	C	"Began" is the verb that accommodates the adverb "badly". The other choices are in the incorrect form of "begin". The action has already started, making the past tense form the correct option.
10	A	The verb that best completes this sentence is "was". The other options do not make sense. The paper had already been written indicating past tense.
11	Are	"Are" is clearly the word that is needed to complete this sentence. "The team and every player **are** happy."
12	will give	Since this sentence is talking about the future, the correct verb phrase to complete it is "will give".

Lesson 8: Tell Me More

Question No.	Answer	Detailed Explanations
1	C	If you look closely at the word "growly", you will notice the root word "growl".
2	B	Since there is nothing being compared here, the best word to complete this sentence is "long". Elongate cannot work because it is missing the necessary ending and would require the form "elongated".
3	B	"Confusing" is the adjective describing the noun, "assignment."
4	C	If you chose "merrily," you are correct. Merrily describes the verb, whistling, telling how he did it.
5	B	If you chose "really," which describes the other adverb, and "too," which describes the adjective "busy," you found both of them!
6	B	Clearly, all these words create sentences that are complete, but only one makes sense. You would sharpen the pencil as it was broken.
7	D	Tasty is the word that completes the sentence and maintains that strawberries are desirable.
8	D	Clearly, angry denotes that one is in trouble. Confusing means understanding a process. Also, if someone is happy or smiling, those emotions do not represent trouble.
9	B	How did the boys enter the room? They entered the room "slowly". "Slowly" is the adverb that describes the boys' movement.
10	D	There are actually two words that describe the pie. "Apple" and "delicious". The answer choice, "delicious" is the adjective.
11	Dear	"Friends" is the noun in this sentence. "Dear" is the adjective that is describing "friends".
12	Mildly	"Disturbed" is the word that is showing action. We then start to look for the word that explains how the disruption occurred. It occurred "mildly", making this the adverb.

Lesson 9: Subordinating and Coordinating Conjunctions

Question No.	Answer	Detailed Explanations
1	B	This is the correct answer because "rather than" is an example of a subordinating conjunction.
2	D	This is the correct answer because "until" is an example of a subordinating conjunction.
3	A	This answer choice is correct because it accurately defines a coordinating conjunction.
4	B	This answer choice is correct because "but" is a coordinating conjunction. The rest of the choices are subordinating conjunctions.
5	D	This answer choice is correct because "and" is the coordinating conjunction in the given sentence.
6	C	This is the correct answer choice because "even if" is a subordinating conjunction. The other choices are coordinating conjunctions.
7	B	This is the correct answer because it accurately gives the definition for subordinating conjunctions.
8	D	This is the correct answer because "since" is the only subordinating conjunction found in the given sentence. The rest of the answer choices are examples of verbs.
9	C	This is the correct answer choice because "yet" is the only coordinating conjunction found in the given sentence. The other choices are not conjunctions.
10	A	This is the correct answer because "as soon as" is the only subordinating conjunction used in the given sentence.
11		LaTonya said that she was getting a new bike <u>and</u> a new purse for her birthday. The underlined conjunction in the sentence is a coordinating conjunction.
12	But	My mom cooked spaghetti for dinner **but** I really wanted lasagna. The "but" is the only coordinating conjunction used in the given sentence.

Lesson 10: Mix Up Those Sentences

Question No.	Answer	Detailed Explanations
1	B	Clearly, this is providing facts about the giraffe. This is an informative sentence.
2	B	There are two ideas expressed in this sentence. Both are complete. This makes this a compound sentence.
3	C	A complex sentence means that there is one complete idea and a partial idea. Did you notice how the sentence reads: I get a stomach ache? This part of this sentence does not leave the reader with unanswered questions, so it is a complete thought or a simple sentence. When we add the partial idea "When I eat too much candy", the reader is left wondering, "What happens when too much candy is eaten?" This is only part of a sentence, or an incomplete idea. These two combined create a complex sentence.
4	A	While this sentence tells two things that some children do not like to eat, it is only expressing one complete thought. This is a simple sentence.
5	C	This sentence is the combination of a complete thought (Laura and Beth were able to go outside). There is also an incomplete thought expressed here: (and play after they finished their homework). The last part of the sentence cannot stand alone because it would leave the reader with who performed this action. The combination of a complete and an incomplete thought creates a complex sentence.
6	A	While this sentence is about two people, it is only expressing one complete thought. This is a simple sentence.
7	C	"Our dogs can do many tricks" is a complete thought. "When they want to" is an incomplete thought. The combination of a simple and an incomplete idea creates a complex sentence.
8	A	"The little bear likes berries" is a simple sentence. It expresses only one idea. "Today is hot, but tomorrow will be even hotter." This is a compound sentence. There are two ideas that are joined by the conjunction "but". "Giraffes are herbivores; a carnivorous animal is a lion" is an example of a compound sentence. There are two complete thoughts joined together by a conjunction. "I think they are coming over, but you might want to call them just to be sure" is another compound sentence.
9	A	The sentence that mentions Jeremiah's love of fruits and Jasmine's fondness of vegetables is a compound sentence. It has two complete thoughts.

Question No.	Answer	Detailed Explanations
10	B	"I had math homework on Monday, a math project on Tuesday, and a math quiz on Wednesday" is the best choice for combining these three sentences into one. There is no need to have three sentences that all start with "I had".
11	B	The baby's bottle was missing, **so** we looked through the entire car. "So" is the transition that shows the cause of looking. It was because the bottle was missing.
12	B	Alexander forgot his glasses on the counter, **but** his mom was able to bring them to school for him. "But" is the appropriate conjunction that shows that the situation was okay because the glasses were delivered to school.

Lesson 11: Capitalization Dedication

Question No.	Answer	Detailed Explanations
1	i	"I" is a proper pronoun. It should always be capitalized, even if it is not at the beginning of the sentence.
2	D	"Mom" is a proper noun. It should always be capitalized unless it has the word "my" in front of it. The correctly written sentence is: I said, "I don't feel well, Mom."
3	B	She said, "Doctor, my child doesn't feel well." This is the correct answer. Given that the person is speaking, the first word inside of the quotation or the dialogue is capitalized. The beginning of the sentence should also be capitalized.
4	B	I told Grandma I was sorry is the correctly written sentence. "I" and "Grandma" are both proper words that require capitalization.
5	B	Dr. and Crane both need to be capitalized. Dr. is a title that is paired with Crane to create a proper noun.
6	C	The first word and the important words in a title are required to be capitalized. The correct capitalization is The Lord of the Rings
7	D	The first and most important words in a title are capitalized.... The title should be written as: The Chronicles of Narnia
8	C	The first word, as well as the most important words in a title should be capitalized. The title should be: From the Mixed-Up Files of Mrs. Basil E. Frankweiler
9	A	Grandma is the first word in the sentence and it is a proper noun. This is the only word in the sentence that needs to be capitalized. The word dad is not capitalized because it is used as a common noun.

10

	Correct	Not Correct
Little House on the Prairie	✓	
A Wrinkle in Time	✓	
The Lion King	✓	
The Call of the Wild	✓	

Lesson 12: Punctuation Education

Question No.	Answer	Detailed Explanations
1	B	The rule in the English language is that if addresses are written on one line, commas must be placed after street address, city, but not after state before zip code. The correct choice is: 1345 Sycamore Street Chicago, IL 123452
2	C	The rule in the English language is that if addresses are written on one line, commas must be placed after street address, city, but not after state before zip code. The correct choice is: 8142 Brown Avenue New York, NY 14353
3	A	The rule in the English language is that if addresses are written on one line, commas must be placed after street address, city, but not after state before zip code. The correct choice is: 800 Heartbreak Lane Las Vegas, NV 83902
4	C	A comma is needed to separate the speaker from the direct quotation or the statement of dialogue that is being said. The correctly written sentence is: "Where is my cookie?" said the little girl. Notice that since the quotation ends in a question mark because it is asking a question, you do not use a comma.
5	A	This sentence has the speaker in the middle of the sentence. The speaker still must be separated from the dialogue. The correctly written sentence is: "Bring me a snack," said the bratty little boy," or I'll bite you."
6	C	The speaker must be separated from the dialogue. The correctly written sentence is: "Please hand me that plate," said the waitress.
7	C	The sentence that is written correctly is: "There it goes again," exclaimed Jason.
8	C	One dentist would examine the teeth. The report belongs to the dentist, so the correct form of the noun is: dentist's.
9	C	The sentence is about one skunk, the word "way" is singular, and needs the singular possessive form of the noun. The correct word for this sentence is: "skunk's"
10	A	Since "parents" is plural, it needs the plural possessive form of the word to complete this sentence. The correct word is "parents".

Question No.	Answer	Detailed Explanations
11	C	"It is only 3:00," replied Leon. A comma is needed to separate 3:00 from the speaker.
12		Jamie screamed, "There is a spider!" The punctuation belongs inside or before the closing quotation mark.

Lesson 13: The Comma and Quotation Dilemma

Question No.	Answer	Detailed Explanations
1	C	This answer choice has a correctly placed comma after "Grant asked." The quotation marks are also correctly placed. Answer choice A is not correct because there are no closing quotation marks after ball and there needs to be a question mark after ball instead of a comma. Answer choice B is not correct because the comma is wrongly placed after Elizabeth and there aren't any open quotation marks in the dialogue. Answer choice D is incorrect because there isn't a comma and the quotation marks are used incorrectly.
2	B	This answer choice is correct because the comma and quotation marks are correctly placed. The answer choice A is incorrect because the quotation marks are around "Amber said." Answer choice C is incorrect because quotation marks surround "He replied,". Answer choice D is incorrect because the whole quote includes suggested Sammie.
3	A	This answer choice is correct because the quotation marks and comma are correctly placed. Answer choice B is incorrect because the quotation does not start with a capital letter, there isn't a comma, and the quotation marks are not properly placed. Answer choice C is incorrect because there aren't any closing quotation marks, and a period is used instead of a comma. Answer choice D is incorrect because the quotation mark is incorrectly placed behind "stated", and a period is used instead of a comma.
4	D	This is the correct answer choice because the quotation marks and comma are correctly placed. Answer choice A is incorrect because it is missing a comma and the quotation does not begin with a capital letter. Answer choice B is incorrect because there is a comma placed after the question mark and the quotation mark is placed incorrectly behind Randy. Answer choice C is incorrect because the comma is improperly placed behind Jill and there are no closing quotation marks.
5	A	This answer choice is correct because it has a correctly placed comma.

Question No.	Answer	Detailed Explanations
6	B	This answer choice is correct because the dialogue is correctly capitalized, and there is correct comma and quotation placement. In answer choice A there is a period after "said" and there should be a comma; also it is not capitalized and there are no closed quotation marks. Answer choice C is incorrect because the comma is incorrectly placed after Walker. Answer choice D is incorrect because the open quotation marks are improperly placed as is the comma; also the quotation does not start with a capital letter.
7	C	This answer choice is correct because it is the only one that has the correct placement of the comma and quotation marks. Answer choice A is incorrect because it does not contain a comma after "birthday" and the closing quotation marks should be placed after the comma behind birthday. Answer choice B is incorrect because the quotation marks belong in front of I and behind birthday. Answer choice D is incorrect because it does not contain a comma after birthday.
8	A	This answer choice is correct because it is the only choice that is correctly punctuated. Answer choice B is incorrect because there isn't a comma after "attention" or after "Williams". Also there aren't any opening quotation marks before "I". Answer choice C is incorrect because there aren't any quotation marks after attention or opening quotation marks before "I". Answer choice D is incorrect because there aren't any opening quotation marks before "May" or after "attention"; the period behind Williams should be a comma.
9	C	This answer choice is correct because the commas and quotation marks are correctly placed. Answer choice A is incorrect because there is not a comma after kitchen, the quotation marks after mom are improperly placed, there isn't a comma after mom and there aren't any open or closed quotation marks before "we" and after "cookies". Answer choice B is incorrect because the period after "mom" should be a comma. Answer choice D is incorrect because there aren't any open quotation marks before "we".
10	B	This answer choice is correct because it gives an accurate description of a quotation.
11	D	This answer choice D is correct because it was correctly punctuated. Answer choice A is incorrect because there is no comma after papers or closed quotation marks. Also there is no open quotation marks before I.

Lesson 14: Impressive Possessives

Question No.	Answer	Detailed Explanations
1	C	"Mine" is the only word that sensibly completes this sentence. My things are all mine.
2	D	The correct answer is: Lydia's things are all hers.
3	D	The correct answer is: Billy and Tim's things are theirs.
4	B	The correct pronouns are needed to complete this sentence. Bobby was doing his homework when I called, so he didn't take my call.
5	A	I was worried when my pencil broke, but Ali loaned me one of his.
6	B	The correct possessive pronoun is "our". The person is speaking from a first person point of view.
7	A	Friend is a singular noun. The possessive form of this noun is friend's.
8	B	"Her" does not require the use of an 's to show ownership. The corrected sentence is: I cannot believe that she lost her ring. (Notice the her's is incorrect.)
9	A	The puppies belong to the dog. The dog is singular, so an 's should be added to show ownership. They are the dog's puppies.
10	D	The tires belong to the bicycle. There is more than one bicycle so it needs to be plural possessive.
11	D	Given the incorrect possessives in the other sentences, the correct sentence is: I forgot to invite Julian to my party.
12	A	The puppies belong to the dog. The dog is singular, so an 's should be added to show ownership. They are the dog's puppies.

Lesson 15: Compelling Spellings

Question No.	Answer	Detailed Explanations
1	B	If you chose B, you picked the right answer. A rule that can help you to remember is that the root word does not change when a suffix or second word is added. When "hiker" is added to "hitch," the result is "hitchhiker." Neither word loses a letter. When the suffix "–ly" is added to "natural," the result is "naturally." Neither the word nor the suffix loses a letter. "Mis-" + "spelled" = "misspelled". Neither the suffix nor the word loses a letter.
2	D	If you chose D, you made the right decision. Words that end in silent –e do not change when the –r ending is added. "Rider" is the correct spelling.
3	D	The misspelled word is thief. The rule, i before e except after c and "eigh," as in "neighbor" and "weigh," doesn't work all of the time. When uncertain, choose "ie" if the sound is "ee."
4	D	"Words that have different spellings, different meanings, but the same sounds" is correct. Homophones are spelled differently. These words have different meanings, but sound the same. For example, meat and meet are homophones.
5	C	C is the correct answer choice. The words flower and flour are homophones because they sound alike but have different spellings and meanings.
6	C	C is the right choice. Each word begins with the prefix "dis-," not "diss-,".
7	C	Answer choice C is correct because it has a "knight," which is a person spelled with kn and "night" at the end as a time of day. Knight and night are homophones because they sound the same. They are spelled correctly based on the context of the sentence.
8	D	If you selected D, that was a good decision. All of the words that begin with the prefix "mis-," keep their original spelling when the prefix is added. ("Misspelled" has two "s"es because "spell" is the root word and has an "s" of its own.)
9	Tommorrow	"Tommorrow" is misspelled because it does not need the double m after the first syllable. It should be spelled t-o-m-o-r-r-o-w.
10	Febuary	"Febuary" is misspelled. This word is missing the "r" following the b. The word should be spelled F-e-b-r-u-a-r-y.

Lesson 16: Syllable Patterns

Question No.	Answer	Detailed Explanations
1	C	There are three syllables in the word telescope: tel-e-scope
2	D	There are four syllables in the word astronomer: a-stron-o-mer
3	C	Grad-u-a-tion has four syllables.
4	D	Appreciated has five syllables. ap-pre-ci-a-ted
5	C	Day only has one syllable.
6	B	El-bow has two syllables.
7	Ex-cit-ing	Ex-cit-ing has three syllables.
8	D	Ex-cur-sion has three syllables.
9	D	Prac-tice has two syllables.
10	D	Favorites has three syllables. They are: fa-vor-ites
11	Two syllables	Ostrich has two syllables. These syllables are o-strich

Lesson 17: What's Your Reference Preference

Question No.	Answer	Detailed Explanations
1	B	Answer choice B is the correct response. Nia must choose a reference source that is based on facts since it is a research paper. The resource must also be about the topic being researched. The other 3 choices have nothing to do with the American Civil War.
2	A	A fiction story about the civil war might give some facts, but Nia might not know for sure which is fiction or which is fact.
3		The answer to this question would be to read an informational book about seashells.
4	C	The best reference to use in locating the meaning of marine is to use a dictionary. A dictionary is a book that provides clear meanings of words. The other resource choices may or may not give the correct definition for marine.
5	C	C is correct. The page you would look on would be words with "ma" because marine starts with the letters "ma". Guide words are used in a dictionary at the top of the pages and the dictionary is arranged in alphabetical order.
6	B	B is the correct answer using a dictionary. Along with meanings, a dictionary provides the sound and/or pronunciation of words. The other choices do not pertain to the reason that dictionaries are used.
7	A	A is the best reference to use in locating more information on handling bees. This choice is specifically about the subject needed to be researched. The other choices are about bees or include aspects of bees but not specifically about bee handling.
8	C	A reference on crafts would NOT be helpful to the situation presented in the text. A mother and daughter baking cookies for a fundraiser doesn't have anything to do with crafts.
9	B	The only reference that pertains to the topic of lions is B, a book on big cats. The other references are not about the specific type of animal, lions.
10	B	Box 1 is more than likely from a dictionary. It provides the meaning of words in alphabetical order.
11	B	A synonym for conceal is "wrap," answer choice B. This is found in box number 2 from a thesaurus. The word wrap is used and next to it are synonyms that include the word conceal.

Lesson 18: Connect the Word for Effect

Question No.	Answer	Detailed Explanations
1	C	Sad is the best answer choice to use in the blank. Marina likes spending time with her grandmother but had never spent more than one night away from her parents. Marina tells the reader that she is not happy. The opening line tells us Marina is going on the trip so she isn't confused. She is sad, not concerned at the thought of not seeing her parents for two weeks.
2	A	The word choice, different, is correct. The second paragraph tells what the boy did that was not the same as last year.
3	B	Ferocious is the correct word that goes in the blank. It goes along with the detail that the author uses to describe the father dragon, "destroy things and fire-breather."
4	B	Noisy is the word used to complete the blank. The last paragraph begins by contrasting the life of the duck inside and outside the shell. Noisy is the opposite of the word quiet.
5	D	Upset is the word to be used in the blank. The blank is followed by the phrase, "unfinished fence." The troll in the story, was working hard. The task remained unfinished. That troll did not feel glad, joyous, or happy.
6	C	Powerful is the best word for the blank based on the context of the sentence. This sentence describes why the ostrich walks instead of flies. The other word choices do not make sense.
7	A	Statement A is the correct answer because it compares an angry child to a lion. Peaceful is not used in describing an angry child. Fast paced rabbit has to do more with speed and not attitude or behavior.
8	A	This statement gives the best detail in describing a sunrise. A sunrise is about color and brightness together, it does not describe warmth.
9	B	The best answer for the blank is "sad." The author tells the reader that the balloon escaped. It wasn't something that Jeremiah wanted to happen. He felt sad.
10	A	Statement A describes the waterfall. The other choices did not describe the waterfall but merely gave an opinion about the waterfall.
11	B	"Time for Fun," is appropriate for the blank since it is about a boy delivering a speech to his friends. The audience in this situation makes it acceptable to talk about recess and fun.
12	B	Rewarding is the best word choice for this title. Since a teacher is giving information to students it should be factual and relevant to the audience. The other three choices are more negative and if that was the case, why give the speech.

Lesson 19: Difference in Spoken and Written Language

Question No.	Answer	Detailed Explanations
1	B	This answer choice is correct because the term "killer" as used in the sentence means something is "excellent".
2	A	This answer choice is correct because the term "out of touch" means "clueless". The other answer choices do not accurately explain "out of touch".
3	C	This answer choice is correct because the term "it's in the bag" can be correctly defined as "having been solved or completed".
4	A	This answer choice is correct because the saying "come on its time to split" can be clarified with the sentence "It is time to go." The other answer choices do not accurately clarify the saying.
5	D	If someone says you are "flaky" they are not saying your skin is peeling, that you are cute, or that you are smart. They are saying that you are unreliable.
6	C	This answer choice is correct because if someone is a "riot" it means that individual is really funny. The other answer choices do not describe "riot" as it is used in the sentence.
7	B	This answer choice is correct because it correctly summarizes the sentence "The gorgeous young woman captured the elite title of homecoming queen". This sentence could be found written but would most likely not be spoken. "A pretty girl won the title of homecoming queen, is a telling sentence."
8	C	This is the correct answer choice because the term "no sweat" means "no problem". The other answer choices do not accurately define "no sweat".
9	A	This answer choice is correct because it correctly uses the term "chicken" in a sentence without changing the context. If someone is a chicken then they are too scared to do something.
10	D	This answer choice is correct because if 'something is grungy' then it is dirty. This answer choice accurately portrays this thought in a sentence. The other choices do not portray it in this manner.

Lesson 20: Same Name, Different Game

Question No.	Answer	Detailed Explanations
1	B	A purse, packet or a parcel would not make sense for the kangaroo's pouch. Clearly, the kangaroo's pouch is a pocket.
2	C	If something is flourishing, it is doing well. This means that it is able to stay alive.
3	B	Ostrich eggs would not be large enough to make statues. They would not be the right texture to make caps or books. The jewelry is the only sensible product that comes from the ostrich egg, since it is an ornament or adds to the appearance of something.
4	B	In this context, the word "arms" means weapons. As a citizen, one can protect them self and their family by "bearing arms" or having weapons.
5	A	In this context, the word "ball" means a fancy dance.
6	B	The robber probably could not bury his money in a bank office. This is referring to the "bank" on the side of a river.
7	A	A person can be called thick, but it is uncommon, so it is more likely that the sentence is talking about a cake batter.
8	B	The kind of bill that is expensive means money owed. You would not refer to a man named Bill as being expensive nor would you reference money as being expensive.
9	A	A die is one of a pair of dice.
10	B	The use of the word "fair" indicates equality or giving the same amount. This means that the cookies need to be divided equally.
11	Pre-	The prefix pre- refers to before, so a pregame occurs before the game.
12	Re-	Re- is a prefix that means again. If someone retells something, they are telling it again.

Lesson 21: Context Clue Crew

Question No.	Answer	Detailed Explanations
1	A	Noonafter is not a time of day. Dawn refers to the early morning. The word aftermoon is misspelled. The correct answer choice is afternoon.
2	C	The trunk of the tree, is not going to be wide. The obvious answer is that it is "not so wide". If it were really tiny, their feet would not fit on it.
3	A	Amy is clinging, and clearly there is fear. Frightened means afraid.
4	C	The man is talking to a child, and "stooped" is paired with the word "down", the man is bending down. The word bent is the meaning for stooped.
5	B	Annoyed means that you bother someone or pick at them. They do not enjoy this attention and it is not desired. Clearly, if you annoy someone, they are irritated.
6	A	Partly and partially mean that it is not a whole, but it is a part of the whole. Someone who is partially blind, can see some things. This is indicated by the reference to being able to see some items in the room.
7	B	She wants her eyesight restored, which suggests that she wants her vision returned to perfect condition. This may not be able to be done, however it is her desire. She wants to be able to see items, regardless of whether they are close or far away.
8	C	Biting off more than you can chew is a figurative way of saying that there is too much to be done. It does not refer to eating.
9	A	The text pairs "accelerates" with too fast, which shows that Andy is speeding up. It also shows that he is frightened. All of this relates to "accelerates" having a meaning of "speeding up". Andy would not be speeding up or going too fast, if he had a wreck or was stopped. Andy would not be frightened or going too fast, if he had slowed down.
10	B	The paragraph provides information related to Andy's lack of listening. He also mentions asking his dad to show him again. Clearly, persuade means that he needs to convince his dad to teach him the basics of bicycling one more time.
11	hard working	If she is a "diligent" worker that wants to make straight A's, this clearly relates to her being a hard worker. Hard workers strive for great success. The meanings "bored" and "fast" do not match her desire for straight A's, Clearly, she is not lazy if she strives for straight A's.

Lesson 22: The Root and Affix Institute

Question No.	Answer	Detailed Explanations
1	A	Given that "wail" is the root word and "ed" is the suffix indicating past tense, the prefix is "be".
2	B	Let's look at the parts of the word in "telescope", there is the prefix "tele" and the root word "scope". The prefix "tele" means over a long distance, and "scope" refers to seeing. A telescope is a device that allows us to get a closer view of objects that are far away from us.
3	A	A suffix is found at the end of a word, and some answer choices can be quickly omitted. Also, "treat" is the root word. This leaves "ment" as the suffix.
4	C	"Coincidence" is a big word. Let's look at how it could be broken down ---- do you see any root words? How about incidence? An incident is something that has happened. To get this root word, "co" must be removed. Clearly, "co" is a prefix that means together.
5	C	The word "tripod" has a prefix. A unicycle has one wheel, a bicycle has two wheels, and a tricycle has three wheels. We are given a clue about the word "tripod". Tri- means three. A tripod has three legs.
6	B	Look at the words "happy" and "unhappy", one means glad and the other one means not glad. The same is true of the words cover and lock when the prefix -un is added. This changes the word's meaning to an antonym or making it mean opposite from the original word.
7	B	B is the best response. The abolitionists were against slavery, the peace marchers are against war, and a person who doesn't like to socialize is antisocial. All of these indicate "against".
8	D	If D is the best choice. "Micro-," means small. Did you notice that all of the underlined words mean "tiny"?
9	B	Distant, long, and far away are all used with the three words that have the prefix tele-. This indicates that the prefix tele- means distant.
10	C	The prefix "un-" means not. Clearly, a jacket is NOT desired in hot weather. The girl was NOT happy when her dog died and the boy was NOT certain.
11		Dis is the prefix for Disagree. Pre is the prefix for Prearrange. Ab is the prefix for Abnormal.
12		The prefix is 'Dis'; The root word is 'agree' and 'able' is the suffix.

Lesson 23: Referring to References

Question No.	Answer	Detailed Explanations
1	B	The definition states "to involve completely: ENGROSS" This closely matches "wrapped up" as used in the sentence.
2	B	The definition states "not before known, heard, or seen : UNFAMILIAR" is how the word strange was used in the given sentence. The other definitions do not apply.
3	C	This question asked about the measurement of time. The only word found in the glossary that was about time was A.M. Times between 12:00 (midnight) and 12:00 (noon).
4	D	This question is about comparing data. The word found in this glossary that addresses comparison of data is bar graphs (a graph that uses rectangles to compare the amounts of data).
5		The two words found in this glossary that are about differences are: distinction: a difference made between two or more individuals, ideas, or events. distinguish: to mark off as different; to recognize the prominent features.
6	C	This answer choice is correct because it is the only word from the glossary that is about an area of study.
7	A	This answer choice is correct because all of these definitions tell the amount of something. (2 a : more than one <several please> b : more than two but fewer than many <moved several inches> c chiefly dialect : being a great many)
8	B	Answer choice B is the only word that is similar to the word fancy as stated in the definitions
9	C	This answer choice specifically answers the question (4 : to visualize or interpret as)
10 Part A	D	Answer choice D states what a group of stars are called. (constellation: a group of stars that is shaped somewhat like an animal, person, or object)
10 Part B	B	Answer choice B contains the two words that is related to things found in the sky from this glossary excerpt. (constellation: a group of stars that is shaped somewhat like an animal, person, or object crescent: the shape of the moon as it appears in its firstor last quarter, with curved edges ending in points)

Lesson 24: Making Words Work

Question No.	Answer	Detailed Explanations
1	A	The words that rhyme are "toil, soil, and boil"
2	B	Maria is waiting for the concert, to began and it makes sense that she would be a bit "uneasy". Happily, easily, and unfriendly are not correct.
3	C	An antonym is a word that has an opposite meaning from another. Laughed refers to positive, happy emotions, and "giggled" is a synonym. "Cried" is the antonym for the underlined word.
4	B	The words thought and sought have the same ending sound as the word brought.
5	B	Homophones are words that have different meanings, origins, or spellings, but sound the same. The words there and their sound the same. There actually refers to a place or location, such as "Let's walk over there." On the other hand, their refers to ownership or possessiveness, such as: "I want to get a car like their new one."
6	C	Kelsey and Maya both want to play with the soccer ball, and they are having an argument. This leads us to note "quarreled" as a disagreement or a fight that has occurred in the past. Fought is the past tense verb for fight, making this a synonym for quarreled. Do you recall that a synonym is a word that has the same meaning as another meaning?
7	D	An antonym is a word that is the opposite or has a different meaning from another word. Clearly, morning is the opposite of night. The words dark and sleep may be features of night, but they are not opposites.
8	A	An antonym is a word that has an opposite meaning from another word. To be wrong is to be different from being right or correct.
9	D	The words slight, right, and night all end with the same sound. They are rhyming words.
10	B	An antonym is a word that has an opposite meaning from another word. One who has a deep feeling is having profound a meaningful emotion. These words are synonyms. The antonym is shallow. Deep indicates far down, while shallow indicates not very deep.
11	Scream	A whisper is very quiet. A scream is very loud. These are words that have opposite meanings. They are also known as antonyms.
12	carelessly	Notice that the word carefully ends in the prefix -ful meaning that it is "full of care". On the other hand, carelessly ends in the prefix -less, meaning that there is no care. Clearly, these words are opposites or antonyms.

Lesson 25: Shades of Words Meanings

Question No.	Answer	Detailed Explanations
1	Cloudy	"Cloudy" correctly finishes the analogy.
2	A	This answer choice is correct because "tasty" can be substituted for "rich with flavor". The other answer choices would change the meaning of the sentence.
3	D	This answer choice is correct because "hilarious" can be substituted for "very funny". The other answer choices would change the meaning of the sentence.
4	B	This answer choice is correct because 'graceful" is the word being described in the sentence "Lily was elegant as she moved across the dance floor." The other answer choices "awkward, rigid, and careless" could not be substituted in the sentence.
5	C	This answer choice is correct because "daring" is the word being described in the sentence "The tightrope walker was very bold as he walked along the high wire a hundred feet up in the air." The other answer choices "timid, cautious, and cowardly" are not being described in the sentence.
6	A	This answer choice is correct because "wasteful" accurately completes the sentence without changing the meaning of the sentence. The other choices would change the meaning.
7	B	This answer choice is correct because "tremendous" accurately completes the sentence without changing the meaning. The other answer choices would change the meaning.
8	D	This answer choice is correct because "majestic" accurately completes the sentence without changing the meaning. The other answer choices would change the meaning.
9	B	This answer choice is correct because "obnoxious" means the opposite of "precious". The other answer choices mean something similar to "precious".
10	C	This answer choice is correct because "smile" means the opposite of "snarl". The other answer choices mean something similar to "snarl".

Lesson 26: Connecting Related Words

Question No.	Answer	Detailed Explanations
1	C	This answer choice is correct because "enraged" replaces "infuriated" in the sentence without changing the meaning of the sentence. The other options all change the meaning of the original sentence.
2	Enormous	"Enormous" replaces "tremendous" in the sentence without changing the meaning of the sentence.
3	D	This answer choice that is the most extreme is "overjoyed". The other answer choices cheerful, happy, and delighted are not as extreme.
4	C	"Murmur" is the only choice that is similar to whisper. The other answer choices cause noise.
5	B	This answer choice replaces "sphere" with "orb" which does not change the meaning of the sentence. The other answer choices change the meaning of the sentence.
6	B	This is the correct answer choice because "slick" is similar to "slippery". The other options are not similar.
7	D	The least extreme answer choice is "competitor". "Enemy, attacker, and rival" are all more extreme in their meaning.
8	C	This is the correct answer because in all of the other answer choices, the words are very similar. In C, dart is used instead of froze, thereby changing the meaning from stop to move quickly. C is the correct choice.
9	A	This answer choice is correct because "potential" is similar to "possible". The other options are different from possible.
10	B	This answer choice is correct because "behaved" is least like "naughty". The other options are similar to "naughty"

Lesson 27: Vocabulary Acquisition

Question No.	Answer	Detailed Explanations
1	B	The question defines the word "denominator."
2	D	The class that you would most likely learn about "mammals" is science class.
3	A	This answer is correct because the "sequence of events" of a story is the order in which events occur in the story.
4	D	This answer is correct because you would most likely hear of "hyperbole" in ELA class.
5	B	This answer choice is correct because if you are asked to estimate, you are to give a number that is close but not exact.
6	B	This answer is correct because if the directions of an assignment tell you to provide "evidence", then the directions are asking you to give proof of where you found your answer.
7	C	This answer choice gives an accurate definition of "moon phases".
8	D	This answer choice gives an accurate definition of "maximum".
9	B	You would most likely learn or hear about subordinating conjunctions in ELA class.
10	A	This is the correct answer choice because if a teacher asks the student to write a verse of a poem, that student would write one line of a poem.
11		If a teacher asks you to justify your answer, the teacher wants you to give proof of your answer.

GMAS FAQs

What will GMAS Assessment Look Like?

In many ways, the GMAS assessments will be unlike anything many students have ever seen. The tests will be conducted online, requiring students complete tasks to assess a deeper understanding of the Georgia standards. The students will take the Summative Assessment at the end of the year.

The time for the ELA Summative assessment for each grade is given below:

Estimated Time on Task in Minutes			
Grade	Section 1	Section 2	Section 3
3	80	75	75
4	80	75	75
5	80	75	75
6	80	75	75
7	80	75	75
8	80	75	75

How is this Lumos tedBook aligned to GMAS Guidelines?

The practice tests provided in the Lumos Program were created to reflect the depth and rigor of the GMAS assessments based on the information published by the test administrator. However, the content and format of the GMAS assessment that is officially administered to the students could be different compared to these practice tests. You can get more information about this test by visiting https://www.gadoe.org/Curriculum-Instruction-and-Assessment/Assessment/Pages/EOG-Study-Resource-Guides.aspx

What item types are included in the Online GMAS Test?

Because the assessment is online, the test will consist of a combination of new types of questions:

1. Selected Response or Multiple choice questions
2. Multi select or two part questions
3. Short Constructed response
4. Extended Constructed response
5. Drag and Drop
6. Hot text

For more information on 2022-23 Assessment year, visit
http://www.lumoslearning.com/a/gmas-2022-faqs
OR Scan the **QR Code**

Why Practice with Repeated Reading Passages?

Throughout the Lumos Learning Common Core Practice workbooks, students and educators will notice many passages repeat. This is done intentionally. The goal of these workbooks is to help students practice skills necessary to be successful in class and on standardized tests. One of the most critical components to that success is the ability to read and comprehend passages. To that end, reading fluency must be strengthened. According to Hasbrouck and Tindal (2006), "Helping our students become fluent readers is absolutely critical for proficient and motivated reading" (p. 642). And, Nichols et al. indicate, (2009), "fluency is a gateway to comprehension that enables students to move from being word decoders to passage comprehenders" (p. 11).

Lumos Learning recognizes there is no one-size-fits-all approach to build fluency in readers; however, the repeated reading of passages, where students read the same passages at least two or more times, is one of the most widely recognized strategies to improve fluency (Nichols et al., 2009). Repeated reading allows students the opportunity to read passages with familiar words several times until the passage becomes familiar and they no longer have to decode word by word. As students reread, the decoding barrier falls away allowing for an increase in reading comprehension.

The goal of the Lumos Learning workbooks is to increase student achievement and preparation for any standardized test. Using some passages multiple times in a book offers struggling readers an opportunity to do just that.

References
Hasbrouck, J., and Tindal, G. (2006). Oral reading fluency norms: A valuable assessment tool for reading teachers. Reading Teacher, 59(7), 636644. doi:10.1598/RT.59.7.3. Nichols, W., Rupley, W., and Rasinski, T. (2009). Fluency in learning to read for meaning: going beyond repeated readings. Literacy Research & Instruction, 48(1). doi:10.1080/19388070802161906.

Discover Engaging and Relevant Learning Resources

Lumos EdSearch is a safe search engine specifically designed for teachers and students. Using EdSearch, you can easily find thousands of standards-aligned learning resources such as questions, videos, lessons, worksheets and apps. Teachers can use EdSearch to create custom resource kits to perfectly match their lesson objective and assign them to one or more students in their classroom.

To access the EdSearch tool, use the search box after you log into Lumos StepUp or use the link provided below.

www.lumoslearning.com/a/edsearchb

The Lumos Standards Coherence map provides information about previous level, next level and related standards. It helps educators and students visually explore learning standards. It's an effective tool to help students progress through the learning objectives. Teachers can use this tool to develop their own pacing charts and lesson plans. Educators can also use the coherence map to get deep insights into why a student is struggling in a specific learning objective.

Teachers can access the Coherence maps after logging into the StepUp Teacher Portal or use the link provided below.

www.lumoslearning.com/a/coherence-map

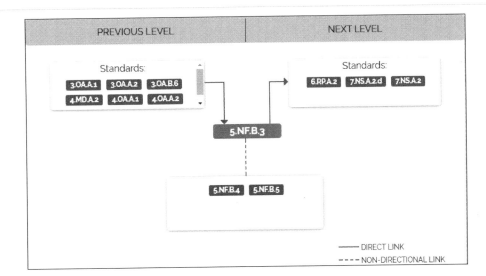

Progress Chart

Standard		Lesson	Page No.	Practice		Mastered	Re-practice /Reteach
GMAS	CCSS			Date	Score		
ELAGSE3RL1	RL.3.1	The Question Session	10				
ELAGSE3RL2	RL.3.2	Tell Me Again	21				
ELAGSE3RL2	RL.3.2	Caring Characters & Life Lessons	38				
ELAGSE3RL3	RL.3.3	Calling All Characters	47				
ELAGSE3RL3	RL.3.3	A Chain of Events	62				
ELAGSE3RL4	RL.3.4	Figurative Language Expressions	78				
ELAGSE3RL5	RL.3.5	Parts of a Whole	87				
ELAGSE3RL6	RL.3.6	Who's Talking Now?	103				
ELAGSE3RL7	RL.3.7	I Can See It Now	117				
ELAGSE3RL9	RL.3.9	Alike and Different	126				
ELAGSE3RL9	RL.3.9	Setting the Scene	138				
ELAGSE3RI1	RI.3.1	Explicitly Comprehension	168				
ELAGSE3RI2	RI.3.2	The Main Idea Arena	176				
ELAGSE3RI3	RI.3.3	Cause and Effect	188				
ELAGSE3RI4	RI.3.4	Educational Expressions	196				
ELAGSE3RI5	RI.3.5	Special Text Parts	204				
ELAGSE3RI6	RI.3.6	What Did You Already Know?	211				
ELAGSE3RI7	RI.3.7	Informational Illustrations	220				
ELAGSE3RI8	RI.3.8	Connect the Dots	227				
ELAGSE3RI9	RI.3.9	Compare and Contrast Important Points and Key Details	235				

Standard		Lesson	Page No.	Practice		Mastered	Re-practice /Reteach
GMAS	CCSS			Date	Score		
ELAGSE3L1a	L.3.1.A	People, Places, and Things	258				
ELAGSE3L1a	L.3.1.A	Replace Those Nouns	261				
ELAGSE3L1b	L.3.1.B	Regular & Irregular Plural Nouns	265				
ELAGSE3L1c	L.3.1.C	Awesome Abstract Nouns	268				
ELAGSE3L1d	L.3.1.D	Show Me the Action	272				
ELAGSE3L1e	L.3.1.E	Simply Simple Verb Tenses	276				
ELAGSE3L1f	L.3.1.F	Make It Make Sense	280				
ELAGSE3L1g	L.3.1.G	Tell Me More	283				
ELAGSE3L1h	L.3.1.H	Subordinating and Coordinating Conjunctions	287				
ELAGSE3L1i	L.3.1.I	Mix Up Those Sentences	291				
ELAGSE3L2a	L.3.2.A	Capitalization Dedication	295				
ELAGSE3L2b	L.3.2.B	Punctuation Education	298				
ELAGSE3L2c	L.3.2.C	The Comma and Quotation Dilemma	301				
ELAGSE3L2d	L.3.2.D	Impressive Possessives	305				
ELAGSE3L2e	L.3.2.E	Compelling Spelling	309				
ELAGSE3L2f	L.3.2.F	Syllable Patterns	312				
ELAGSE3L2g	L.3.2.G	What's Your Reference Preference	316				
ELAGSE3L3a	L.3.3.A	Connect the Word for Effect	321				
N/A	L.3.3.B	Differences in Spoken and Written Language	326				
N/A	L.3.4	Same Name, Different Game	329				
ELAGSE3L4.a	L.3.4.A	Context Clue Crew	333				
ELAGSE3L4.b	L.3.4.B	The Root & Affix Institute	337				
ELAGSE3L4.d	L.3.4.D	Referring to References	341				
N/A	L.3.5.A	Making Words Work	347				
N/A	L.3.5.B	Shades of Word Meanings	350				
ELAGSE3L5.c	L.3.5.C	Connecting Related Words	354				
N/A	L.3.6	Vocabulary Acquisition	357				

Lumos Learning
Developed by Expert Teachers

Grade **3**

GEORGIA
Math
GMAS Practice

UPDATED for 2022-23

ONLINE

2 GMAS Practice Tests

7 Question Types

COVERS 25+ SKILLS

Available

- At Leading book stores
- Online www.LumosLearning.com

Made in the USA
Columbia, SC
11 March 2023

13628742R00217